Mumonkan
The Gateless Gate

Published by The Buddhist Society
Patron: His Holiness the Dalai Lama
Registered Charity No. 1113705

Published by The Buddhist Society, 2023
© The Buddhist Society, 2023
Text © The Buddhist Society

ISBN: 978-0-901032-66-9 (The Buddhist Society)

A catalogue record for this book is available
from the British Library

Edited by Michelle Bromley and Eifion Thomas
Designed by Avni Patel

Printed by TJ Books Limited

The Buddhist Society
58 Eccleston Square
London
SW1V 1PH
T: 020 7834 5858
E: info@thebuddhistsociety.org
thebuddhistsociety.org

Mumonkan
The Gateless Gate
by Mumon Ekai

with commentary by
Soko Morinaga Roshi

THE BUDDHIST SOCIETY TRUST

CONTENTS

Foreword

Soko Morinaga Roshi (1925-1995) played an important part in the transmission of Zen to the West. He was both loved and admired by his students in England. On his various visits to the Buddhist Society in London, and to the Buddhist Society Summer Schools, he gave many talks.

This book is compiled from Soko's recorded talks on the *Mumonkan*, *The Gateless Gate* by Wumen Huikai (1183-1260), the Zen classic that covers the forty-eight cases that play an important part in the study and practice of those who undertake the practice of Zen Buddhism.

In person Soko was tall, warm, and positive, quick and precise in his movements, but graceful and very natural at the same time. He was informal, but not in the least casual. His presence commanded respect but he didn't demand it in any way. He was curious about all things English: oak trees, stately homes, the punk movement. Our history, geopolitics, (some of it to the dismay of our own teacher) as an Island people close to a continent seemed to parallel Japan with its proximity to Korea, China, and Asia; the politeness such as there was here, he enjoyed, as well as English customs and our monarchy.

His voice was rich, and he enunciated his Japanese very clearly. It was a pleasure to hear him speak, which he did with comfortable and unforced authority. There was nothing slow or ponderous about him, on the contrary he seemed animated by a dynamic energy that touched us all, in some way. Many who attended his Teishos were deeply moved, others inspired, few were unaffected. He seemed to us young students of Zen the embodiment of everything a Zen Master should be.

The only reason for the existence of the Zen tradition is to help us wake up, and to bring into full awareness the original insight of the founder of Buddhism, Gautama Shakyamuni, who passed it on to his disciple Mahakasyapa, who in turn passed it down through the succeeding generations to us, through the line of succession. This insight into the true nature, once recognised, carefully nurtured, and cultivated has the innate power, to not only transform individuals, but also whole societies.

The story in the case of Soko Morinaga and the transmission of Zen to the West can of course be traced as far back as Gautama Buddha but for our purposes the story begins with

Hakuin Ekaku 白隱慧鶴 (1686-1769) who reformed and transformed the Zen tradition in Japan.

Gasan Jitō 峨山慈棹 (1727-1797) became Hakuin's disciple late in life after a bruising encounter with the master, and it is from Gasan Jito who continued the reforms, that the whole of Western Zen can be traced, both here in the British Isles and in America.

Inzan Ien 隱山惟琰 (1751-1814)

Taigen Shigen 太元孜元 (1768-1837)

Gisan Zenrai 儀山善來 (1802-1878)

Kosen Sōon 洪川宗温 (1816-1892)

Imakita Kosen 今北 (1816-1892) of Engaku-ji, a child of the Meiji, was, however, eager to introduce Zen to a much wider audience. He was a remarkable figure, a man of his times, well-educated and a

Confucian scholar whose book, One Wave in the Sea, was translated by Soko Morinaga Roshi into modern Japanese (Tokyo: Hakajusha, 1987), English by Janine Anderson Sawada.

Imakita Kosen encouraged his Dharma heir Shaku Soyen to attend the World Parliament of Religions in Chicago in 1893, where Shaku Soyen met Paul Carus, dubbed the 'Ashoka of American Buddhism' by Miriam Salanave. Carus enquired of Shaku Soyen if he knew of someone who could help in his work in translation and Shaku Soyen suggested that his young lay disciple DT Suzuki (1870-1966), then in his early twenties, might be able to help.

It was the same DT Suzuki whose speech on Zen forty years later in 1936, before the World Congress of Faiths in Old Queen Mary's Hall in London, so affected Christmas Humphreys that he immediately became a Zen student and adherent. It was Irmgard Schloegl's attendance at Christmas Humphreys' Zen Classes at the Buddhist Society that inspired this Doctor of Geology to drop her academic career and go to Japan to study and train in Zen. She undertook her training in Daitoku-ji Zen Training monastery under two successive masters, both of whom were in the direct line of Dharma heirs of Shaku Soyen.

The circle was complete when Irmgard met Soko Morinaga the 'grandson' of Shaku Soyen in Daitoku-ji where he was head monk, and they became friends, she referred to him as her 'Dharma uncle' with this Imakita's wish for Zen to be introduced to the West came a step closer.

Soko Morinaga ordained Irmgard Schloegl decades later in England and inaugurated the former home of Christmas Humphreys, as Shobo-an, 'Hermitage of the True Dharma'; and as she began teaching regularly, it seemed in the mysterious way that Zen seems to work, that a seed planted in the late 19th century had begun to germinate.

So, it is with gratitude to those that have kept this tradition alive, that we make this little offering, in the hope that it will perhaps encourage some to undertake training in this art of arts, and science of sciences, also, just another wave in the great ocean of spiritual life and being.

Desmond Biddulph
President, The Buddhist Society
London, 2021

Preface

It has been most rewarding to bring to publication Soko Morinaga Roshi's Commentaries on *The Gateless Gate*, the koan collection by Mumon Ekai.

But how did it come about?

Some decades ago, while living in Brussels I happened by chance to come across a book entitled *The Buddhist Handbook* by John Snelling. The effect was immediate and despite never having had any previous contact with Buddhism, I resolved to seek further. At the back of the book was the address of The Buddhist Society, London and I wrote at once to join. By return I was given information about The Buddhist Society's Summer School and signed up to attend.

By good fortune Soko Morinaga Roshi had commenced a series of Teishos on the *Mumonkan* at the Summer School. The forty-eight cases or koans by Mumon have traditionally been used in Zen training.

A Teisho is when a Zen Master selects a koan or classical Zen text and uses it to introduce his students to his own experience/spirituality of Zen. The Teisho presents pointers to Zen trainees, giving them direction in their own practice. It is magnificent if the words of the Teisho make a connection with the Zen student's own heart, but this is not likely to happen if the student only attempts an intellectual understanding. In addition, the Teisho can give impetus to shattering the excrescences that mount up as we go through life.

Soko Roshi came over each year from Japan to give these Teisho at the Summer School. Of course, at that time never having engaged in Zen training or zazen I was at a loss to fully comprehend the talks. Nevertheless, a chord was struck and I returned each year.

Meanwhile I also joined the Zen group under the guidance of Venerable Myokyo-ni who had trained in Japan at the same monastery, Daitoku-ji, as Soko Roshi.

It was last year while looking through back copies of the journal *Zen Traces* that I once again came across the Teishos that Soko Morinaga Roshi had given at the Summer School so many years ago. It was a glorious re-encounter. How true are the words of Soko Roshi in his commentaries to these koans. 'The benefit of reading such a koan text – and the comments on it – is that we set our own understanding against it, and then can transform our own understanding.'

On rediscovering this text, it was difficult to believe that it had not been published, so I set about getting this done. Help was at hand, Fairlight Zen Temple had copies of the tapes of the talks which needed review, and The Buddhist Society Trust also warmly welcomed this project for The Buddhist Society. Crucially we needed editorial expertise to bring the spoken word to the written word rather than a transcription. Michelle Bromley offered her services and the project was airborne. Weekly zoom meetings with Michelle were events to anticipate with joy as progress proceeded, and we wrestled with difficulties.

This important book of commentaries by Zen Master Soko Morinaga brings to light that, 'In the Zen transmission, the aim of the training is experiential direct understanding.' The voice of Soko Morinaga rings out loud and clear. From the journey he has undertaken, there are wise words in profusion for those that wish to follow.

Zen students everywhere can come to understand that 'there is no need to be taught the truth, important is only that within ourselves we eradicate and get rid of what is mistaken.'

It is with gratitude that we bring this book to a wide audience.

Eifion Thomas

Introduction

Throughout the eighties and nineties Soko Morinaga Roshi made annual visits of several weeks each summer to Shobo-an, the Zen Centre in London. During his stay he would also lead the Zen class and hold lectures at the Buddhist Society's annual Summer School. It was during these visits that he gave teisho on all the forty-eight koan cases of the *Mumonkan* which have been collected together in this volume. His long-standing and close association with Shobo-an went back to the period at Daitoku-ji when he and the Venerable Myokyo-ni both trained under Oda Sesso Roshi.

Soko Morinaga Roshi (1925-1995), coming of age in the unsettled times of post WW2 Japan, found himself drawn to Zen practice. He began his training under Goto Zuigan Roshi at Daitoku-ji and received Dharma transmission from Oda Sesso Roshi who succeeded Zuigan as Abbot of Daitoku-ji. In 1965 Morinaga Roshi became the abbot of the temple of Daishu-in in Kyoto, where he opened the Zen meditation hall to lay people in the area and to foreign students. For some time he also served as president of Hanazono University in Kyoto, the principal training university of the Rinzai School in Japan. In keeping with the tradition of the teachers of his lineage, he was keen to make the teachings of the Buddha available to a wider audience outside the temple walls. He travelled to many parts of the country to lead meditation retreats for monks and laypeople. But as well as Japanese students, he also trained European and American students, two of whom built Daishu-in West in California as a Western counterpart to Daishu-in in Kyoto.

Ven. Myokyo-ni, Irmgard Schloegl (1921-2007), was trained at

Daitoku-ji monastery in Japan, where for twelve years she worked under two successive masters, Oda Sesso Roshi and Sojun Kannun Roshi. It was while training under Sesso Roshi that she met Soko Morinaga who was also training with Oda Sesso Roshi and was the head monk of the monastery at the time. Throughout her time in Japan, Morinaga acted as guide and spiritual adviser. On her return to England in 1972, he visited regularly and continued to support her in establishing the Zen Centre. During his visit in 1984 he ordained her as the Ven. Myokyo-ni and inaugurated Shobo-an as a Rinzai Zen Temple. He was, as Myokyo-ni said, 'a Kalyamitra, a good friend and teacher, to the Zen Centre,' and was affectionally referred to as 'uncle.' She was abbess of the Zen Centre's two training temples, Shobo-an and Fairlight, over which she presided until her death in 2007.

Mumon Ekai (Chin. Wumen Huikai) (1183-1260) was a Chinese Chan master of the Song period. His major work the *Mumonkan (Wumenguan)*, *The Gateless Gate*, is a collection of koans he compiled and to which he added comments and verses. Koans or gong-an, are brief stories or dialogues and encounters between masters and students from the past, or sometimes phrases from the sutras. Many erudite articles and books have been written on koans – their history, development and use in Zen training. At the same time, the word 'koan' itself has now found its way into Western dictionaries and is even referred to in popular culture. However, to a non-Buddhist reader koans still seem either mysterious or completely illogical, and to the Zen student they present a challenging problem that has to be worked with. Koans have been used as a teaching technique to try and help the student to go beyond conceptual thinking and to make an intuitive leap beyond contradictions and dualistic thinking. But rather than say more about them, it is better to let the reader get an impression of koans, koan study and the Mumonkan itself, by reading the Roshi's commentaries.

The Roshi's commentaries presented here are far more comprehensive than just an interpretation of the koans. He places them in both the historical and spiritual context in which they originated. He introduces us to all the old masters involved, relating their histories, idiosyncrasies and training methods. Many analogies in his teishos also come from his own experiences as a novice and monk, and later as a roshi; but he also draws on his observations of modern society. More importantly, however, he brings out the deeper meaning of the koans by making them relevant to our daily lives. Throughout these commentaries, we get to know both the Roshi's serious and his humorous side, and strongly sense his warmth and sheer joy of living.

As he puts it: 'Zen is not something that can be labelled as Zen – it is here and around us. What exists, what is, is the only reality, is the very reality in which we live. Therefore, when reading koan texts you have to read them in relation to that reality. In order to help us to do that, the patriarchs presented us with a variety of such problems. A koan is not an end in itself, it is merely a means or a trigger to encourage us to see reality as it is. So, what do these koans and the commentary really mean to you? Some may consider them as a kind of ragbag, others may find them to be useful information, and still others may take them as interesting curiosities that have little, if anything, to do with our own life. Yet the forty-eight koans in the *Mumonkan* relate directly and personally to your lives. Even the story of a Chinese monk from a thousand years ago, who raised a finger – if you do not take that incident as here and now, in this place, for yourselves, then it will not amount to Zen training.'

Michelle Bromley

Acknowledgements

Over the years many people have been involved in the preparation of this book, which has now finally culminated in its publication for the benefit of Zen students everywhere and a wider readership. Foremost, much gratitude goes to Soko Morinaga Roshi who for many years dedicatedly visited and offered much support to the nascent, and then under his encouragement the growing and flourishing, Zen group at Shobo-an.

For the majority of the teishos presented here, Professor Martin Collcutt of Princeton University kindly served as interpreter. His academic background in Japanese cultural history and his personal and long-standing involvement with Morinaga Roshi and his teachings, made Professor Collcutt's participation invaluable at the Summer School.

For the few occasions when Prof. Collcutt was unable to attend, Yoko Ocuda, a Japanese student of Ven. Myokyo-ni's, helpfully stepped in and acted as interpreter. She also worked with Myokyo-ni on the translation of Torei's *Inexhaustible Lamp*.

Soko Morinaga Roshi's commentaries on the forty-eight koan cases of the *Mumonkan* were originally published between 1984 and 1994 in *Zen Traces*, the in-house journal of the Zen Centre. The teishos were given during that same period at The Buddhist Society Summer School. The translation of Mumon's Cases, Comments and Verses were done by Ven. Myokyo-ni in preparation for the Roshi's teishos. Much gratitude goes to the many people at Shobo-an who at that time, over thirty years ago, patiently transcribed the tapes, typed them out and prepared them for *Zen Traces*.

Finally, thanks are due to Eifion Thomas who became reacquainted with these wonderful teachings in the back issues of *Zen Traces* and, recognising and appreciating their significance, wished to make them available for a larger readership. He has overseen the editing and publication of this very important book.

CASE 1 · JOSHU'S 'MU'

A monk asked Joshu, 'Does a dog have Buddha-nature?' Joshu said, 'Mu.'

In the study of Zen, the barrier of the patriarchs must be passed. If you desire this mysterious insight (satori), the workings of the heart must cease completely. Unless this is accomplished and the barrier has been passed, you resemble ghostly sprites leaning on grasses and clinging to trees. What is this barrier of the patriarchs? Just this 'Mu', and so it is called 'The Gateless Barrier of Our School.'

Those who have passed the barrier have become familiar not only with Joshu but with all the successive patriarchs, can walk hand in hand with them, mingle eyebrows with them, see with the same eye and hear with the same ear. Is this not wonderful? If you wish to pass this barrier, you have to concentrate your whole body with all its three hundred and sixty bones and joints and its eighty-four thousand pores into this 'Mu', and hold it before you day and night without ceasing. Do not take it as nothing or as something – neither as 'is' nor as 'is not.' It then becomes like a red-hot iron ball which you have swallowed and which now sticks in your throat – you cannot bring it up nor spit it out.

All the useless knowledge you have up until now accumulated, and the erroneous things you have learned, throw them all away in one go! After a long time, it will ripen naturally in the unity of inside and outside. Then, like a dumb man in a dream you will know for yourself but cannot communicate it. Your whole activity is suddenly vitalised and moves, startling heaven and shaking the earth. Or it is as if you had laid hands on the general's great sword. If you meet the Buddha, kill the Buddha if you meet the patriarchs, kill the patriarchs. You have thus entered the great freedom though you stand on the shore of birth and death. Within the six realms of being and the four modes of birth, the Samadhi of Play (*yuge sammai*) opens. So again, how to work on this 'Mu'? Put your whole energy, your utmost effort into it – and if you do not give up on the way, another lamp of the Dharma will light up.

THE VERSE
狗子佛性
全提正令
纔涉有無
喪身失命

The dog – Buddha-nature!
Quite at ease and with true authority.
But if you become involved in 'yes' and 'no', however little,
you lose both body and life.

SOKO ROSHI'S COMMENTS
For listening to teisho, both body and heart need to be relaxed, ready and open to receive. When a cup is full, or the heart is filled, there is no room for anything new to enter.

I became a monk because I had lost the sense of any purpose to my life and was spiritually drifting. Since then, forty years have passed. As I see it, these days sadness, grief and pain have by no means disappeared. Every day brings both happiness and pain; however, they are not problems. If you look out at the landscape, there is no problem; there are just trees, grass, clouds. Yet people create problems out of these, like it is cloudy, or that trees are growing too close, or perhaps even the fact that grass is too green! In a letter I recently received, the writer said that he could not grasp how Buddha-nature can be inherent in trees or grass. Why? If trees and grass, or a desk are endowed with Buddha-nature, why is it that these, unlike human beings, unlike the writer himself, do not feel anguish?

My answer to the person looking at the trees, at the grass, or at the desk, would be that if they really want to make a problem out of it, this is the way to do it: not to wonder why trees, etc., do not feel pain or anguish, but rather to ask why it is that I, endowed with the same Buddha-nature as they have – why is it that I feel anguish? Why don't I think of my own situation or my own heart, rather than that of the trees, grass or the desk? Why, for example, instead of really trying to understand myself, do I try to understand Zen Buddhism or the Buddha-nature of the desk? This same mistake is what our koan today is concerned with.

Master Joshu (778-897) lived to the ripe old age of a hundred and twenty, and is perhaps the greatest Chinese Zen patriarch. He did his novice training at Jizo-in, the 'Temple of the Magnificent Buddha.' At nineteen he first met his teacher, Nansen, who was by then already an old man. Tired and resting on his bed, he received the young novice. Nansen asked Joshu, 'Where have you come from?' 'I have come from Jizo-in, the Temple of the Magnificent Buddha.' Nansen asked him, 'Have you seen a Magnificent Buddha?' On being asked this question, most people would immediately start thinking, chasing thought after thought, frantically trying to come up with some clever reply. Now as Joshu had been a novice in Jizo-in, the Temple of the Magnificent Buddha, he had of course seen this beautiful Buddha image. Most people would think that this question referred not to the Buddha image in the temple, but that Nansen was asking about the Buddha in the heart. They would then feel self-satisfied at having seen into the deeper meaning of the question and be pleased with their understanding. In Japan, such persons are considered fools! For thinking along such lines, one arrives at a dead-end.

Joshu, however, replied immediately, 'I have not seen a magnificent or resplendent Buddha, but I am seeing a reclining Buddha.' On hearing this, Nansen was so astonished that he sat up and asked, 'Are you under the guidance of a teacher?' Joshu bowed and said, 'Although it is cold, I'm glad to see that the master seems to be very well,' and from then on, Joshu stayed and practised under Nansen for forty years. For the next twenty years after Nansen's death, between the age of sixty and eighty, he wandered around from monastery to monastery, continuing his practice. At eighty, he settled at the Kannon Temple where he devoted himself to guiding others till the end of his life, at the age of a hundred and twenty.

In the first encounter, the first *mondo*, between Joshu and Nansen, Joshu was not yet enlightened. However, he had already reached a level of spiritual attainment where he was no longer taken in by concepts and so was not tricked or caught by the notion of a 'Magnificent Buddha.' He did not think of a teacher other than Nansen, who was there directly in front of his eyes. Most likely, if he had been in front of a dog and had been asked about his teacher, then he would have perhaps taken the dog as a teacher. At the age of nineteen, Joshu already knew that you live in this moment, wherever you are, whatever you may be doing, in whatever situation. And in Zen practice, too, the main focus is on a way of life in which you live from moment to moment.

One day a monk asked Joshu, 'Does a dog also have Buddha-nature?' Perhaps this foolish monk remembered the Buddha's teaching that Buddha-nature is in everything. If Joshu had said, 'Yes, a dog has Buddha-nature,' then the monk's next question would have been, 'Why is the Buddha-nature imperceptible in here, yet bounding around on the rocks, or lying there under a tree?' This is the same as wondering why a desk does not feel anguish though it has Buddha-nature.

Joshu cut through this question with his 'MU!' ('No!') This story became famous throughout China. Over the one thousand and two hundred years that have passed since then, it has been used as a koan in both China and Japan, and now I am giving teisho on it here in England. If Joshu were here, he might say, 'Bungler!' For really, what is the problem? Generally, we think Joshu responded to whether a dog has Buddha-nature or not. But actually there was no problem, though you may find this difficult to understand. So, I am just making it even more difficult. The monk asked, 'Does a dog have Buddha-nature?' Ask yourself first, 'Does a dog have Buddha-nature?' When we ask ourselves who really lives a life that is less admirable than that of a dog, then the Buddha-nature is probably there too. In that case the flavour of this koan will surely seem very different to you. As explained before, Joshu's response of 'Mu' ('No') does not mean that Buddha-nature does not exist, or that the dog does not have Buddha-nature. In whatever miserable or hopeless circumstances, or however desperate things may seem for us, these instantly may be changed into situations which present no problems, if only we give up conceptualising and rationalising.

Never think about what Joshu's reply 'Mu' means. If you treat it as a philosophical question or examine it analytically, it is just so much nonsense. Fundamentally there is no problem. Sit with complete peace of mind, look at things with complete peace of mind, eat with complete peace of mind. Be disturbed or upset when confronting a difficult problem, but be so with complete peace of mind. In pain or suffering, cry with complete peace of mind. And if you feel joy then do so with peace of mind

Although I'm talking to you of this now, some forty years ago, I also could not do this, and so I practised and sat zazen with the utmost effort. I wanted to attain enlightenment and thought that satori was a state in which I would achieve perfect purity without any sense of delusion. That kind of thinking is not really mistaken, but however much one may meditate, one cannot attain it, and the more determined one is and applies oneself, the further away it seems and the less one can achieve it. There was not enough time for zazen during the day and so I would sit at night after everyone had gone to bed. But at that time, I was the monk responsible for waking the others in the morning. Worried that with even a small amount of food I might fall asleep, I stopped eating. The result was that rather than falling asleep I felt faint throughout the night and could not continue, and so for three mornings in succession, I was some thirty minutes late because I had either fainted or fallen asleep on the cushion. Soon after that it was my turn to become *jikijitsu* (Zendo Head-monk). The head monk of the monastery and the head monk of the zendo take care of the affairs of monastery and meditation hall respectively, and the head monk asked me rather angrily whether I was really determined to practise, and nearly expelled me from the meditation hall for neglecting my duties.

However, Master Sesso knew why I had failed to rouse the monks for three mornings and forgave me. Even after this, I continued to sit zazen all night. Then the others began to take notice and from then on, I no longer missed out on waking the monks in the morning. Thus, I have come to realise that *shugyo*, practice, is something which cannot be done on one's own, but needs to be supported and sustained by people and things around you. Practising along those lines over a long period of time, I became absolutely exhausted. Although bodily sitting, the spirit to really drive through to satori seemed to have vanished.

Until then, my zazen had been driven by my will. Whenever I was looking at something, hearing a sound, smelling something, or feeling something touching body or heart, everything in my practice was supported by my will. But because of the extreme exhaustion into which I had fallen, my will vanished. From head to toe, all that was left was exhaustion; what was sitting on the cushion was just sheer exhaustion.

Then something very strange happened. I cannot remember when, but in the dark of night, what until then had seemed like a miasma or fog around this exhaustion suddenly lifted. I could hear the slightest sound and could see even in the dark; and all I heard, saw or felt was extremely clear. Yet there was no one who listened, nor was there an 'I' as somebody who was feeling. Now, this is talking after the event and is just an attempt to convey some sense of what happened; however, it cannot be described accurately. But I would stress again, that it was not myself hearing, seeing or touching.

And now returning to ordinary life, and the present again. We think of ourselves as being the bodies that we inhabit, and we think of everything outside our bodies as somehow opposite to or in contrast to this self; outside existence, 'it,' is not 'me.' Isn't this how we sometimes think of ourselves, as being in opposition with something? A self that one can think of as being opposite to something, as separate, is not oneself. In Zen training we are constantly cautioned, 'Look at yourself – see yourself.' But the self that one can see consciously, in conscious awareness, that is not the self. What I saw when I was utterly exhausted, what was seen even in the dark, was seen because I was no longer there, and with the self no longer there, objects were not 'other' than myself; and in that sense, everything had become myself. Shakyamuni Buddha became enlightened while looking at the morning star on the 8th of December. One Zen Master expressed that as, 'When the Buddha saw the light of the morning star, he thought that he himself was shining.' Perhaps you understand what experience he referred to. It is not that you cannot see, it is not that you cannot hear – you can hear very well and see very well; but within that perception there is no seeing or hearing self, and so the division between seer and the seen, or the listener and the heard, does not exist. There is no difference between the dog and the human being, and there is no difference between that which is Buddha-nature and that which is not Buddha-nature. There is no lump or substance of self, so there is consequently no lump or substance apart from the self either. Everybody today believes that everything moves by cause and effect. However, the categories of cause and effect do not really exist. Even in joyful, unpleasant and unhappy circumstances, in the absolute state this is also so, even while circumstances change from moment to moment. Living, in this way, this is 'MU.' It is not that there is nothing. Being able to live this way from moment to moment, or changing and responding from moment to moment, the more you try to explain it, the more difficult it becomes. So, all I can say is, suffer without any problem, feel joy without any sense of a problem. Or as I said above, cry with peace of mind, feel sadness with peace of mind, laugh with peace of mind. And if you cannot do so, then, like I did, sit zazen until you fall off your cushion.

Mumon, the compiler of the *Mumonkan*, trained under Master Getsurin. Given this Mu-Koan, he worked on it for six years, but could not see into it. He came near to despair, but found that continuous zazen (sitting meditation) made him sleepy, and so he resorted to constant walking meditation, morning, noon and night, around the cloisters, and through the corridors of the monastery. If he, nevertheless, became sleepy, he banged his head against one of the pillars, and then continued walking. One day, on hearing the sound of the bell for the midday meal, he had satori. The clarity of the sound of that bell went straight to his heart; he heard the bell without ears, and was taken with great joy.

Later, when he himself taught others, he always gave this as the first koan. His koan collection comes down to us as *Mumonkan*, the *Gateless Gate*, and the first koan in it is Joshu's 'Mu.' By a strange karmic connection, the name of Mumon's temple, Ryusho-ji, is the same as that of the temple in which I myself and Myokyo-ni practised together in Kyoto.

Mumon begins his commentary with the statement that if you want to find and practise true Zen, then you have to pass through the barrier established by the patriarchs. However wonderful it may seem to us, our own conception alone is not sufficient. Only by our own initiative, our own individual effort, can we achieve true happiness allied with universal truth. And only when individual experience and universal truth tally is the resultant happiness lasting. Contrary to this, an individual opinion that does not accord with universal truth can but procure short-term, temporary satisfaction, but cannot give life-long permanent joy and happiness. By demanding that the gate has to be passed through, Mumon was not setting up Zen as an authoritarian system. There is nothing authoritarian about it. The patriarchs established this gate in order to enable followers to bring together both their personal experience and universal truth.

Mumon then continues with, 'Give up the workings of the heart.' This, however, does not mean to enter some kind of blind state, becoming unaware or vacant. From my own personal experience, which I have related, I realised that what I perceived through the eyes and ears, through the senses, stood in the way of satori. By trying to see the own true self, what I saw with the eyes or heard with the ears or felt with the heart, was a kind of differentiation. I was not able to find the true self because of the difference I perceived between myself and others, and could only see things in contrast to myself. But from my experience arose the true realisation of self, with the direct perception of the dissolution of self. However deeply you may know the separate or partial self, to the very end it will always remain only a personal understanding, rather than a truly universal understanding. A well-known Japanese poem says, 'In the ancient capital Nara, the Sarusawa pond is beautiful. The pagoda casts its reflection into it. When you clap your hands, the birds rise startled and fly away. The carp in the pond, thinking it is feeding time, crowd together, and come close. The waitresses in the teahouse nearby think a customer has arrived and come out with a cup of tea.' This is according to personal experience – the birds, the carp, the waitresses, none are mistaken; however, none of them have heard that sound purely. They have all heard it, or perceived it, as it were, through their own spectacles, according to their own understanding. But the sound of the bell that Mumon heard, the scenery that I myself saw in the darkness of night, this pure realisation or experience, undiluted by personal understanding, is what is meant by giving up, cutting away the workings of the heart.

If one does not pass through the barrier, or one does not give up the workings of the heart, however superb or high a degree of experience or knowledge one may achieve, if it is not at one with universal experience, as Mumon says, it is like ghosts and sprites clinging to trees and bushes. Thus, if by oneself, by one's own efforts, one seeks to establish one's own individual way of life, then almost unconsciously one is led by and influenced by something or somebody else, and tends to grasp or cling on to, or seek support from that. This, of course, indicates that one is not living fully by oneself. Though in all Western countries stress is placed on personal independence and on individuality, nonetheless, there will be some who are perhaps rather weak in the face of authority, others who are responsive to it, and still others who react against authority. But those who really have passed through the barrier of the patriarchs and who have cut away the workings of the heart – the sense of differentiation – even though they respect authority, they are not overawed by it. With a heart full of this respect, they still remain free themselves, their own persons.

In Zen training we are ever exhorted to seize the chance for realising the truth. So, what is this wonderful gateless gate of the patriarchs? The single character 'Mu' of Joshu, this koan, is the 'gateless gate.' Mumon says that because it is so fundamental, he put this koan first in his collection. If you can truly pass through this gate, not only will you directly encounter Joshu, you will always go hand in hand with all the patriarchs, be able to see as one with them, hear as one with them, feel as one with them. In the texts, this is called 'mingling eyebrows' with the patriarchs. But do not be taken in or get captivated by such quaint expressions. For here it simply means becoming one. Nor try to envisage encountering Joshu who died more than a thousand years ago. The important thing is that your personal experience should mesh with universal reality or truth. Then if things that you are looking at, at the moment, are things that the Buddha may have looked at, or the patriarchs may have seen, what you feel at this instant is the same as other people are feeling. If you can maintain this way of understanding, would this not be a quite wonderful way of living? And the opposite of this: husband and wife married for thirty years, and although side by side in bed may yet be thinking of completely different things, seeing things in completely different ways and consequently feeling lonely and isolated. Joshu says that this experience of being in accord with universal truth is the most wonderful thing. So, in that case, do you not sincerely wish to pass through this barrier? Mumon is here encouraging and urging us. For if this result can be achieved, then do you not want to try for it with all your might?

Do we not find or make problems for ourselves every day? Although there really is no problem, yet until or before reaching the stage of no longer having problems, we have to deal with problems. To begin with, every day a new problem crops up. Not just every day, but morning, noon and night, new problems keep coming up. In my case, on becoming a monk, for the first time in my life, there was only a single problem, morning, noon and night. Throughout the whole year, I directed my energies towards this single problem – the gate of the patriarchs. Therefore, Mumon says that when you have this desire, the determination to break through the barrier, then you simply throw away everything, the three hundred and sixty bones, and the eighty-four thousand pores, your eyes and your ears. All your energy is thrown into the koan, and you simply must become this 'Mu.'

Mumon further warns that you should not interpret this 'Mu' in an abstract or nihilistic way, nor should you see it as dualistic, 'being' versus 'non-being.' Now, the real and basic function of a Zen Master is to cause people to go astray. Scholars explain ideas and thoughts in great detail in order to get people to understand things, but this kind of knowledge slowly moves away from the truth. Now, the real function of a Zen Master, on the other hand, is to cause people to go astray. Then getting lost, they gradually draw closer to the truth. But nowadays people have weaker resolve, become easily confused and run away. I also now have to resort to explaining things more explicitly.

When the monk asked, 'Does a dog have Buddha-nature?', Joshu answered, 'Mu.' What Joshu meant by this is that the dog does not have the Buddha-nature that you think it has. He would like you to think that you all have been scolded or told by Joshu, 'Mu!' Told to give up and throw away your own individual notions of Buddha-nature. Now, thus emptied, listen to what I say. This beautiful flower here has a clear shape and form, but even as you are looking at it, it is undergoing transformation from moment to moment. Surely you all will agree to this?

The leaves of an oak are different from the leaves of a chestnut. From the leaves alone we can know the one is from an oak tree, and the other is from a chestnut tree; so, then we conclude that oaks have these kinds of leaves, and chestnuts have those kinds of leaves. Of course, each individual leaf also has its own characteristic leaf pattern, but each of all the many, many leaves is undergoing this moment-to-moment transformation. The same applies to our own faces, bodies, hearts and spirits. Certainly, there are momentary characteristics, individual ones and features that are common to all, but at the same time they are all undergoing a moment-to-moment change. Suppose a woman sits alone in a room, quite naturally and relaxed. Then her husband enters and she speaks with the voice of the wife and looks with the eyes of the wife, and assumes perhaps the appearance and facial expression of the wife. But, if from behind her a child calls 'Mummy!', her face and voice and gestures and body are those of the mother as she turns around and says, 'What is it?' Intrinsically, everything is subject to transformation, is changing. There is nothing which has a fixed, unchanging form. This is the meaning of the term 'formless'; it really means of no fixed form. If we return to the flower mentioned above, however beautiful, it will wither. The flower has no attachment that makes it cling to the moment of perfect beauty and no dread of or resistance to withering. But we human beings desire to preserve and to hold onto the moment of perfect beauty. The inescapable fact, however, is that we all are subject to ageing. This is *munen* – regret, remorse. Nothing has a place in which to remain, to abide. Everything is subject to change. It is not a question of our will, but simply the work of nature.

In our koan, then, the working of non-attachment, of no-fixed-form and of non-abiding, of not having a permanent and stable resting place, this is the Buddha-nature at work. Even though you may not sit in meditation for years as Mumon did, or I myself, or walk and walk until you are exhausted, you can and should always see that things do not have fixed forms and thus be aware of non-attachment. In your daily lives, too, you can and should check to see that your heart is not stuck to and held by things. But do not try and achieve this by the force of your will either. What we humans can do by willpower is to cause things to become fixed even though they are intrinsically moving, changing; to cause things that in themselves have no sense of attachment to become attached; or to try to put a stamp of permanence on things which really have no fixed form – that is all human willpower can do. It has been said again and again, we do not have to consciously become empty – we *are* empty from birth. The problem is simply that we have lost this emptiness of heart (*mushin*) by adding unnecessary knowledge. In his commentary Mumon therefore likens the koan to a red-hot ball which you cannot swallow and cannot vomit out. Concentrate all your energies, and thus get rid of all the bad habits and experiences that you have accumulated in the past. Mumon urges us on, saying, 'All the useless knowledge you have up to now accumulated, and the erroneous things you have learned, throw them all away in one go!'

Working with 'Mu' is thus not simply a chanting or repeating 'Mu, Mu,' whether loud or in one's heart. Just smash any fixed form;

check to see whether you are bound by attachments or not, and check to see whether you are clinging to something or not. Mumon then explains that, like this red-hot ball, you make use of the lack of fixed form, of non-attachment, and of impermanence, to achieve 'Mu.' And once having realised 'Mu,' it will then no longer be necessary in each instant to recall non-attachment, no fixed form, and impermanence.

'MU!' That is sufficient.

Thus, pursuing one's training over a long period, the kind of training that one has achieved through willpower, or things that we have built up through conceptualising, all of these will naturally and easily pass through the heart. At that moment there is then no opposition, no duality between self and other. Everything becomes one. As Mumon says, 'After a long time it will ripen naturally in the unity of inside and outside.' Then you will also realise that you are in fact living in harmony with everybody, with all other sentient beings. That experience is like a dumb man who had a dream. Because he cannot speak, he cannot relate what he saw in his dream, but he knows it, and quite unconsciously smiles. In Chinese, being able to live in this way is expressed as 'startling heaven and shaking the earth.' This is not an exaggerated statement; it is quite natural when living in harmony with heaven and earth.

It is like taking the sword of some powerful general who was never defeated in battle. Then if you meet the Buddha, or the patriarchs, you will not be led astray by them. Whatever authority you may confront, while you respect that authority, you remain free. That is the meaning of Mumon's, 'Kill the Buddha, kill the patriarchs.' Do not mistake this and think you should go and kick a statue of the Buddha. What you are killing is not the Buddha or the patriarchs, but the mistakes within yourself. Mumon says 'You have thus entered the great freedom though you stand on the shore of birth and death.' By 'birth and death' he is referring to suffering. When you are born, you cannot make any choices. No one can choose their parents, nationality, or their sex. Yet we constantly pick and choose. For those who believe we human beings can choose, existence is painful. We cannot choose or select our death either. So, what he is saying is that in this life which is often not as we would like it to be, we can yet live easily and readily. Now you understand that if one is not present oneself, then things go smoothly. So, it is not a matter of getting others to do as we wish; we must not attempt to manipulate situations. For freedom is not making others do what we wish them to do, or shaping our environment to our liking. Rather, it is the freedom to live easily within this environment which we cannot force to function according to our own desires. The Six Realms of Being and the Four Modes of Birth are Buddhist technical terms. Here Mumon's meaning is that in whatever environment we may be in, we can live the freedom of children at play. Now what do you think is the meaning of playing like children – the Samadhi of Play?

A child playing with a golf ball is simply enjoying himself. He doesn't attach any particular value in hitting the ball with a club, he just does it for pleasure, and he enjoys it. But we tend to think of things in terms of value and permanence. And yet, for example, when cooking a meal, however delicious, we will not put it into a museum or expect it to survive for a thousand years. It is quickly eaten and what returns to the kitchen is a dirty plate. Then we think that in doing such unrewarding work our whole life flows away – is this what life is all about, then? Should I not be doing something that is of greater value? So, we reduce our understanding of life to a value judgement, such as cooking food, and in return getting a dirty plate. Or else we may think that though kitchen work is not enjoyable I must do it, because it is my duty to feed my family. Then it grates. But if without thinking along such lines one simply enjoys what one is doing in the kitchen, that is the Samadhi of Play. And not just simply in the kitchen, but if in every situation or relationship, we can meet, discover and find this playfulness, that is the life of a Buddha. But how, Mumon asks, do you enter this state? And he repeats again that by means of this koan 'Mu' we can enter it.

Good or bad, rich or poor, self or other, if you think of these even for a fraction of an instant, then 'Mu'! That is the way to work through the barrier. Then just as when darkness vanishes the instant a candle is lit, so likewise reality will open up in front of your eyes.

Mumon also composed a verse starting with, 'Dog – Buddha-nature.' But for your sake, I suggest you substitute 'myself – self – me' for 'dog.' This then raises the problem of the nature of reality, of everything. It is a world in which there is no duality or opposition. But the moment you judge or evaluate in dualistic terms, this world in which there are no opposites, the life of Buddha-nature and of your own life will split asunder. It is not that life ends; but rather that you are then no longer able to see reality for what it is.

CASE 2 · HYAKUJO'S FOX

Whenever Master Hyakujo assembled his monks for teisho, there was an old man who always followed everyone to listen to the Dharma. When the others withdrew, he also withdrew. Unexpectedly one day he did not leave. The master then asked, 'Who is the one who again stands before me?' The old man replied, 'Actually, I am not a human being. In the past, in the time of Kasyapa Buddha, I lived on this mountain. At that time, a monk asked, "Does an enlightened person also fall under the law of cause and effect, or not?" Because I replied, "He is not subject to cause and effect", I have fallen into the body of a wild fox for five hundred births. Now I beg you, Master, to reverse this by a turning word and kindly release me from this wild fox.'

Thereupon the old man asked, 'Does an enlightened person still fall under the law of cause and effect, or not?'

The master said, 'He does not obscure cause and effect.'

At these words, the old man experienced great enlightenment. Bowing, he said, 'I have cast off the body of the wild fox. I will remain at the back of this mountain. May I please request a funeral in accord with the precedent for deceased monks.'

The master ordered the head monk to beat the clappers to announce that after the meal everyone was to attend a monk's funeral. The monks all discussed this. In the entire assembly all were well, and in the Nirvana Hall (infirmary) too no person was ill. What did this mean?

After the midday meal it came to pass that the master led all of them to the bottom of a rockface behind the mountain. With his staff he poked and brought forth a dead fox. Then he performed a cremation ceremony.

Towards evening the master ascended the rostrum and explained what had happened earlier. Thereupon Obaku asked, 'The old man made a mistake with his answer of the turning word and was thrown into the body of a wild fox for five hundred years. On the other hand, what if his answer had not been wrong, then what?'

'Come forward,' said Hyakujo, 'and I will explain.' Obaku came forward and gave the master a smack. The master clapped his hands and laughing said, 'I thought that the barbarian had a red beard, but there is another barbarian with a red beard.'

MUMON'S COMMENT

Not falling into cause and effect, why sinking into a wild fox? Not obscursing causation, why released from a fox's body? If with regard to all of this you have the single eye, then you are able to realise how the former Hyakujo was able to roam freely through five hundred lifetimes (as a fox).

THE VERSE

不落不昧
兩采一賽
不昧不落
千錯萬錯

Not falling, not obscuring,
Two sides, one coin,
Not obscuring, not falling,
A thousand mistakes, ten thousand errors.

The protagonist of today's teisho is Master Hyakujo. Among the many patriarchal Zen Masters, and in China alone there were one thousand seven hundred of them, Master Hyakujo has a prominent position. In Zen temples in China, there is, of course always an image of Sakyamuni. But in addition there is also an image of Bodhidharma, flanked on his right by the image of Master Baso, and on the other side by the image of Master Hyakujo. In Zen temples in Japan, we worship Bodhidharma every morning, along with, Master Rinzai, the founder of the Rinzai school, Master Hyakujo and Master Kido, who was influential in the transmission of Zen from China to Japan.

Thus Master Hyakujo outshone all others, even though his teacher, Master Baso Doitsu, had the largest number of disciples out of all the patriarchal masters. Those who attained satori under him and became excellent roshis or good teachers (*chishiki*) numbered ninety-four. Three among these are called the Three Sages: they are Hyakujo, Nansen, who was the teacher of Master Joshu and Master Chizo of Seido. The reason why Master Hyakujo is so highly respected is because of the high spiritual state (*kyogai*) he attained and because he was an outstanding teacher, but that is not all.

Buddhism came to China in the first century CE, and in the following centuries sutras were translated and interpreted, temples were built, statues of the Buddha crafted and Buddhist art flourished. At the beginning of the sixth century, Bodhidharma came to China from India and transmitted the true spirit of Buddhism. Though he himself never used the word Zen, people in later times referred to the true spirit of Buddhism taught by Bodhidharma as Zen. Those monks who trained in the spirit of Bodhidharma did not at first form any groups. They trained separately in the various temples that they happened to belong to. Therefore, the lifestyle of the Zen monks was not clearly defined. It was under these circumstances that Master Hyakujo for the first time set down rules for the life of the monks.

Even today in China and Japan, the rules established by Master Hyakujo play a pivotal role in the life of Zen monks. These rules are necessary for Zen training, but they also embody the fundamental spiritual state according to which experienced monks function. Joshu's koan 'Mu' exemplifies this fundamental spiritual state that Zen trainees have to attain. And those who have attained this state have to function in accordance with it in daily life. Zen monks function as Zen monks, and ordinary people function as ordinary people, according to the spiritual state of the heart they have attained. Therefore, the theme of today's koan looks at the subtle functioning in accordance with the spiritual state attained through Joshu's 'Mu.'

One day, a training monk asked Hyakujo, 'What is the most wonderful thing in this world?' To this Master Hyakujo answered, 'Sitting alone on Mount Daiyu.' This story is taken from the *Blue Cliff Records*. Daiyu, the name of the mountain, means great and wonderful. People who read the words 'Sitting alone on Mount Daiyu' in Chinese characters get the impression of something great and courageous. They feel as if they were sitting alone on top of the Himalayan mountains with the whole world in their belly. But this is not the true meaning of these words. 'I am here now. What else can be more wonderful than that?' That was the spiritual state Hyakujo was in.

I am giving a teisho here and now. You are listening to the teisho here and now. There is nothing more wonderful than this situation. If I put it like this, there may be some among you who think that what is wonderful is listening to the teisho. But that is not so.

When this teisho is finished and we have rested awhile, the bell rings. We all go to the dining room to dine. I am dining in the dining room here and now; and you are also dining in the dining room here and now. There is nothing more wonderful than that. But again, if I put it like this, you might think that what is wonderful is doing something together. But that is not so.

In his spiritual state, Master Hyakujo recognises nothing more valuable than that he is here now, whether he is in heaven or hell. And for him, there is no heaven or hell. Those who look at Hyakujo from the outside might think that now Hyakujo is happy, or now Hyakujo is unhappy. But that is nothing more than judging something from the outside. For Hyakujo himself, there is neither happiness nor unhappiness. The Buddha-nature of Hyakujo shines here and now, and that is all. The koan of Hyakujo's Fox arises from that spiritual state Hyakujo has attained.

Another famous story about Hyakujo exemplifies the importance he placed on work. Naturally, the way the heart functions is reflected in the way the body functions. He did not stop working even when he was eighty years old. His disciples worried about him and felt concerned that he was still working. Not having arrived at the spiritual state of their master, they thought that Hyakujo was making an effort to be an example to them. But actually this was simply Hyakujo's natural spiritual state, as natural as water running from a high place to a lower place.

To prevent Hyakujo from working, the disciples hid all his tools one day. So Hyakujo did not work that day, but neither did he eat. Again the disciples became concerned about Hyakujo because he would not eat, and they begged him to eat. Hyakujo's answer has become very famous in the Zen school: 'If I don't work for one day, I don't eat for one day.'

When I told this story to a young Japanese student, he said, 'Then Zen is the same as Communism.' He probably remembered the words, 'He who does not work shall not eat.' But that is a completely different. Hyakujo did not say to other people, 'If you don't work, you should not eat.' If people start saying that to one another, then quarrels will arise. Hyakujo simply did not want to eat when he had not worked. This came from his fundamental spiritual state, the circumstances of the heart.

One day in this state, as Hyakujo walked around the mountain at the back of his temple where he worked all day, this story of the fox must have occurred to him.

Please divide the English translation you have of this case into three parts. Part One ends where the fox asks Hyakujo, 'Please cremate my body as a monk.' Part Two ends with the words, 'And so he had the body of the fox cremated.' The rest makes up Part Three of this case.

I am going to start the comments on this case from the beginning of Part Two. If you had read the case from the beginning, you might have thought that what happened on Mount Hyakujo was so miraculous that it could not happen in this world. But there is nothing miraculous in this world. All the miracles happen in peoples' minds. Hyakujo must have come across the body of a dead fox on the mountain at the back of the temple, and out of the great compassion of his heart, he made up this story for his monks.

Therefore, after lunch he told all the monks in the temple to gather in order to attend a funeral for a monk. Everyone was puzzled, as there was no monk who had been ill and died. Master Hyakujo, taking all the monks with him, climbed the mountain at the back of the temple. He pulled out the body of a dead fox from behind a rock and cremated it in the way that monks are cremated when they die. That night he called all the monks and told this story.

Now I will comment on Part One of the case.

Master Hyakujo said, 'You might have not noticed that every time I gave teisho, there was an old man sitting behind you at the back of the hall. When the teisho was finished, the old man always disappeared. But one day, after everybody else had left the hall and returned to the zendo, this old monk stayed behind. I asked him, "Who are you?" He answered, "I am not a human. I am a fox now. But a long, long time ago I used to be the head priest of this temple. One day a training monk came to me and asked, whether after you attain satori through training, you still fall under the law of cause and effect?"'

Here I'd like to add a comment. In the long history of human beings, people have always made efforts to go from hell to heaven, from misfortune to happiness. In ancient times in India, it was thought that there were many other places apart from hell. It was believed that, depending on how we spent our life, we could be reborn as an animal, as a hungry ghost, or as fighting demons. This is called the constant revolving on the wheel of life and death. This was simply a figment of the imagination, like a ghoul or a ghost. But those who believed in it had a strong desire to escape this continuing cycle on the wheel of life and death. People nowadays might not believe in this revolving on wheel of life and death, nonetheless, they may have fears, that their actions today may affect their life in five or even ten years' time and this idea instils fear in everyone's heart.

This fear felt by everyone, is represented by the question of this monk who asked, 'Can you escape the law of cause and effect, if you train and attain satori?' To that the old man had answered, 'If you attain satori, you can escape the law of cause and effect, you will not fall under the law of cause and effect.' But his answer seems to have been wrong, and he was fated to be reborn as a fox for five hundred lifetimes.

Therefore, the old man asked Hyakujo, 'Please help me with your strength to escape from being a fox.' And the old man, then assuming the role of that monk who had asked him that very question, asked Hyakujo, 'If you attain satori, will you still be subject to the law of cause and effect?' Hyakujo answered: 'You would not obstruct the law of cause and effect.' On hearing this, the old man attained satori, and was able to escape from the body of a fox. And he said, 'I am now back to being a monk. The body of the dead fox is on the mountain at the back of the temple. Please cremate it in the way that monks are.'

Hyakujo then said to the monks, 'That is why, after lunch, I took you all and climbed the mountain for the funeral of this fox.'

This is a rather alarming koan. What do you think it means, not being able to obstruct the law of cause and effect? Does that mean that there is no point in training and you have to give up all your hopes, because your fate is absolutely inevitable? No, that is not it. But then what is the true meaning of these words? What was it that Hyakujo wanted to convey? Not what he meant by these words, but the life he suggested through them.

This is one koan. The next koan: If you say that if you train and attain satori, you are not subject to the law of cause and effect, is that really wrong? Is it the right answer to say if you trained and attained satori, you would not obscure the law of cause and effect?

Supposing there was a mountain at the back of my temple, Daishu-in, and a monk was living there as a fox. A long time ago, he was reborn as a fox because he said, if you trained and attained satori, you would not obscure the law of cause and effect. He came to me and I told him that if you trained and attained satori, you would not be subject to the law of cause and effect and he attained satori. Now I am giving to you another koan on top of Hyakujo's koan, as a present.

When Hyakujo told all the monks this story that evening, there was a monk called Obaku among them. He was to become the teacher of Master Rinzai, who established the Rinzai school. He had already attained satori, but he was cultivating his spiritual state on Mount Hyakujo. As soon as Hyakujo finished telling the story, Obaku came forward and asked the question, 'If this old man who gave a wrong answer had given the right answer, what would he have happened then? Would he have remained a human instead of becoming a fox, or would he have been reborn in heaven?' This is indeed a wonderful question. Obaku's ear was not deceived either by the words that no one can set aside the law of cause and effect, or that you can set aside the law of cause and effect.

Obaku was not bound, and he was not caught by the fishing net that Hyakujo had cast at the monks, and being free, he had grasped the core of the story. That is why Obaku was able to ask such a question. Hearing this, Hyakujo was delighted, because he had found a wonderful opponent in playing a game. So Hyakujo told Obaku to come closer, which is like being told to come closer by a lion. If you go closer, you will probably have your head bitten off! But Obaku turned out to be an even stronger lion. As soon as he got close to Hyakujo, Obaku hit him before Hyakujo could hit Obaku.

There was once a training monk who, having heard this story, hit Zuigan Roshi during the interview. Zuigan Roshi, used to sit with his legs crossed when he gave interviews. The training monk who came for the interview had not been able to answer the koan for some months, so he copied Obaku, because he did not have the answer. Because he hit him so hard, Master Zuigan fell over backwards. Zuigan then chased him out of the room. This is the wonderful function of Master Zuigan.

When Hyakujo was hit by Obaku, he knew very well why he had hit him. Therefore, Hyakujo did not say, 'And then what?' Instead he was so delighted that he burst out laughing and said, 'Here is someone equal to Bodhidharma.' The English translation of the Chinese literally is, 'I thought only that barbarian had a red beard, but here is another one with a red beard.' The translation I have given you is very free, but points to the meaning. As the words imply, Hyakujo recognised Obaku's spiritual state; indeed, he gave the authentication. But why? What was it that Hyakujo saw in Obaku that so delighted him in being hit by his disciple? It was not Master Hyakujo, his teacher, that he hit. Then what was it that he hit? What was it that he struck? Unfortunately, I cannot give you the answer because this is the third important koan.

However, I have already given you a clue to this koan at the beginning of this teisho – 'Sitting alone on Mount Daiyu.' There is nothing more wonderful than that; being here and now. And that wonderful moment is not limited to this present moment, but continues on like that into the next moment, and the next. Neither being subject to the law of cause and effect nor not being subject to the law of cause and effect, can interfere with it. Neither happiness nor unhappiness can intrude. There is no chance for either hell or heaven to intrude. There is no illusion whatsoever. Simply living in this moment here and now, and that moment continues for ever. Healthy people in the state of health, ailing people in the state of illness; the foolish and the wise, the beautiful people and the plain; the low-ranking and the high. The Buddha-nature shines in all as they are, here and now, each in their own spiritual state.

You might get the wrong impression and think that the Buddha-nature would not shine, even if you didn't function in some way. The Buddha-nature shines as you talk and as you listen. The Buddha-nature shines as you eat, as you work, and as you sleep. The Buddha-nature shines when you are immersed in the samadhi of the loo, and when you are immersed in the samadhi of the bath. Mumon adds in his comment that if a person lives such a life, they could live a wonderful life even if they met the fate of being reborn as a fox five hundred lifetimes.

Now that we have come to the end of this teisho, why don't we call Obaku back?

CASE 3 · GUTEI RAISES A FINGER

Whenever Master Gutei was asked to say something [about Zen], he merely raised one finger. Latterly he had a young attendant, who on being asked by visitors what the master taught as his essential teaching, likewise raised his finger. On hearing about this Gutei cut off the boy's finger with a knife. Crying in pain, the acolyte turned and fled. Gutei called after him. The acolyte turned his head and Gutei once again raised his finger. The acolyte was suddenly enlightened. When Gutei was about to die, he spoke to the assembly, saying, 'I received one-finger Zen from Tenryu, and for my entire life I made use of it without exhausting it.' When he finished speaking, he passed away.

MUMON'S COMMENT

The insight of both Gutei and the acolyte, does not depend on raising a finger. If you are able to see into this deeply, then Tenryu, Gutei, the acolyte and you yourself are all strung together on a single thread.

THE VERSE

俱胝鈍置老天龍
利刃單提勘小童
巨靈擡手無多子
分破華山千万重

Gutei made fun of old Tenryu,
The young boy sustained the thrust of a single sharp blade,

The river-spirit raised his hand and with a little effort
Breaking apart the many ridges of Mount Hua.

SOKO ROSHI'S COMMENTS

After I gave the talk yesterday afternoon, I became a little bit worried
that you may have misunderstood what I had said. Sure enough, after
the teisho, one person, representing several others, came to tell me
how they had felt on hearing my story, and wondering whether they
had understood it correctly. He said, 'When we heard that story, we
thought that you had to undergo great hardships in order to become
a roshi, and that it was not possible to become a good roshi without
undergoing such hardship.' So I told him that they were mistaken,
and that I would explain it to them in detail at today's teisho.

When you hear someone tell a story like that, it always sounds
very difficult. The day before yesterday, during our afternoon talk,
I explained to you verbally how you should walk. At that time, I just
gave a rough explanation, but if I had explained it in detail physiologi-
cally or in terms of the force of gravity, I could have written a book on
it. And yet even a child can walk! You would get stuck in your training
if you started feeling that it was very hard, and then you wouldn't be
able to continue in your training. On hearing my story, you may have
thought that I had been through a very hard training, but I myself do
not feel that I have gone through a hard training. All I have done is to
follow the training from moment to moment. If you saw a man on top
of a high mountain as you stood at the bottom, you might think that
he must have gone through great difficulty to get up there. But all he
did was to walk step by step to get there. If you stopped comparing
where you are with the top of the mountain, and just walked step by
step, then you would find that what had soared above you the day
before is now below your feet.

Once there was a young man training at the monastery of Daitoku-ji in Kyoto who had come from Guatemala in Central America. Round about mid-November, he began to grow paler and paler, because the December Rohatsu Sesshin was approaching. He had heard from other monks in the monastery how terrifying the Rohatsu Sesshin was. So every day, he went round asking the monks, 'Do you think that I will be able to sit through the Rohatsu Sesshin?' No one, of course, could answer such a question, as that was his own problem.

In the end, on the last day of November, just one day before the Rohatsu Sesshin started, he came to consult me, because he couldn't stand it any longer. At that time, I was the *jikijitsu*. He asked me the same question; he wanted to know whether I thought he would be able to sit through the Rohatsu Sesshin. I asked him, 'Can you sit through one period?', and he answered 'Of course, I can.' So I replied, 'Then you should be able to sit through the Rohatsu Sesshin. At the Rohatsu Sesshin, you do not sit through for one week. You just sit through for one period. When you have sat through one period, cast away that one period, and then sit for another one period. Do not think of the sitting periods that are to come. If you find that even one period is too long for you, then just sit for that single moment. Sit for the single moment, and then again, sit for the single moment. That moment is not any moment. The whole history is contained in that single moment. Without this single moment, ten thousand years would not be able to come into being. If you were able to sit for the single moment, you would be able to understand the Zen saying, "Ten thousand years lie in a single moment of profound contemplation – you live ten thousand years in a single moment."' He decided to put the advice I gave him into practice and was able to sit the Rohatsu Sesshin through to the end.

When the Rohatsu Sesshin finished, he came running to me delighted and told me excitedly that he had been able to sit it through. This is one form of satori. The Japanese word satori means 'to obliterate the distance between oneself and the other.' He may not have been able to close the distance between himself and the Rohatsu Sesshin completely, but he had certainly diminished the distance.

When you see me meditating absolutely motionless from nine-thirty to eleven, you may feel that there is a gap between you and myself. However, I am not sitting motionless for an hour and a half. What I am doing is sitting for that present moment only. You may stretch your legs and move your body during the *kinhin*, but if you learn to sit moment by moment during the whole period, the gap between us will diminish.

On encountering a misfortune, there are some people who think that such a misfortune only happens to them. But, in fact, it is something that everybody encounters, though at a different time and in a different place. If someone who happens to be on holiday passes by you when you are working, does that mean that he is fortunate and you are unfortunate? That is not so. You may have walked past him as he worked when you were on holiday.

It is not by doing something special or different from others that we become a better person. Rather it is by doing the same thing as others, but doing it more wholeheartedly that we become a better person. A person who learns and ponders the same things as others, but experiences it more wholeheartedly, values each and every moment of their lives and develops compassion, which is the love of the Buddha. What closes the gap between oneself and others is the realisation that whatever one experiences is also experienced by others. It is a big mistake to think that what you experience is something very different from what someone else experiences, or to think that what someone else experiences is something very different from what you experience.

My teacher, Master Zuigan, never praised any of his disciples. However, on one occasion, he agreed with what I said. When I first started training, I felt hopeless about my ability to do the training, and despaired. Most people, when they start Zen training, alternate between feeling that they have become a wonderful person and thinking that they are utterly hopeless, and, like the waves, these feelings toss them to-and-fro. Everyone here must have felt the same way at one time or another. I, too, was suffering from a sort of inferiority complex, feeling that I was no good. Finding me in such a state one day, Master Zuigan said, 'How is it going? Are you going to give up training?' and I answered, 'No, I am not going to give up training, because, hopeless as I am, if I managed to go through this training, that will be a proof that anyone can go through this training.' That was the only time that Master Zuigan smiled and said, 'That's a very good idea.' And here I am now giving you a teisho, so don't give up!

Each present moment contains a vast length of time, and each of you contains everyone else within yourself. No matter how small a thing is, it contains everything in itself. There is no distance in between things. The ultimate state of satori is not to understand this in your mind, but to experience feeling it in your heart.

I have not been saying these things just as an answer to the question that you asked me yesterday afternoon, but also as an overture to today's koan on Master Gutei. Master Gutei is not as famous as Joshu or Hyakujo, whom I commented on in the previous two koans. Master Gutei lived in China in the ninth century. The only thing that he did during his teaching life was to hold up one finger. He was living in a little temple in the mountains without having attained satori. He seems to have been a serious-minded person, for he chanted a formula in a sutra called the *Gutei Butsumo Sutra* (*Jundei Kannon Sutra*) every day. That is why he was called Master Gutei. The real name is not known.

One day, a training nun came to his temple. She did not take off her hat as she should have done as a matter of courtesy. She kept it on and walked around Master Gutei three times, then stood arrogantly in front of him. So Master Gutei said, 'Why don't you take that hat off?' She answered, 'If you could say that one word, then I will take off my hat.'

Master Gutei was a Zen monk, so that one word must embrace the whole world. It must contain the true essence of Buddhism. Master Gutei could not say that one word, so the nun was about to walk away quickly, looking as if she felt that it was no use staying with a fool like this. It was dusk, and so it was getting dark. Master Gutei couldn't help saying, 'Why don't you stay for one night, as it is getting dark.' But the nun answered, 'If you could say that one word, then I will stay.' Again, Master Gutei failed to give the answer, and so the nun went away.

That night, Master Gutei could not sleep. He said to himself, 'Outwardly I may look as if I were a fine monk, but inwardly I am hopeless. I am now living in this temple, but I am not qualified to be a head priest. Tomorrow at dawn, I shall start out on a training journey, carrying my luggage.' Having decided to do so, Master Gutei eventually fell asleep, and in a dream, he saw someone like a god, and this god said to him, 'There is no need for you to start out on a training journey, for a living Buddha is coming here very soon.' So he decided to wait for him.

Then a monk called Master Tenryu came to the temple on a journey. Master Tenryu was the Dharma-heir of Master Daibai Hojo, and Master Daibai Hojo was the Dharma-heir of the famous Master

Baso Doitsu. When Gutei saw Master Tenryu, he thought that this must be the living Buddha. Assuming the role of the nun, Master Gutei asked him the question that the nun had asked him, 'If you could say that one word, then I will take off my hat.' Master Tenryu held up one finger. When Gutei saw that finger, all doubts disappeared, and he attained a wonderful satori.

This is the crux of today's koan. You must not ponder on the meaning of Tenryu's finger. The important thing is that you face up to this question as if it were directed to you here and now, instead of thinking that these things happened in the ninth century. Everything is contained in that one word – the whole universe, the long history, yourself and others. That one word must not be what someone else has said, but a word that has welled up from the depth of you heart.

Since I arrived in London, I have shaken hands with some people. I have said, 'How are you?' and they have said, 'Very well.' Then I have said, 'Is that true?' Have you understood what I was getting at? They were telling a lie. They said, 'Very well,' but on being asked, 'Is it true?', they said, 'No, I'm not.' If you gave such an answer, the nun would never stay for one night at your temple.

Please recall what I said at an earlier teisho. Do not think that in Zen training there are special words that only the Zen monks can understand. I may be wearing something different from you, but if I don't eat, I will get hungry; when I do eat, that is bound to come out somehow. I experience the same sorts of things as you do, I think about the same things as you do, and I cry and laugh in the same ways as you do. I have trained for a long time, and so I have experienced some things that if you knew about them, you may think it terribly hard, but I have not become anything other than a human being. Still, I don't think that I have trained in vain, because now I am laughing, crying, living in health and coping with illness with my heart always at ease. If that nun came to me when I lay fast asleep and kicked the pillow off from under my head and demanded me to say that one word, I could answer without a moment of thought. After he gained satori, Gutei answered every question throughout his life by holding up one finger.

One young disciple training under Gutei imitated what he did. Among my own disciples there is also one disciple who is good at imitating the way I speak, and another who is good at imitating the way I walk. This young disciple also imitated Gutei by holding up one finger. If someone said, 'Hey, novice, is the Master in?', he would hold up one finger. If someone else asked, 'Novice, where are you going?', he would hold up one finger.

Gutei happened to hear about that and he called the novice to his room and asked him, 'What is the true essence of the Buddha-dharma?' The novice, out of habit, held up one finger. At that moment, Gutei grabbed the finger and, taking a knife out that he had hidden down his sleeve, he cut that finger off. The novice was startled and started running away, when Gutei accosted him in a firm voice, 'Novice!' When the novice stopped and turned round, Gutei held up one finger.

That is the story in *Mumonkan*. However, when Master Zuigan commented on this case in his teisho, he put it differently. When the novice started to run away, Gutei called to him to stop. The novice stopped and turned round in spite of himself, and Gutei asked him fiercely, 'What is the true essence of the Buddha-dharma?' The novice held up one finger on impulse, but his finger wasn't there anymore, and at that moment he gained satori. Either story will do, but I introduced Master Zuigan's version because I found it very powerful.

The end of this koan tells the story of Gutei on his deathbed. As Gutei was about to take his last breath, he called all his disciples round him. He showed his finger to everyone, saying, 'I used this all my life, and yet I could not exhaust it. Look at this well.' And then he breathed his last. Please don't just be impressed by the way he died. No matter how much satori one has attained, one might still die in great pain. The wonderful thing is that Gutei had just one treasure, and he used it throughout his life but could not exhaust it.

What is the treasure that one uses all one's life and yet, no matter how much you use it, you cannot exhaust it? It is no use travelling all over the world in search of this treasure. Gutei had it, I have it, and you all have it. The only difference is whether you use it or not.

Something that you use all your life and yet cannot exhaust, something that does not wear out even if you use it throughout your life. What is that? It would be a great mistake to think that saying it was the Buddha-nature would suffice. The Buddha-nature is just a name. It must be alive and functioning. The Buddha-nature must be alive and functioning – what does that mean? The whole of life is contained in this word. Everybody is contained in oneself. All one's life is contained in this present moment. In each step we take, everything is contained. What is important is to experience that feeling.

The thing is to live this moment, here and now. Yesterday, I told you the story of Hyakujo in which he is asked, 'What is the most wonderful thing in this world?' and he answers, 'Sitting alone on top of Mount Daiyu.' The crux of this case is that each of you live in that spiritual state. We will finish here today.

CASE 4 · WAKUAN'S 'WHY NO BEARD?'

Wakuan said, 'Why does the Barbarian from the West have no beard?'

Training must be real training, satori must be real satori. Once the barbarian's true face has been intimately seen into, it has been attained. But when you explain what you have seen, you have already made it into two.

癡人面前
不可説夢
胡子鬚無
惺惺添懵

Do not tell your dream
To a fool.
The barbarian without a beard –
Adding obscurity to clarity.

The Chinese expression above, literally translated as the 'Barbarian from the West', means foreigners to the west of China, probably referring to India. Because Bodhidharma, the first Zen patriarch, came from there, he is known as the Barbarian from the West. Wakuan asks, 'Why does Bodhidharma not have a beard?'. You have all seen pictures of Bodhidharma and will know that he is always portrayed with a beard. Chinese, Koreans and Japanese do not have heavy beards, and from their point of view, not only Bodhidharma, but western barbarians in general are rather hairy! In Zen paintings someone with a heavy beard is likely to indicate Bodhidharma. And yet Wakuan asks why Bodhidharma has no beard!

In Zen stories, and in koans, whoever is introduced, be it a Buddha or one of the ancient patriarchs, they always refer to ourselves. So, ask yourself why it is that you do not have a beard? And women, who do not have beards, may ask themselves, why it is that they do not have any hair – or why do I have no eyes, no ears or no nose? In the *Heart Sutra* it is said that there are no eyes, no ears, no mouth, nothing! So, when chanting the *Hannya Shingyo*, the *Heart Sutra*, we are reminded of it again.

Tozan, one of the great Chinese masters, entered temple life at the age of seven. He was first taught the *Heart Sutra*. In Japanese temples, too, it was the custom to instruct very young novices by knocking the *Heart Sutra* into them, word by word. Tozan probably also learnt it this way. But when he came to the section 'no eyes, no ears, no mouth,' he was stunned. He touched his eyes, his ears, his nose, to check, and then asked the instructor, 'But surely I have eyes, a nose, and ears; why is it said that I do not?' Unfortunately, the instructor was not enlightened, merely someone with a shaven head and wearing a robe. Startled by this question, he realised that he could not help this young novice and advised him to see a monk who had attained enlightenment.

Tozan then practised for years and came to realise that, in fact, he had no eyes, no ears, no mouth, etc. He became one of the founders of the Soto Zen tradition which Master Dogen introduced to Japan. Dogen said, 'To know Zen is to forget oneself.' This is a well-known saying, but few people realise that it means one does not have eyes, ears or nose, etc. Rather, it is usually understood as forgetting oneself by an act of will. But one cannot do that. One cannot, by using one's own will, make oneself into nothing – in fact, there is nothing! It is not that one wills oneself to forget oneself, or to drop oneself, one is intrinsically in that state from the beginning. It is not that one gets rid of one's eyes, mouth, or ears by willing it! Originally, from the beginning, they did not inherently exist, have not been there. It is we who create them, make them up by our own will.

A young man once came to me and told me he was having difficulty with his parents and was very unhappy. He cried and said he wanted to do his best for his parents. This took place between him and me. His parents were not present; he could not see them face to face, nor hear them, he only felt deep love towards them. Back at home, however, actually being with his parents in the flesh, the same difficulties persisted. The same also applies to other relationships. A woman came to see me who had just quarrelled with her husband. Having married for love, while talking to me that love welled up naturally and she planned to cook a really good meal to await him when he came home tired from work. But when her husband arrived, all those good resolutions were forgotten, and again they quarrelled. Do you remember similar situations in your own life?

When we create images in which the other person has such eyes, or that kind of nose, and such a character, then we cannot improve our relationship with that person. But is such a construct that we have built up ourselves the real person we have dealings with? Yet not only do we define those we have dealings with like this, we also define ourselves in that way. I have this face, this body, this personality, these abilities. If this sticks to you, you carry it around with you whatever you do.

Another time, a mother came and brought her child with her.

'This child is lazy and stupid from birth.' Have you ever seen a lazy baby? Or a child so stupid that by the time it is three it cannot master some speech? Have you seen a child that only complains and never does anything? It is not so from birth. But the parent has decided that is the way the child is.

So, in the case of 'no beard' or 'no hair,' it is not enough to try to approach it conceptually. Think of yourself as an infant. If it is difficult to put yourself into this situation, imagine looking at an infant. As we grow older, we tend to be less interested in things, and accordingly simply label them as valuable or as of no value. An infant, however, does no such thing; it is fascinated by everything that is around, even in dust or rubbish, and grasps for it. Some infants when learning to crawl, push backwards when trying to move forwards and so get further away from what they want to reach, and begin to cry. However, they will not give up! They try again and again with the same result, backwards rather than forwards, not just for a day, or a week, but struggling on and on until eventually they are able to move forward. If a reporter came to interview such an infant and asked it 'How's it going?', it would probably reply, 'Oh, it's very, very tough!' But in time the child learns to move forward, to grab hold of things, and to stand up. Yet it does not then congratulate itself and boast that it has made a tremendous advance. Rather, it lets go of what it had attained and gives itself to the next 'practice', learning to stand up by holding on to what is at hand. And once it has learned to heave itself up, again it lets go of what it had clung to in order to stand up, and now tries to walk.

In the development of a child there is no sense of limit, of having achieved my aim and this is where I stop. Rather, a fascination operates in the child from moment to moment. Of course, the child is not able to walk immediately and so it cries, but then tries again, just as when it was learning to crawl; and again after repeated efforts it manages to walk. A child neither feels that it cannot change, nor that it must try to change. But once we have grown up, we all want to change ourselves, yet we do not change. Now you are reading in familiar English, but you do not understand. A newly born infant does not have any language. From its point of view, strange shapes appear and peer down at it. They then say that its nose looks like daddy's, the eyes are like mummy's, the slight turn of the mouth is exactly like granny's; hearing such and other things and repeating, the child begins to learn to speak. We all were like that; why then have we frozen up like ice? Why is it that we have come to have fixed ears, eyes, noses that we cannot change? In defining oneself and others, and then defining the relationship to each other, what originally was free is made into some difficult relationship. Thus, when Wakuan asked 'Why does Bodhidharma have no beard?', he was urging people to find in themselves the Bodhidharma that does not have eyes or ears or a mouth, the Bodhidharma within oneself, and also the Bodhidharma within this or that person. When we have achieved that, then we can freely change relationships. Everything that comes out of this is of itself limitless.

In autumn, the farmers burn off all that is left on their fields, and so leave them fallow during the winter. Nor does anybody believe that the grass has gone for good; in spring, with warm rain and mild breezes, it begins to grow again. Whatever face we may have, whatever state or ability, whatever our relationships with others, it is like the grass in the meadows – it does not end. Put a match to them and burn away eyes and nose and ears, everything, and become 'MU!' At that instant new grass begins to emerge. That is the original working of the Buddha-nature.

Mumon then added a comment, *shugyo* – training – must be real training, or training directed at real things. Conceptualised, intellectualised practice is no good, nor is a practice that is only an imitation, a style. Satori, too, must be real, direct satori. A true satori is one which is useful to us in our daily lives. It is not something that can be reduced to some kind of knowledge, or something that can be bandied about by means of words. To achieve satori, we have to see, at least once, the face of Bodhidharma without a beard, or eyes, or mouth. However, we should not then jump to the conclusion that we now have got it! Seeing the face of Bodhidharma makes Bodhidharma an outside object, and that is not the true Bodhidharma in oneself. When you say, 'I understand, I have grasped that beardless Bodhidharma,' then at that moment oneself and Bodhidharma have become separate. Meeting Bodhidharma directly is the instinctive, the spontaneous working of the Buddha-nature within, not being taken in by somebody's face, not being captivated by one's own condition, simply and naturally reaching a point where one can look at things as they are, or hear them as they are.

Mumon also composed a verse which in a sense is a response to Wakuan. 'Hi, Wakuan, you shouldn't tell fanciful tales to foolish people, you only cause them to go further astray.' Tales of Bodhidharma without a beard will only obscure things, cloud the vision of those who are moving into the light. So, in place of Mumon's verse, I am offering you another: 'Do not steal up to a sleeping child and yell at it, "Sleep well!"'

Do you understand? If not, treat it as a koan and work on it until you do.

CASE 5 · KYOGEN'S MAN UP A TREE

Master Kyogen said, 'It is like a man up a tree, holding onto a branch with his mouth, his hands not clinging to any branch, his feet not resting on any limb. Under the tree there is someone asking the meaning of Bodhidharma's coming from the West. If he does not reply, then he disregards what the other asked; if he does answer, then he injures himself and loses his life. What is correct now, what answer can you give?'

Even if there is the eloquence of a flowing river, all is to no avail. Even if one can expound upon the entire great treasure-house of the (Buddha's) Teachings, that too is of no avail. If you can clearly answer this from within, then you now give life to the way that was dead before and destroy the way that previously was alive. If, however, you are unable to do this, then you have to wait for Maitreya to come and ask him.

香嚴眞杜撰
惡毒無盡限
唖却納僧口
通身迸鬼眼

Kyogen was truly fabricating,
His evil poisons are without limit,

He immediately silences the mouths of the monks,
The whole body sprouting demon's eyes.

You all look as if you were getting rather tired from the efforts you have been making to concentrate during zazen. If you get tired as a result of making such efforts, you may be making the wrong kind of efforts. At the beginning of this Summer School, I told you that when you sit zazen, it is not you that sits. I told you not to try to concentrate with your willpower or try to do zazen for a long time with your willpower. Sit down on the cushion in the correct posture, and then give yourself into the care of something that is not yourself. After that, that something other than yourself which you don't know, will do the sitting; and that something that is not yourself is in fact the genuine self.

Try to be more resourceful when you go for a walk in the afternoon during the lunch break. I can see you walking around the grounds from my window. It is very interesting to observe so many ways of taking a walk. However, most of you, particularly those who belong to the Zen group, walk looking very serious. You look like Indian ascetics, or philosophers deep in thought, or Chinese martial arts practitioners.

However, I have noticed one lady who walks in a delightful way. She swings her arms, and at first I thought that she was doing it deliberately. But it seems that she does it all the time. Her whole body moves rhythmically in a lively way. She holds her neck up, and she is always smiling. She walks rhythmically, turning her head to take in all the scenery around her. She walked like that on the first day, and on the second day, and on the third day, and this morning as well. I could not help facing her with palms together and praying that she would continue to stay in the spiritual state that she is in now throughout her life, both in happiness and unhappiness.

Verbally, it may sound paradoxical, but to concentrate means to be delivered, to be set free, so another name for satori is deliverance. The Japanese word for deliverance is *gedatsu*. The first Chinese character *ge* means untying the knot, and the second Chinese character *datsu* means to be set free. The sitting posture of zazen looks very rigid, with your legs crossed and your hands folded, but inside there is the deliverance of the heart.

From my window, I could also see children playing outside, and it reminded me of my childhood. During the summer vacation, I would leave home immediately after lunch and go somewhere where my parents couldn't find me, and return home in the evening when I got hungry. Then my mother would always ask me, 'What have you been doing all this time?', and I would always answer, 'I haven't been doing anything.' You also must have similar memories of your childhood, and so you know that when you said that, you didn't mean to tell a lie. Children are never aware of what games they are playing. That is because they are not playing games with their willpower, consciously trying to concentrate on them. Children spend their life from moment to moment in samadhi. I hope that by tomorrow, you will have learnt how to concentrate while being delivered at the same time.

We are always tied down by something or other in our lives. We can never live without being tied down to certain circumstances. People usually call these circumstances happiness or unhappiness. But what we call happiness or unhappiness is in fact the spiritual state that we are in, depending on our circumstances.

Now, let's begin today's case on Master Kyogen. Master Kyogen began his training under Master Hyakujo, but Master Hyakujo was already very old when Kyogen started his training, and he died shortly thereafter. So Kyogen went to Master Isan, who had inherited the Dharma from Master Hyakujo. Kyogen was very intelligent by nature and was very learned. When he was training under Hyakujo he was already well-known for his excellence throughout the Zen communities in China.

When Master Isan saw that Kyogen had come to continue his training under him after Hyakujo had died, the first thing that Master Isan said to him was, 'I understand that you are able to give ten answers if someone asks you one question, and a hundred answers if someone asks you ten. But I do not intend to ask you about anything that you have learned from outside yourself. I would like you to say the one word from before you came out of your mother's womb.'

This question may sound strange to you, but please recall what the nun said to Master Gutei in the Case 3, 'If you can say that one word, I will take my hat off.' Kyogen must have given him various answers. When he said, 'mu' (nothing), Master Isan must have said, 'Joshu has said that.' When Kyogen said 'ku' (emptiness), he must have said, 'That's in the *Heart Sutra*.'

Many of you here are probably married, but if you weren't, suppose that you were in love with someone and said 'I love you' to him or her, and your lover said, 'Many people have said that over centuries, so I want to hear something that only you can say to me.' What would you say then? Or suppose that your child said that he could not trust you unless you said that one true word, then what would you say to your child? Or suppose that your true friend was in deep despair, and he needed a word that showed your friendship to them. Then what would you say to them? It must not be a word borrowed from someone else, but something that you yourself have thought of.

Kyogen no longer could think of anything to say to Master Isan. He did zazen every day and pondered, he read many sutras and pondered, and went to Master Isan and gave him answers. But Master Isan always said, 'That is something you have learnt from outside yourself.'

In the end, Kyogen went to Master Isan and said, 'I just cannot think of that one word. Please, out of all your love as a teacher, tell me what that one word is.' Kyogen was earnest, but in fact what he said revealed contradictions, because Kyogen was asking his teacher to tell him what no one could tell him. Rightfully, Master Isan answered, 'I can tell you that one word, but if I did, that would be my answer, not yours.'

Therefore, Kyogen gave up training under Master Isan. He gave up trying to attain satori. Kyogen thought that he was carrying so much more karma than others that he could not possibly attain satori during this lifetime. But he thought that, even if he were not able to attain satori during this lifetime, he could still lessen his burden of karma in this life and attain satori when he was reborn in the next life. This way of thinking is typical of someone who is in doubt as to what he should do. But Kyogen was very earnest, so he left Mount Isan in tears.

Kyogen decided to go to the grave of the excellent National Teacher Echu, who had been a disciple of the Sixth Patriarch, and he swept and cleaned the grave every day. On the surface, he thought he had given up attaining satori, but deep down in his heart, he was still yearning for that one true word, and so it matured without his being aware of it.

One day, when Kyogen swept and cleaned the grave and threw the sweepings into the bamboo grove, a pebble in the garden waste hit a bamboo stem and made a sound, and on hearing that sound he attained satori.

This story is well-known and considered as a good example of how a Zen monk attains satori. However, if you could attain satori just by hearing a sound, anyone who can hear should be able to attain satori. Another monk attained satori when he saw a peach blossom. If you could attain satori on seeing a flower, everybody here should be able to gain satori at once. The important thing is that until that very moment when something triggers satori, something has been maturing or fermenting inside you for a long time.

The sound of a pebble hitting the bamboo was a sound that Kyogen had never heard before in his life. It was nothing but a sound made by the bamboo. If we put it in philosophical terms, we could call it pure experience. But what we call it is not important. What is important is whether or not that experience – of seeing it directly, hearing it directly, and touching it directly – has the power to change your life. After he experienced this, Kyogen was no longer the person he had been before he had that experience. Today's koan was born from what Kyogen experienced.

Ever since he left Mount Isan in despair, Kyogen had been on the edge of awakening. It was when he was pushed to the limit, that he happened to hear the sound that the bamboo made and gained satori. We seem to be seeking satori earnestly all the time, yet, in fact, we are often deceiving ourselves. Kyogen demonstrated this extreme situation to his disciples who were often deceiving themselves. Suppose that you were holding on to a branch of a tree by your mouth only, neither are your hands holding on to a bough or your feet touching a bough. You often see a similar sight at a circus, don't you? If you were in such a situation, and someone under the tree asks you for the truth of the Buddha-dharma, what would you do? Even if you were able to expound brilliantly on all Buddhist sutras, if you opened your mouth to do that you would fall from the tree and die. How would you answer? Hakuin put it into a question like this, 'Suppose that a terrifying demon got hold of you at the scruff of the neck, and threw you into a hole in which a fire was roaring – what would you say? How could you escape? How could you save yourself?'

Are you not pondering on this koan as if facing your actual death?

Actually, there is a terrifying demon behind each of you, and he has you by the scruff of the neck. He will cast you into heaven or hell, depending on the mood he is in. There is a demon behind me, too. He may have already cast me into the hell of cancer – I don't know, because I haven't seen the doctor. If I found out that I had cancer and that I would die very soon, what sort of peace could I maintain in my heart? That is the question that the koan is asking.

We live every day in changing circumstances. I have told you many times that it is an illusion to think that you could pick and choose what circumstance you live in. The graver the circumstance, the less possible it is for you to choose. What help could we get in such circumstances? That is what the koan is asking.

When I was still young and inexperienced in the training, I was very surprised when I heard one roshi say that if someone asked him the meaning of Bodhidharma's coming from the West, he could answer it straightway at any time. Anyone can give a teisho on the meaning of Bodhidhama's coming from the West if they have time to prepare for it. But I doubt if I could answer it at all times. If I were asked the question when I had a stomach ache, I may not be able to answer it, but I might be able to answer the question if I were in amenable circumstances, but not otherwise.

Yet I feel grateful to be able to say that now I am able to maintain the peace of my heart, because I no longer have to answer that question myself. Something other than myself that is in me is ready to answer it very freely for me. If 'I' tried to hear the sound of the bamboo, I wouldn't be able to hear it. If 'I' tried do see the flower, I wouldn't be able to take in even its colour. But now that I have learned not to see with my own eyes or to hear with my own ears, something other than myself will always see and hear.

A few years ago, an eighty-year-old Japanese historian came to see me. He had been born into one of the most famous aristocratic families in Japan. But at the age of eighty, he was still very unhappy. He openly cried, saying that he could not put up with the unhappy situation he was in any longer. Why was he so unhappy? He was born in an aristocratic family, so he was not brought up and looked after by his own mother. Moreover, when he was still very young, his mother got divorced from his father and left home. Apart from exchanging greetings in the mornings and in the evenings, he had very little contact with his father.

There were several people in charge of his education, and he learnt many poems and songs from an early age. He was by no means stupid, so he studied hard at the university and gained much knowledge. He had experienced and learned many things, but there was one thing that he had neither experienced nor learned, and that was the experience of coming into touch with something directly with a bare heart. He could not come into touch with things or people with his heart bared. Whenever he saw a flower, it reminded him of a famous poem that he knew and it interfered and prevented him from coming into touch with that flower directly. Whenever he met someone, the knowledge he had of some wonderful image from literature or art would interfere and prevent him from coming into direct contact with that person. He had many wonderful friends, but never experienced the contact of the heart. He married four times, but he failed to build a relationship with his wives with a bare heart. He said to me, 'There is not much time left for me, but before I die, I would like to experience being in touch with something or someone directly with a bare heart.'

Can you understand such pain as he felt? When you are still young, perhaps this sort of suffering doesn't strike you as much. When I was young, I thought that you lived your life to gain things. I thought life meant making efforts to gain physical strength, making efforts to gain friends, gain a family, and gain social status. But when I was round about forty, I realised that life meant losing more and more things. You forget all the things you have learnt. The body you've trained grows weaker. Your eyesight and your hearing deteriorate. Your teeth fall out. Your friends die and you lose your job. Your children leave home, and even your wife or your husband may die.

When he reached this state, this historian felt that he wanted just for once to experience being in touch with something with his bare heart, whether it brought him happiness or unhappiness. That is the question that Kyogen's koan is asking you. How can you live your life with a bare heart, irrespective of happiness or unhappiness?

CASE 6 · THE BUDDHA HOLDS UP A FLOWER

Once when the World-honoured One was at Spirit Mountain he held up and showed everyone in the assembly a flower. Everyone was silent. Only Kasyapa's countenance broke into a smile.

The World-honoured One said, 'I have the Treasury of the True Dharma Eye, the subtle heart of nirvana, the true form of no-form, the mysterious Dharma Gate, not relying on written words, a special transmission outside the teaching. I give and entrust it to Mahakasyapa.'

MUMON'S COMMENT

Golden-faced Gotama treated people as if they were nothing, he repressed the virtuous and made them worthless, sold dog-meat labelled as sheep's head, regarding this as more or less unique. But if at that time in question, the whole great assembly had smiled, how could the Treasury of the True Dharma Eye have been transmitted? And supposing that Kasyapa had not smiled, how would the Treasury of the True Dharma Eye then have been handed down? If you say that there is a transmission of the Treasury of the True Dharma Eye, then the Golden-faced old man would be shouting lies at the village gate.

THE VERSE
拈起花來
尾巴已露
迦葉破顏
人天罔措

Holding up a flower,
The snake reveals its tail,
Kasyapa's countenance broke into a smile,
People and demons are bewildered by this display.

SOKO ROSHI'S COMMENTS

The texts used in teishos are taken from Buddhist Sutras, and from the writings or records of the Zen patriarchs. Teisho is different than a lecture. The latter usually puts emphasis on either historical or on analytical presentation, or gives a close textual explanation of the material. Teisho, however, is not so much a lecture on a particular subject, or an effort to clarify a particular text, but rather presents a problem that may be reflected on by the listeners and is presented to you to ponder on. It is not to be understood through knowledge or learning. Taking up and pondering the problem that is presented, or a problem that presents a difficulty to you, may be used to try to open doors within yourself. So, the nature of teishos is such that, if you try to grasp them logically, they will defeat your understanding.

Some years ago, I was talking at the Buddhist Society, and I said, 'That which is standing before you is not a human being, but soap that was made in India, packaged in China, and labelled in Japan; so do not try to remember what I say to you.' What I said then, and repeat now, is that if there is a resonance between what I say and something that is moving within your own hearts and, if you can use both of these together and wash them away, that is the way I would like you to use what I say.

Nobody is so foolish as to think the soap they have bought is too precious, and so hang it around their necks to walk about with. The purpose of soap is to wash it away with the dirt on your body. So I hope you will find a meaning other than approaching what I say with, 'Oh, that is fine' or 'I know that', but perhaps find something that does not correspond with what you think, or that does not add to your knowledge, but which presents some kind of obstacle to your understanding. Then when you grapple with that, some better understanding comes out of it. That is what I am hoping for. If you get rid of one false view or misunderstanding, and only replace it with another, then nothing has been achieved. I hope that you have now got a sense of what teisho is about, and what it means.

The case that is being presented today for teisho is the Buddha's address to his assembled disciples. The place or location is on a small peak, sometimes referred to as Vulture Peak, where the Buddha, in the closing years of his life, liked to deliver talks to his followers. When the Buddha was about to mount the raised platform to give his talk, a nobleman presented him with a golden flower. The Buddha ascended to his seat and silently held up the flower.

His followers probably thought that in his lecture today the Buddha would talk about the flower he held in his hand, and they were silent. Only one of his disciples, Kasyapa, smiled the moment he saw that flower. The Buddha, seeing that smile, said, 'I have something wonderful, and I now transmit it to Kasyapa.'

Giving the flower to Kasyapa, the Buddha said, 'I have the Treasury of the True Dharma Eye, the subtle heart of nirvana, the form of no-form, the mysterious Dharma Gate.' First of all, I would like you to focus on the phrase 'Treasury of the True Law Eye' – *shobogenzo*. This is based upon four Chinese characters – *sho, bo, gen and zo. Sho* is correct, true; *bo* is law, Dharma; *gen* is eye; and *zo* is a treasure-house or storehouse.

The most vivid or the most powerful impression that you tend to take from it, is of *shobo*, of true Dharma. However, the most important one of these four characters is *gen* – eye. *Ho* (*bo*) – Dharma or law refers to everything in the world around us, not just objects which have form, but also formless ones which lie behind them as rules or principles. If you look at a tree that is bare, do you see the movement of spring, summer, autumn and winter within it?

So 'law' is not just the bare tree without leaves, but the rules or principles according to which it moves and functions and has its life. The 'true' of 'True Dharma' does then not really refer to 'Dharma,' but rather to 'eye'. In the Dharma, there is no true and false. True and false are in the human eye. So, the eye of the true law, the *sho - bo - gen*, is the eye which sees this form and the principles which lie behind form, truly and at all times.

The final character, *zo* – storehouse, has the meaning of infinite or infinity. It is a treasure-house which contains all things; however much or however often you may use them, they are never exhausted. Thus the eye which sees things truly is not an eye which sees something truly just at this moment, but which saw truly in the past, however long ago, and which will see truly in the future. And the 'subtle heart of nirvana' tries to give some idea of the condition or state of the eye that sees the law truly.

To elucidate this eye, referred to in the phrase *shobogenzo*, Buddhists frequently use the image of the mirror. A mirror reflects what is before it, just as it is; it truly reflects colour and form and does so at this moment. If you move it one way or another, up or down or anyway, it will always reflect truly whatever is before it at that instant. How can the mirror do this? Because a mirror itself has neither colour, nor a pre-established form. Nothing is inscribed on it. Thus, a perfect mirror reflects things truly, because in reflecting, it is not drawing things to itself, nor enlarging or expanding itself, nor adding anything to itself. This quality of the mirror, of not having anything and yet being able to reflect everything perfectly, is what is meant by nirvana. This term has the meaning of stillness or quiet, as well as of *mu* – emptiness. It may also be used in the sense of not being born and not dying. It is thus something that carries on infinitely through all time, and which always and constantly reflects things just as they are.

And the phrase translated here as 'subtle heart' is the ability or the state of being able to do that, to reflect things truly. In the term *myoshin*, 'subtle heart', the character *shin* stands for *kokoro* and means heart. When we translate this as 'heart', we tend to think only of our own hearts. But though the mirror may be reflecting whatever is before it, and reflecting it perfectly, nobody would mistake the reflected object for the mirror. When people experience suffering, or any kind of discomfort, they tend to think this expresses their own feelings, or actually is themselves. Yet, in fact, it is just an image of something that momentarily has been reflected in the mirror, in the heart. Therefore *myoshin*, the subtle heart, does not refer to that series of reflections as they occur from moment to moment, but is the basic essence of the heart, of the *shobogenzo*.

Someone feeling pain, or having experienced a series of hurtful events or distressing relationships during their life, will think that the human heart and human relations are somehow soiled, unpleasant or stained. Equally, people who are lucky in their friendships and family relations, and who only experience pleasant and joyful relationships, will naturally consider this to be the nature of human life. Both are mistaken. It is exactly the same mistake as when looking at a mirror and seeing it reflect something dirty, to think that the mirror is dirty; or thinking, that because it reflects flowers, or something beautiful, that the mirror itself is beautiful. Both are precisely the same misunderstanding.

So we must not think that the intrinsic essence of human beings is something that we were born with, and carry through life, and die with. We have to see it as the expression within us of a power or a force that is to be found everywhere, throughout the universe, in all things. This is what is referred to by *myoshin*, translated here as 'the subtle heart of nirvana.' From there, it is natural to ask: What, then, is the basic form, the original form, of this *myoshin*, this subtle heart? The Buddha expressed this as *jiso muso*, translated here as the true 'form of no-form.'

Do you understand that? Can you really grasp that idea? Do you know what soap-less soap is? This is not a perfect example. But think of water – what form does water have? When this question is asked, the only answer you can give is that it does not have any form; but surely you are convinced that water without form does not exist. Water that is flowing in a river takes the form of the river, and water that is in a cup assumes the form of the cup; water in the ocean has the form of the ocean. But whatever form the water may take, that is not the original form of water. This is what is meant here by 'form of no-form' or formless form. However, water cannot become like iron. Perhaps, when it is frozen, it has a somewhat similar form. The potentiality that underlies all human beings, animals and plants, the whole universe – that potentiality is the formless form. And this implies that this formless form can assume the form of anything – is free to take any form. So, what the Buddha meant was that he possessed this mysterious, marvellous, wonderful form; and what he said before the assembly was that he was giving this exactly as it was, transmitting it exactly as it was, to Kasyapa.

This story is found in the Sutra called the *Mombutsu Ketsuji Sutra*. From a very early period, this Sutra has been considered apocryphal and Buddhist schools other than the Zen School disregard it. The

Taisho Daizo Kyo – the Great Treasury of Sutras – was compiled in the Taisho era (1912-26) in Japan. It is an enormous collection of all the Buddhist scriptures. At the editing stage, the inclusion of the above Sutra was considered, but in the end it was decided not to include it. Thus, the accepted view is that this Sutra is spurious and is being used only by the Zen school in order to establish its tradition and authority.

However – and it is very important to get this across – the reason why Zen Masters have prized this Sutra and this story, has nothing to do with its historical accuracy or inaccuracy, nor with the fact that it may have been used to emphasise a legitimate transmission in Zen. It has another purpose. When, at the beginning of this teisho, the meaning of a teisho was explained, you surely must have understood what a teisho is pointing to. So, the reason why Zen Masters prized this particular story and this Sutra, is that it is a marvellous soap, because it is a soap that removes the most fundamental grime!

The basic teaching of Buddhism is that, in all of us, in all beings, there is Buddhahood, or Buddha-nature; and, in this present case, the Buddha-nature is expressed by the term *shobogenzo*, the treasury of the true Dharma eye, the subtle heart of nirvana, the form of no-form. But if this marvellous Buddha-nature exists, not just in one person, but in everyone, then why is it that people get confused, or lose the awareness of it? Why is it that some people, for example, suffer so much? Or why is it that there are people who cannot pick themselves up again when they suffer? And, if the Buddha-nature is in everything, pervades everything, is in all of us, why is it then that we have to engage in training, in *shugyo*; why is that necessary? Is it because, although we say it exists in everybody, it actually is only in some specially selected group, or specially selected individuals? Perhaps it is that the Buddha gave the transmission rather secretly or quietly to Kasyapa, for him and a small group of his disciples, so that it passed to them, but somehow it did not get handed to you?

What then is the basic form, the original form, of this Buddhahood, which the Buddha offered to everyone, but which some people do not see? This is the problem that the text we are looking at confronts us with. Can you respond immediately, individually, to this problem? If you cannot answer, then grapple with this problem until you can.

All of us human beings are very adept at carrying problems, or bearing problems, and then somehow escaping from them. People I talk to, and especially Zen groups, seem to love carrying problems, and showing them off, but mostly they do not try desperately or hard enough to resolve their problems. The koan that is offered here in the *Mumonkan* is not like an accessory to walk around with, a pretty something. It rather presents something that really is very hard to see, and to deal with, something in the nature of a crisis. It is just the same as grime or dirt that has to be washed away with soap. Everybody needs to resolve this problem individually, and thus we should implant this doubt, this problem within each of us. The problem must grind inside each of us in such a way that sleeping and waking, whatever we are doing, we cannot escape from it.

The Chinese Zen master Mumon added his commentary to the case for that purpose, to further twist or force people to grapple with the problem. Right from the start, Mumon's commentary is not a kind of interpretation of this original problem. He added it to further confuse, or further force those who are grappling with it, to think. As I said at the beginning, I am not a human being, but just a bar of soap; or, in another way, I could be seen as a devil dressed in the robes of a monk! I have the function, the role, of putting people in the position where they are forced to grapple with this problem and cannot escape from it.

Now to Master Mumon's Commentary. The golden-faced Gautama

is a reference to the Buddha. And so, as if he were all by himself, he impudently, or perhaps arrogantly, or selfishly, did something. The English translation reads, 'He treated people as if they were nothing, he repressed the virtuous and made them worthless' – or another way of putting it would be, 'it was as if he turned black into white.' Or, and again as the English translation of the commentary says, 'He sold dog-meat labelled as sheep's head' – it was as if he held a sign up saying 'Sheep's Heads' but instead of that he cheated people by selling dog's flesh. This Zen style of putting things is not to be taken as if Mumon were criticising the Buddha. For example, the Japanese use extremely polite language with people they are not very well acquainted with; but within informal situations, if a very good friend says something particularly fine or splendid, instead of praising him, they are more likely to say something derogatory or perhaps even slap his shoulders. I suppose it may be the same in England!

So, there are different ways of expressing one's respect; one of them is through words that are overtly respectful; but another way is to make fun of the person, to deprecate, or perhaps to make light of them in some way. In our case, Mumon is not just looking at the Buddha; he is also looking at those people who, when hearing the Buddha's words, do nothing, or do not even try to think about doing something. Therefore, with his disciples gathered around him, the Buddha seemingly staged a kind of performance of handing the flower and the transmission to Kasyapa. Most people would think that in this action something special was going on. But from Mumon's point of view it was nothing special at all, just a silly, meaningless performance.

When the flower was held up, Kasyapa alone smiled. Therefore, the Buddha went through this performance. Now what would the Buddha have done if everybody had smiled, or laughed, when he held up his flower? Or, on the other hand, what would the Buddha have done with the treasure of the eye of the true Dharma – *shobogenzo* – if, when he had put on this performance for Kasyapa, Kasyapa had not reciprocated, had not smiled? How then would the Dharma have been transmitted, and what would the Buddha have done with it? You may now wonder what Mumon's words really mean. Is it a question of the true Dharma being some kind of distinct thing, like a stick, which the Buddha transmits to someone? Or is it that if you do not get the true Dharma directly from the Buddha in some way, that you do not have it, or that people do not have it?

The basic teaching of Buddhism is that *shobogenzo*, or *busho*, (Buddha-nature, Buddhahood) is intrinsically within all beings. However, those who really see, can really grasp it, and reveal it themselves fully and completely, their number is small indeed. Knowing something and believing something are two very different things. All know they must find or grasp happiness for themselves. Yet, knowing that, people somehow tend to believe that they need to be given this happiness as a kind of present from someone else.

As an analogy, however delicious a meal may look, unless one eats it oneself one does not really, fully know it. Everyone knows that having one's mother eat the meal for one because it is too troublesome to move one's mouth oneself, that really doesn't make any sense. Everyone really knows and totally believes that, and no one assumes that they will be satisfied by proxy. But with regard to one's own peace of mind, or tranquillity of heart, there is always the tendency to make this very mistake.

And it is because of this that we are gathered here. Of course, it is not bad that you have come here, but the fact that we are together here should not lead you to assume that I will somehow make you happy, or that through me, you will find happiness. Rather than coming here and gathering around me, each of you must grasp that for him or herself. What I can teach is simply that the Buddha is within each of us. But just as in the case of eating that meal for yourselves, so in the case of seeing into your own Buddha-nature you have to reveal it yourself and live it yourself.

In this connection, I would like to tell you a story. At last year's Summer School, I found a girlfriend. She was five years old. This year, I am only here for the first week of the Summer School and then leave for Japan. She is coming to the second week, so we cannot meet; and secret love is just like this! However, when I was in London, she sent me some flowers with her mother; and from her father I heard this story. The uncle of one of her friends had recently died. Her friend said to this little girl, 'My uncle has died, and now he must be in heaven with God.' The moment she heard this the little girl said, 'God is not in heaven, in that faraway place. He is in me, and in you and in the flowers around us. If you don't understand me, go and ask my mother.'

When I heard this story, I felt very happy, overjoyed, because it meant that her father and mother did not confine their practice just to Summer Schools or Sesshins. They were striving to realise their practice and the implications of their practice in their daily lives, and so the little girl had been able to say what she had said to her friend.

At the moment that little girl perhaps believes more deeply than her father and mother, that Buddhahood or Buddha-nature is inherent in everything. If, being a small child, she causes trouble, or mistreats things, or abuses things in any way, all her parents have to do to deal with the situation is to simply remind her that there is Buddhahood in those things too. Or if she grieves or feels despondent or desperate at times, all her parents have to do is to remind her that she too shares this Buddhahood. But to somebody who does not really believe it, who is not convinced of it, but simply believes it in a kind of intellectual way, such a reminder would be quite useless.

The reason, then, why Mumon raises this problem of what would have happened if everybody had smiled, or what would have happened if Kasyapa, had not smiled, is to force everybody to grapple with this problem of finding and realising Buddhahood within themselves. Mumon goes on to say that if this *shobogenzo*, this eye of the true Dharma, is something that can be handed around from one person to another like a parcel or a present, then the Buddha is tricking us, or is tricking those who were around him. By this, Mumon is stating that, even though not received directly from the Buddha, this Buddha-nature is within everyone.

Now, if we try to believe, or believe, that this Buddha-nature is indeed within us, but does not function, does not come into operation, then this belief becomes impossible to hold. As above, if there is Buddha-nature within everyone, why is it that some people are subjected to anguish and suffering? Why is it that some people seem somehow to be hated by others, and other people seem to be so easily loved? Why is it that when most people naturally want to try to be happy, so many others find themselves, or put themselves, in situations where they are desperately unhappy? Well, in order to force people to really think about this very intense and personal problem of self-realisation, of Buddhahood, Mumon by way of twisting and grinding the knife still deeper into the problem, ends his comment by the suggestion that if the Buddha-nature exists in all beings, why was it that in that situation the Buddha only passed the flower to Kasyapa?

This is a problem that people have suffered over and wrestled with, for centuries; and one of those who wrestled with this most vigorously, and painfully, was the Japanese Zen Master, Dogen. He is probably known to you as the founder of Japanese Soto Zen, and the founding abbot of the great monastery of Eiheiji.

Dogen was born in the year 1200. It was a time of confusion, violence and warfare in Japan. His father was a political figure of the day, and in order to increase and extend his power he made several political marriages. Each one was with the daughter of a man who held the greatest power in the land. He finally aimed at the very pinnacle of power by adopting a young woman, and making her the consort of the Emperor, hoping that through the child that would be born, he could exert influence over the Imperial house. He was a very adept, scheming politician, who used every possible trick in the book to try to swim successfully in that age of confusion and warfare. On the other hand, Dogen's mother was a young woman whom his father had married last. Like her husband, she was a member of the nobility. She was extremely beautiful, but was subjected to a whole sequence of hardships; she was an unhappy, or ill-starred, beauty. Before Dogen was ten, both his parents were dead, and Dogen was made a monk; not of his own volition, he was just put into a monastery.

There during his novitiate, he heard repeatedly from his teachers, 'Buddha-nature is in everyone.' But the innocent boy could not help realising that he was surrounded by warfare, and he could not help wondering, if Buddha-nature was inherent in everybody, why his own father should have been such a scrambling and scheming politician, nor could he understand why, to build up his political career and enhance his power, his father should have married so many women and made them so unhappy. And Dogen found it hard to understand why his mother, whom he had loved as a small child, had been subjected to so much pain and suffering.

Dogen then began to ask those monks whom he had contact with and who had a reputation for wisdom, 'Why is it that, if Buddha-nature exists as you say it does, why is it that such things happen? Why is it that, if this Buddha-nature exists, human beings still have to go through a process of training, of *shugyo*? Why should it be necessary for them?' But no one could answer his question.

Just at this time Zen was being introduced to Japan from China. Dogen went to one of these new Zen temples, but he could not get a satisfactory answer there either – an answer to his particular problem. But he did find something. He noticed that, in contrast to the temples of the older forms of Buddhism, these new Zen temples had a very vital, lively, energetic feel to them. He therefore decided he would continue to wrestle with his problem in Zen training, and did so until the age of twenty-three, when he went to China with his teacher.

In China, Dogen put himself through a very intense spiritual training. On returning to Japan after about four years, he said something in his first lecture that was startling. 'I went to China, wandered from temple to temple, and eventually came to a temple that was headed by the monk Rujing (or Nojyo in Japanese). Under him, I finally realised, without explanation, that the eyes are horizontal and the nose is vertical.'

Another way of putting this is to say, willows are green, and flowers are red. If you hear such phrases without some depth of experience, you are likely to dismiss them as being flippant or silly. But they are simply the very tip of the iceberg. That willows are green and flowers are red, or that the eyes are horizontal and the nose is vertical, is a statement of how difficult it is to look at things precisely and clearly, exactly as they are. Nor is it something that you can understand by piling up explanations. Rather, it is something you grasp without any explanation at all. It is that you can realise the eyes and nose of Buddhahood within yourself, that the eyes are horizontal and that the nose is vertical, and recognise that directly and clearly. Dogen went on to say that having recognised that the eyes are horizontal and the nose is vertical, he could not be fooled after that; he could not be tricked or cheated by anybody. Being tricked or cheated is not being cheated by somebody outside yourself; fundamentally you are deceiving yourself.

And Dogen followed up this rather surprising statement with another startling remark. 'Having experienced all this in China, I returned to Japan empty-handed.' What he meant was, 'Truly, truly, empty-handed, with nothing in my hands, I returned to my native land.'

When Dogen left for China, perhaps he thought that the reason why he could not solve this problem, this great doubt that he was grappling with, was because he lacked knowledge, or that his training was still inadequate and undeveloped. Or because, in comparison with Chinese temples and the richness that they had to offer, there were fewer temples and fewer masters in Japan. So, he almost certainly set out for China considering the situation in Japan as inadequate. Those were probably his sentiments when he undertook his journey. However, when he got to China and pursued his training there, he began to realise that, in fact, he was bearing much more than he had realised.

I, myself, wear spectacles. Dogen probably did not have the same kind of spectacles; but probably he had invisible spectacles of a different kind that coloured his vision in a variety of ways. Or, like young people with a Walkman around their necks, perhaps Dogen had the equivalent of several hundreds of those! And he saw things that were not really there, or heard things that could not be heard. Probably he did not even really see what was actually there, and did not really hear what was to be heard. What he did in China was to dump all that baggage; so, although he had expected to return to Japan loaded with all kinds of things, he actually returned empty-handed. And out of that emptiness, with those empty hands, Dogen spent the rest of his fairly short life – he died in his fifties – creating his great work, the *Shobogenzo*.

Buddhahood, the Buddha-nature, exists; for some it functions miraculously, to a very high degree; for others it seems to be veiled. And each of us must work and practise until we realise the problem as our problem. Dogen resolved the problem for himself. Generations of Zen Patriarchs have resolved it. But that is the meal that they have eaten. Each one of you has to go to the table for yourselves.

Mumon then puts this in the form of the verse that you see at the end of the case. When the Buddha held up the flower, however small the flower might have been, it showed the truth of everything. It is just like the tip of the tail of a snake sticking out from a hole; from it you are able to know that it is a snake, and the size of the snake. And that is why, on seeing that single flower, Kasyapa could smile – just as a mirror reflects a flower. However, the monks gathered around did not understand what was going on. Now, although it is said 'the monks gathered around,' of course what he is talking about is this group of people gathered here now.

In Zen, something that happened two thousand five hundred years ago is something that is happening now. What happened in India is what is happening here. If there are those here and now who, unlike Kasyapa, cannot yet smile when the flower is held up, then give yourselves with a will to your training. And in Mumon's comments is the appeal that if you don't yet have Kasyapa's insight, you should grapple with this problem until you reach the point where you can truly know that the Buddha-nature is within you, and that it can be used, be put into practice. However, the Buddha-nature is not of much use if, for example, it fizzles out when you try to sit quietly when you are around noisy people. It's easy enough when things are going well, but if it shrinks in other situations, then it is really not strong enough. But I want you to work for a Buddha-nature which will also function when things seem to be going against you. Then you can recognise and use the fact that setbacks themselves have value; or that the person who seems to have turned against you has value.

CASE 7 · JOSHU'S WASHING THE BOWLS

A monk asked Joshu, 'I have only just joined the monastery. Please, Master, teach me.' Joshu asked, 'Have you had breakfast?' The monk replied, 'Yes, I have.' Joshu said, 'Go and wash your bowls.' The monk had Satori.

Opening his mouth, Joshu showed gall, heart and liver. If on hearing (him), the monk did not get it, he calls a bell a pan.

只爲分明極
翻令所得遲
早知燈是火
飯熟已多時

Only because it was very clearly shown,
Was attainment late in coming,
Knowing that flame is fire,
The meal has long been cooked.

The famous Chinese patriarch, Joshu, has already been 'introduced' when commenting on the first koan of the Mumonkan, but I would like to add some more details concerning him. At nineteen, Joshu became the disciple of another famous Chinese patriarch, Nansen, and remained with him until Nansen's death by which time Joshu was fifty-seven and had found his own enlightenment. On Nansen's death he mourned for three years. The following twenty years he wandered around China from Zen monastery to monastery, with the intention that should he meet someone who, though a hundred years old, yet knew less, he would teach him, but if he met an eight-year-old child wiser than himself, he would bow his head and ask for instruction. He was eighty when he finally settled down in a temple, opened his gates and began to accept disciples. He died at the age of a hundred and twenty, much revered by both monks and lay people. Though Joshu lived twice as long as most people, yet the depth of his understanding was many thousand times that of an ordinary person. And so, when we today read the statements, that Joshu left us, however brief they are, there is within them the crystallisation of the depth of all his wisdom.

Many of the young people who come to my temple today tell me that they want to practise Zen because they want to experience many different things. And when I ask them, what they have done so far, it appears they have already done a great variety of things. In recent years, the number of such students seems to have greatly increased. In one case I asked, 'Is there anything you have not experienced? For example, staying put in a single place and really trying to experience something deeply?' But they all go around looking for one new thing after another and think they have really experienced each one of them. But actually they have only passed in front of the gates. The important thing is not how many experiences you have had, or how different these experiences are from those of other people. What really matters is to experience what everybody else experiences, the most commonplace things, but to do so more deeply. It is not important to know many things, or to know more than others know, but to understand more deeply what everybody else understands. Because knowing more deeply, understanding more fully becomes a tremendous source of strength in your life. This is why Joshu stands out, even among the patriarchs, as one of the truly great Zen Masters. Now, we can look at this koan.

A monk came to Joshu and asked, 'I have only just joined this monastery, and my practice is still immature. Please teach me, what is the essential point of the Buddha's teaching?' Now, a monk who asks such a question is not a novice, not of shallow understanding. I do not know how it is in Britain, but in China or Japan, those learned or of great experience do not show it; they are deliberately humble about themselves and what they know. This monk had in all likelihood been around many monasteries and carried with him solid experience. He would thus also have considerable self-confidence with regard to his practice and depth of insight. This is implicit in the question he asked Joshu. The time was probably in the morning, for Joshu said, 'Have you had your breakfast?' The monk answered, 'Yes, I have.'

Now, most Japanese Zen teachers consider this response as very deep and interpret it as such in their teisho. There was really no reason for Joshu to be concerned whether the monk had had his breakfast or not. However, Joshu was the kind of person who in short and simple expressions could include a great depth of meaning. His question, 'Have you had your breakfast?' may perhaps be seen as implying, 'Have you attained satori?' The monk would almost certainly have picked up this deep implication, and replied very directly and firmly, 'Yes, I have' – 'I have tasted satori.' Joshu continues, 'If you have eaten, then go and wash your bowls.' This statement is usually also interpreted in this deep sense. In a Zen monastery it is the practice to wash up the bowls then and there in the Zen hall as soon as the meal is over; the bowls are not piled up and carried away to a sink.

Now, the usual interpretation of what Joshu was saying is, 'If indeed you have eaten, if you have savoured satori, then go and wash your bowls – polish that satori and go.'

With regard to this understanding – and I want to make this very clear – this is not my interpretation, but what other teachers present in their teisho. Of course, it is not bad; I am not saying that they are mistaken, but it is shallow. Do you know why? Because it is a conceptualisation, something from up above the ears. What is actually meant in real terms is, 'If you have attained satori, wipe it off, wash it off.' For it is inconceivable that Joshu should have directed this monk by means of concepts and ideas, rather than on the basis of direct experience. So, what Joshu was showing was not an abstraction but reality, and he showed it directly. If you really want to undertake true Zen practice, then when eating your morning meal, eat it totally and thoroughly, and when you have finished, then wash your bowl cleanly. I hope you may fully understand the splendid quality of Joshu's teaching.

I have referred to grumble-bags in the past. You are already being taught the meaning of Buddhism and Zen practice in a variety of courses. I would like to stress that the thing to do is to just practise without any grumbling. If a banquet is spread before you and you sit down to it, this is not an occasion for complaining, commenting or criticising, but simply one for eating. But I wonder whether the food provided on your tables is perhaps not too lavish and too much. What I can see on your tables are lots of plates piled high with all kinds of delicacies. In this situation, is it not the case that though you give up grumbling, you do not know where to begin?

Young people who come to me often say, 'I am ready to begin and very willing to exert all my effort, but where should I start?' Trevor Leggett once told me a relevant analogy about Judo. If you are not familiar with Judo, think of it as a form of Japanese wrestling. Now, in learning Judo, you have to practise various throws, and there are hundreds of them. Practising one after another, you gradually learn and remember a number of them. But in the actual situation of a contest, however many throws you may know, the throw that you can successfully use against your opponent at the actual moment is only one. And that one changes from moment to moment in the match. If somebody tries to remember all the throws that have been learned, and then wonders which one to apply at that particular moment – well, it is obvious that rather than throwing he will be thrown. Someone who has really mastered the throws in Judo forgets them at that moment in the contest. He goes into it having eaten his breakfast and cleanly washed his bowls. Therefore, however brief the opportunity may be, he is able to apply the throw that just fits that moment.

However much we may strive to gain satori, we have to get up in the morning and eat breakfast. And when we are tired, we must sleep. From second to second, there is never a moment when something does not need to be done. And from second to second there is something that you are always confronting, as in the Judo contest when moment to moment, there is an opportunity for perhaps a successful throw. And this applies to the life of everybody, without exception. Everybody knows it, everybody experiences it, yet not everybody can act accordingly and make the most of it. Why not? Because whatever we are doing, we try to evaluate, to judge and categorise the situation as 'good, is worth doing' or as 'uninteresting, a waste of time.' If a Judo player would think only in terms of the great throws and not bother with the little, lesser and easier ones, he would be no good. And likewise, one who thinks he will use just one single throw that topples his opponent over at once, he, too, is not going to amount to much. Even though a fairly simple throw may at the moment seem of little importance it can lead to an opportunity for a big throw because the moment is constantly changing. The person is not choosing the technique, but the changing situation is offering or providing an opportunity.

In life it is the same. We cannot plan to live this way or that way. Real life is actualising, making use of opportunities that are presented to us from moment to moment. It is not something striking or flamboyant, but rather it is the accumulation of seemingly trivial experiences. This is the way of truly and fully knowing oneself and realising one's potential. In Joshu's very simple phrase, 'If you have eaten, go and wash your bowls', limitless words are contained. In place of Joshu, I now add a few of my own: If you are happy, laugh, if sad, cry. When you are young behave as the young; and when you are old, act as old people do. Live as fully as you possibly can the life of the moment. And when you die, die.

Don't you all feel that somewhere inside you there is something special about Zen training? A moment ago, discussing Judo, I talked about ordinary practice and competition. But in Zen there is no such division because Zen is human life itself. Do we have time for preparation? In the theatre there is time for a rehearsal, and then there is the performance in front of the audience. But in life there is no time for rehearsal and there are no preparatory periods which allow you to think that now, while you are young, you can prepare yourself, and that the real thing – or problems or whatever it is – will emerge when you are older.

So, for all of you gathered here, practising and sitting zazen, it is not that by doing this you prepare to fulfil your future life. You have to know that the moments of the Summer School are those moments of life that cannot be wasted. When you are sitting zazen, enlarge your possibilities and yourself through zazen. And when you are going for a walk, in and by that walking fully become that walking as much as possible. Please, whether talking or eating or whatever you do, treat each second as an opportunity for that growth, make use of each moment to grow and reach full maturity.

The form or manner of that maturation is probably different from what most of you have in mind. When thinking of maturation, you tend to think in terms of self-expansion or enlargement in some way, and you think that what you have inside you somehow expands or inflates. Not at all! It is rather that what you meet enters you. I have been using a lot of analogies from Judo. Now, in Judo the ideal is not throwing somebody by or with one's own strength, but rather the opponent falls by his own strength. Today there are many people who suffer because they feel loneliness, or pain of some kind, and so they hope that they will somehow be succoured, fulfilled or completed by something from outside themselves. But by thinking in this way, they close the doors of their hearts; then if something is being offered, if an opportunity presents itself, they do not let it enter. If you are lonely or want to be fulfilled, if you want to do the utmost to help yourself, then you must open those doors. If you do, then you can be filled – not just by the kindness and help of others, but by what comes to you from looking at trees, at flowers or birds, or at nature around you.

And so just as Joshu taught, when you are eating, eat; when you are washing your bowls, just wash the bowls. And likewise, when on your walk you see a tree, fully and completely respond to it, or on seeing flowers, respond to them fully and completely. If you encounter something that creates happiness, allow it to fill you. If you meet something that people would describe as unfortunate or unhappy, allow that to fill you too. For somebody who does that, the normal distinctions that people make between fortunate and unfortunate, happy and unhappy, such distinctions do not exist. This does not mean that one doesn't shed tears, or no longer feels pain. Like anybody else one grieves and suffers anguish. But there is a way in which you can be filled while crying; or while suffering sadness, you can be filled. I have taken so much time on this point because I want to stress that practice is so commonplace that people find it very difficult, if not impossible, to do. For though human beings are not particularly diligent about things, yet they are strangely attracted by what is difficult or hard to understand.

At this point Mumon adds his commentary, 'Joshu opened his mouth and showed his gall-bladder, heart and liver.' What Mumon is saying is that Joshu, in the simplest words, showed reality. It is hard to know how that monk understood Joshu's words. Mistaking the depth of Joshu's meaning beneath these simple words is like looking at a deer and seeing a horse, or looking at a bell and seeing a pot. And Mumon adds further that, because Joshu's answer was in a sense so obvious, so commonplace, the understanding of it takes a long time.

People are slow to grasp a meaning that is transparent or simple. Thus, they think heaven or paradise is a place far away from where we are living, and they are convinced that practice is something very different from daily life. This is like failing to recognise that the flame burning there in the candle before the Buddha is intrinsically the same as the fire that burns down a house and causes grief and loss to a family. Though the latter is a terrible disaster and the former, the candle flame, is a source of light, love and clarity, fundamentally the fire is the same. If you can understand that the daily life of common suffering is the same as, and comes out of the same process as, the splendid path of enlightenment and satori, then you will realise it was long ago, way back in the past, that you entered that splendid world. And then you will also realise that the ordinary life you have come to accept is really something superbly splendid.

Although many people have both the desire and the determination to really devote themselves to practising, they are not quite sure where to apply their energy. For those people Joshu showed precisely and very clearly what needs to be done. But just because he said and showed it so clearly and simply, most people find it hard to recognise. So, they tend to plan for themselves in their own way and think that practice lies in that direction. But by doing so they only pile up difficulty upon difficulty, making it ever harder for themselves. And though people are in theory attracted by difficult things, they quite noticeably fail to deal appropriately with their own difficulties. They tend to chop and change their plans, which simply results in a succession of changed courses, plans or timetables.

It is like a mother who cannot but see her child as beautiful. But more explicitly, like a mother who instead of feeding a hungry child, spends her time devising ever more elaborate and splendid dishes for it. Please do not laugh at this example; I myself have made just this mistake all too frequently. We call it the 'Hungry Ghosts of Practice', those who would like to eat but are unable to do so. In Buddhism it is said that although the Hungry Ghosts are desperately hungry, the moment food is put before them and they reach out for it, the food bursts into flames. It is not that the food ignites and turns into fire; food is food. But in the eyes of the Hungry Ghosts it appears as fire. Therefore, although starving, they are unable to eat, and although their throats are parched and water is nearby, they cannot drink because they see the water as flames. In spite of the fact that in our daily lives our practice is step by step, we, nevertheless, all too easily, become these 'Hungry Ghosts of Practice', and then we cannot see the reality of what is in front of our own eyes.

When Dogen went to China (see Commentary on Case 6 – The Buddha's Flower), he was just such a Hungry Ghost seeking the

Dharma. He was twenty-three when in 1123 he set out together with his teacher. On arrival at the port of Ningpo, Dogen continued to live on the ship for some weeks, going ashore for short excursions only, looking around, studying Chinese and getting used to life in China. It was well over a month when on one of his forays he happened to meet a Chinese Zen monk. Having looked forward to such an encounter with tremendous anticipation, he invited the monk back to the ship and, entertaining him as best he could, asked him all kinds of questions.

'Where have you come from?'

'From Ayuwan-shan monastery.'

'How far away is it?'

'I got up early this morning and have only just arrived. Tomorrow is the fifth day of the fifth month when we have a special feast day. I am sixty, and until now have not been able to attain much. Now at last I was appointed cook (*tenzo*) of our large monastery, and I want to produce the best food possible for our monks. That is why I got up early this morning and came down to Ningpo to try to procure some mushrooms. Having got them I must return immediately, or I won't be back by nightfall.'

But Dogen, anxious to hold on to this elderly monk and get as much information as possible from him, pressed him, 'Do stay here for the night. I can put you up and feed you, and please tell me more about life in your monastery and in Chinese monasteries in general.'

'No, thank you. I must return tonight or I won't be ready for tomorrow's work.'

Dogen insisted, 'Of course it is possible for you to stay. Even if you are returning late, there are plenty of younger monks who can take charge of the kitchen in your absence.'

However, the elderly monk stuck to it, 'No, it's my job and it is for me to do.'

On hearing this, Dogen, not so much reasoning but rather with something that came out of his heart relating to that great doubt that he was carrying with him, said, 'Forgive me, but you are no longer young and you can't expect to live much longer. This being so, why do you make such a big issue out of mere kitchen work? Why don't you, at your age, devote yourself to meditation and more intense practice instead?'

What Dogen was thinking and implying was that this elderly monk was not really devoting himself to practice. But the monk said, 'You, young fellow, having just arrived from abroad, don't have the slightest inkling of the meaning of the Buddha's path, of training in the Way of the Buddha.'

Dogen asked, 'What then is zazen and the Practice in the Way?'

The old monk replied, 'That you have to find out for yourself. No doubt you will travel around widely here in China, wandering from one temple to another. If there are karmic affinity links and these bring you at some time to our monastery, Ayuwan-shan, then we can talk there. But now it is getting late and I must leave at once.' This came as a shock to Dogen and left such a lasting impression that after he had returned to Japan he recorded this encounter in his *Tenzo Kyokono, Precepts for the Cook in a Zen Monastery.*

Dogen travelled widely in China, visiting many monasteries, staying for a while and then moving on again. During such a visit, Dogen was absorbed one day in reading the teachings of the Zen Masters – perhaps such a central text as the *Hekigan-Roku* or the *Mumonkan*. An elderly monk came up to him and asked, 'What are you doing there?' Of course, the monk could see what Dogen was doing and need not have asked. But Dogen replied simply and directly, 'I am reading the records of the patriarchs.'

The old monk asked further, 'And having read them, what are you going to do with them?'

'I want to know the quality of the practice of the great masters, so that I can apply it in my own practice.'

The old monk stepped closer and said, 'Well, if you do that and apply it in your practice, what will it lead to?'

'I hope to attain enlightenment here in China and bring it back to my own country and offer the benefit of it for helping many people.'

The monk came still closer. 'Doing that, what in the end are you going to make of it?' Dogen could not reply.

If you ponder these two incidents concerning Dogen, and apply them to my comments above, you should be able to derive a rich meaning from it. The reason why we cannot do the simplest and most direct practice is because unconsciously we apply values to what we are doing. Or else we always think in terms of results – how beneficial something is, of what use is it, or what has been the value of a particular action?

Without a doubt we all live within the law of cause and effect, *inga*; and we live within history which is the continuation, the repetition of cause and effect. At the same time all of us desperately hope to be able to transcend the law of cause and effect. But there is only one way of transcending it, and that is to perfect each single second.

CASE 8 · KEICHU'S WHEEL

Master Gettan asked a monk, 'Keichu made a hundred carts. Dismantled into wheels, axle, etc., what is there?' (i.e. where are the carts?)

To get this clear, eyes like shooting stars, energy flashing like lightning.

機輪轉處
達者猶迷
四維上下
南北東西

Where the wheel of energy rolls
Even the expert is bewildered;
(For it rolls) above, below, and in (all) four directions,
South, north, east, west.

Gettan appears at the start of this koan, talking to a monk. He was a Zen Master four generations prior to Mumon in the Dharma lineage. Gettan is not particularly famous among the Chinese Zen patriarchs, but his koan contains a very important meaning. One day, Gettan tossed this problem at his assembled monks. In the translation it seems to be just one monk. It would help you, however, not to think of just that single monk but of the whole community, and not just only of Gettan's disciples, for he is tossing it at all of you. Now, the text says, 'Keichu made a hundred carts.' Every Chinese would have known Keichu as the greatest cart-maker in Chinese history. If you dismantled all those carts into their separate components, then where would the carts have gone?

Now, do you not think that this is a strange question? I shall rephrase the koan so you may find it easier to understand. I was riding on the Underground in Tokyo and at one station the doors opened and a young mother came in leading her small son. The moment they had entered the train, the little boy began bombarding his mother with questions, 'What's that? What's that? What's that?' Each time his mother very patiently replied, 'That's a bench...a window...ceiling... floor ... the strap to hang on to ....' This went on for a while. Suddenly the little boy burst into tears, 'There's no train!'

You have noses, eyes, ears and mouths; I am shaven, but you have hair upon your heads; in your stomachs are all kinds of things; and then there is character and heart, abilities and human talents. Examine, look within at each of these – dissect them and then ask, where are you, yourself. Or where have you come from? Probably all you can offer is a medical explanation of how you were born. But such an explanation will not satisfy your hearts. If, for instance, an autopsy was to be conducted on your body, then where have you gone? What really is life? What really is death? Unless you can truly answer this, can clearly see the answer to these questions, you cannot concentrate fully on what is happening second by second.

I have talked about the koans and said that the perfection of moment-by-moment activity is the height of practice. Here at the Summer School, you can begin to realise this and put it into practice.

Those of you who have children have left them at home, and while you are here, it is pointless to worry about them. And those of you with jobs, have taken time off to come here, and have been liberated, are freed, from your work. There is no need to plan things for tomorrow. When the appropriate time comes, tea is served. About the time that you begin to feel hungry, there is food in the dining room. There is a bed for everybody; and when you feel like having a bath, or going to the toilet, you can do so. And in these surroundings, in this situation, each of you is able to savour things in this moment-by-moment way. Looking around, I feel that almost everybody has returned to childhood; and what this means is that your Buddha-nature is operating more visibly than usual. But to my way of thinking, this is not the fruit or the result of practice. The main reason for this is that you are on holiday! And in a few days this holiday will end. It is not that your problems have gone away, but simply that for a week you have been able to forget them. And at the base of all problems is the problem of life and death. Therefore, those who have been able to resolve this problem for themselves can be on this holiday forever. And they are different from people who are planning and preparing for something to be done in the future. Being able to make the most of, and to perfect this present moment – is this not transcending the chain or law of cause and effect? Listening to me, some of you may think, 'Well, that's fine, a great ideal, but I can't realise it.' True, often you do not realise it; but actually there are times when you can and have done so. In a good environment some are able to realise this even without any training.

I once had a letter from a young girl who had just passed her entrance examination to the university of her choice. Entering a Japanese university, especially the high-ranking ones, is extremely difficult. To get over the hurdle of entrance exams, students have to plan their days around their studies. So, this girl was now completely liberated from the grinding and scheduled study she had been engulfed in. As a reward, her grandparents offered her the use of their summer cottage. While there on holiday, she wrote to me. 'The mountains are shining. The leaves of the trees are shining. The water in the stream nearby is shining. I have never seen such wonderful scenery.' She used the word 'shining' to convey the sense of being filled completely by whatever she encountered moment by moment, whether it was the trees, or the leaves, or the river, all nature around her. Now, this was not the first time that she had been to that cottage; she had seen the same scenery many times before, but that particular spring it shone for her in a way she had never experienced. I put the letter between my hands and alone in my room prayed that in time to come whenever she looked at the same scenery and it no longer shone but appeared dark and gloomy and threatening, she might again see in her mind the trees and all as it shone for her that spring. And that she would realise that it is not human life which is dark and threatening, but that her heart temporarily was in such a state. For if human life were dark and the human heart not to be trusted, and everything were untrustworthy, it would have been impossible for her to have experienced that shining day. If at this Summer School you did see shining trees, leaves or grass, then please do not doubt that there is a way of having a permanent holiday in your lives.

In his commentary to this case, Mumon added that if you can really see this problem directly, then whatever you encounter, you will immediately penetrate to its essential nature. And whatever situation you find yourself in, or whatever may happen, in one single instant you will blend into that. He mentions shooting stars and flashes of lightning – things that are tremendously fast. But this does not mean just fast. What it means is that, whether you encounter a person or a situation, you instantly become one with it, so that there is no room for the entry of anything extraneous, for any outside thoughts or doubts whatsoever.

The English translation of the verse doesn't adequately convey the original Chinese, so look at the translation, but heed my comment all the more. When you have a doubt, if there is an answer, a response to that doubt, then the impact goes particularly deep. In that sense, this is really a wonderful translation! Thus the verse suggests somebody who really and truly has insight into the problem of life and death, sees it clearly, and fully understands it. The power of response and the functioning of such a person is like that of a ground ball (wheel); when rolled, whatever it encounters, it will just continue to roll easily. Even someone of considerable practice will not be able to keep up with this free responsiveness and functioning. The functioning and responsiveness of a person who has seen and clearly understood the problem of life and death moves perfectly everywhere. As in the last line of the verse, it moves freely in all directions; freely and at will throughout time and space.

But when I say this to you, I am sure your heads are now expanding, and spreading out into some realm of infinity – but that is the basis of your mistake; because having this infinite expansiveness, really means being and dealing with the moment that is now in front of you. Here, Mumon is talking about this infinity of space, and the freedom to operate within it, not only in spatial terms; for it does, of course, also imply the freedom within time. Let me repeat: anywhere, anytime, means 'Just now! Just here!' However, on the basis of this teisho alone, you have not resolved your problem of life and death; so, I am giving you some homework. How to get a clear understanding of life and death? I do not mean explaining this in words, but in actual practice, what is it?

Now, to continue our discussion of Master Gettan's Koan. You, who are gathered here at the Summer School, have come with a variety of different viewpoints and inclinations. Some of you will have certainly come for a kind of holiday, but also hoping to learn something of Eastern culture and Eastern religion. Others regularly sit zazen and treat this Summer School as a sesshin, and as an opportunity to press on with their practice. There will also be some who are carrying a burden which they find impossible to discard. You all have various reasons for being here, and different attitudes. I, giving teisho, have but one single objective – to do this as sincerely as I possibly can; particularly today, as I am going to talk about the problem of life and death.

This is a very subtle problem, and perhaps for some people an extremely painful one. I heard that in Britain people do not like to hear or talk of death. And yet the problem of death lies at the root of our everyday lives. Even though it may not be our own death, or that of someone very close to us, yet we are constantly confronted by death – of people we know or love or of relatives. Also, the death of pets, dogs or cats or small birds. Death is an ever-present reality. We cannot live without thinking about death. And however seriously one may ponder things, ignoring the reality of death is a mistake. This may not be very easy to accept; but think that today your lives will end. However unpleasant this thought may seem to you, if you ponder it, then the dimension of understanding you derive from life will become much wider and deeper than you normally experience. All cultures, over and apart from worldly matters such as success, growth, or development, have also always been searching and enquiring into death.

The other day I talked about the Chinese character *bu*, translated as 'martial.' In the martial arts (*budo*) in Japan, the first things taught are techniques and methods of winning. However, after these techniques have been absorbed by their students, the great teachers have always taught that beyond this it is not a question of victory, but the understanding of death which lies at the root of the martial arts. So, the deepest understanding of Japanese martial arts lies in the resolve to die. The practice of living splendidly is at the same time a practice of the acceptance of dying splendidly.

When we really think about or wrestle with this problem of death, then our lives change. For somebody who believes that they have a tomorrow, then whatever they do today tends to be linked to tomorrow, in terms of success, result, or achievement of some kind. Death, however, is like a vast black hole that drinks in, absorbs and takes away success and failure, good and bad. When people who have been living with small concerns or petty notions of good and evil, or with small degrees of personal affection, are confronted with this black hole, they see into a completely different realm. Confronted by it, their own small successes and achievements are somehow immediately obliterated. And in this new world that has opened up before them, they can only think of how to live this very instant.

This is the problem that is raised by this koan. Look again at the text. If we took off the wheels, and removed the axle – where would the cart have gone? When you read these words, they may seem like nonsense to you. However, what lies behind them is the problem I have been talking about. If this koan is read without appreciating the problem that lies behind it about which I have been talking, then it is easy to see why Zen koans may be misunderstood as simply playing with words. Plenty of people come to my temple believing exactly that and assume sanzen interviews to be just a kind of play. Not that sanzen and koans are play, but that such people are only able to see them as play.

If, for example, you study the theories of swimming, using this wooden floor here to practice on, however you learn to move your arms and legs, if you then jump into the water, you still won't be able to swim! If you want to learn to swim, you have to get into the water. And if you don't want to see sanzen as play, then you must not separate sanzen from your daily life. However much I may emphasise this, the tendency still is to take sanzen as something apart from daily life. And so, when for example, their child has died, or they are confronted with the death of a parent, or when, on television, they see suffering and death caused by famine somewhere in Africa, or on the news they hear of the tension between the United States and the Soviet Union, people tend to think that Zen practice is a kind of game.

I would like to tell you the story of a woman I knew. From about the age of forty she had become a kind of servant or attendant to my teacher, Master Zuigan, and stayed with him for the rest of his life. For women of that time in Japan, she had received the best possible education, and until the age of forty had devoted herself to the education of young women. But on meeting Master Zuigan, she was so impressed that she gave up her work and moved into his temple. From that time on, she only dressed in the kind of baggy trousers worn by working women in Japan. She never wore make-up and seemed to have put all her previous feminine interests behind her. And she really dedicated herself to her practice, just taking care of Zuigan, washing his clothes, cleaning and scrubbing, and in order to provide him with a few fresh vegetables, she tilled a little plot out in the garden. She was serious, hard-working, and genuine in all she did, always. To live beside such a woman is extremely painful!

When I became the disciple of Master Zuigan, living beside this really powerful, tremendous woman was very difficult. She was a truly great person. She was sixty-four when Master Zuigan died and I took over the Temple. So as not to get in my way, or create any difficulties for me, she left and found a room in another temple, and lived there until her death. She kept a strict routine, got up daily at four o'clock, and while still dark, she cleaned her room. At first light she went out to sweep yard and garden. Nobody was watching her, she could have done as she liked, taken things as easily as she liked, yet she continued exactly as she had when with Master Zuigan. And in the evening, she would ponder on the teishos that Master Zuigan had given on the *Mumonkan* and the *Hekigan Roku*, or listen to broadcasts on Confucian ideals and study these.

To any observer, this woman lived the finest and truest life you could possibly conceive of. But towards the end of her life, she came to me and told me that she had not been well recently. She had seen a doctor and had tests done in hospital, and it transpired that she had cancer. Ever since she had heard this, she had become very frightened. Partly it was the fear of dying, but partly also doubt.

She had spent years in Zen training beside Master Zuigan and she felt that a person who had been deeply immersed in, and derived something from Zen training, should be able to die splendidly. So, she was troubled that if she died in an undignified, uneasy, tortured way, this would not just be shameful for herself, but would be a reflection on the teacher whom she admired so much.

Now, this grief or problem was characteristic of her. However much she tried to escape from it, it remained with her day and night. So she had come to ask me about it. 'I have tried,' she said, 'I have practised to my utmost, but I still have doubt about death. Where then is the mistake in my practice – where has it gone wrong that I should still feel this? If my practice had really borne fruit, surely I should now be able to face death with more equanimity and peace?' When I heard this, I realised that in her practice she had really gone to the very depths. Until then, I had been impressed by her seriousness, by the earnestness with which she had lived her life; yet at the same time I now was hoping that this sort of unrelenting seriousness of hers could be pushed or driven one stage further. So, I told her that in my own practice and experience, death is not something that comes when this physical body begins to break down. Though we may not be aware of it, death is with us second by second. Our lives are truly sequences of discontinuity – repetitions of being born and dying each moment. However, we fail to see that, and instead believe our lives to be a continuum.

What I would like you to do in future is not to ask yourselves at each stage whether something is right or not, or whether you are correct or not; but whether you are able to die splendidly each instant and each day. That is the question you should be asking. Dying today and being born tomorrow; and when you die tonight and are born tomorrow, you are not born as a small baby but as an old woman, nearly eighty, suffering from cancer. Nor is she someone who earlier was young and healthy. It is a mistake to compare one's past with one's present, or one's situation when healthy with now being sick. Everything from the past that could be used for comparison has all been swallowed up in the black hole. And what is born now is something completely new and afflicted with cancer. None of us, when born as infants are able to choose anything. We come into the world, into conditions that were provided for us; and that self – ourselves – that is born every day, is also born without being able to choose the conditions that we live in. But we live in this instant, with and in the midst of the totality of the conditions that are provided for us. Living today, and dying, and then tomorrow being born and dying. And not only that, but dying in this room and being born in another room. Dying here in the zazen room, being reborn in the dining room; dying there and being reborn perhaps in the room of a friend. Born when you are out walking in the countryside; and when that is over, dying there and being born in the zendo.

Anyway, I talked to the old lady along these lines, telling her to recognise the reality of birth, death and birth in each instant. If you talk like this to people who are well and healthy and getting on with their work, they might laugh. But to an old lady of eighty and suffering from cancer, this is not a joke. So, she put it into practice with great determination. Her features were rather childlike, but because of her very strict and determined attitude throughout her life, a quality of sternness and severity was imprinted on that childlike face of hers. She had made such great efforts and had constantly asked herself whether what she was doing was right or not, and had tried to do what was right. But after talking with me and putting into practice what I had suggested, her face again truly became fully and completely that of a child. She began to live a life which has no future, and so when she was washing her clothes, or the dishes, or tidying up around the place, she was doing it not because it was right, but because she enjoyed it, and she could not live or be without doing things in that way.

Towards the end, she was taken into hospital. Whenever I visited her, the doctors and nurses told me they had never seen such a patient. One of the doctors said to me, 'Tell her that it is she who is the patient and the one who is sick, and that she is not to worry about whether I am tired or not!' 'What you have said is the greatest mistake,' I replied, 'Any patient who worries about where it hurt yesterday, here or there, and worries because of the pain from head to foot – that is being in hell! But because she has forgotten herself, she is able to smile and express concern for you.' The doctor was greatly moved, 'What a real insight you have opened up for me.' For the old lady, the doctors and nurses and those who came to see her were all visitors whom she might never meet again.

Just at that time, not being able to cancel my previous engagements, I had to go to the United States. So, a monk, my oldest disciple, visited her in my stead. On my return, he told me about her death. Her last words were, 'I have lived a very difficult life, and now I'm going into the forest to play with a ball.' The monk when he told me this was himself in tears. This woman had really reached the very deepest point – that living and dying is like a child playing. In Zen this is called *yuge sammai –sammai* is samadhi, the deepest level of meditative understanding, and *yuge* means play or game; the Samadhi of Play. This, I must stress, does not mean living lightly and it does not mean treating things frivolously. What it means is perfecting this instant, each instant, and perfecting the circumstances of the daily life we live. In this, there is no element of attaching value to what one does; nor is there any element of concern for what others may think of us, or how other people may evaluate what we are doing. Nor is there any feeling of 'It's not this I want, but that,' or of, 'If only I were young,' or, 'If I were a man,' or, 'If I were a woman' – there is absolutely nothing of this kind. Only here, now, in this place, realising and perfecting things fully, and then living this realisation as a sequence of perfected moments. Only then, and through this, is it possible in the truest sense to live life and death. In Zen, clarifying life and death is not a question of academic explanation. Making life and death clear in Zen is living life and death, knowing that in one's daily life death is always there. It is not that at some moment death suddenly visits. Meeting the death of someone who is very close to you, if it comes as a shock, it means that you have not really recognised that it was always there. If you really live death within your daily lives, you realise, too, that somebody who has died is also living. But do not think of this as living on in the form of a ghost; for living life and death, finding death within life, living life within death, this is the Buddha. It is not this nose, or ear, or this body.

I mentioned Dogen before. In his famous book, the *Shobogenzo*, Dogen says, 'The person who can see Buddha within life and death does not experience life and death,' he is not subject to life and death. Somebody who does not see Buddha, but sees only life and death, that person is subject to birth and death. Because getting upset and worrying about death is failing to see the Buddha here in the moment-to-moment experience of life and death. If you really live this life and death from instant to instant, then life and death, living and dying, are simply the breath of the Buddha or the beating of the heart, the heart of the Buddha. You should be able to understand this. This may be a little heavy, but I have been talking about the most fundamental problem. What I could say about it, I have said. From here on, it is your problem; and I would like you to experience it, or try to experience it, not on the wooden floor, but in the water!

CASE 9 · DAITSU CHISHO

A monk asked Master Koyo Seijo, 'Daitsu Chisho Buddha meditated for ten *kalpas* in the meditation hall but could neither see into the Buddha-dharma nor complete the Buddha Way. Why not?' Seijo said, 'Your question is most appropriate.' The monk persisted, 'But why could he not complete the Buddha Way by practising in the meditation hall?' Seijo replied, 'Because he did not become Buddha.'

MUMON'S COMMENT

You may know the Old Barbarian, but you are not permitted to understand him. If an ordinary man knows him, he is a sage – if a sage understands him, he is an ordinary man.

THE VERSE

了身何似了心休
了得心兮身不愁
若也身心俱了了
神仙何必更封候

Rather than putting the body at ease, put the heart at ease.
With the heart at rest, the body knows no grief.
If both heart and body are wholly at ease,
To praise such a sage is presumptuous.

SOKO ROSHI'S COMMENTS

When somebody trusts you, do you not feel joy? And when not trusted, are you not sad? We all hope to be trusted by others, but the one we least trust is ourselves. Do you not feel that your faults or weaknesses are always glaringly visible? And, aware of them, you feel that you cannot improve, so always think of yourselves as something that is imperfect. To the degree that there is weakness within us, we tend to become assertive with others, overriding our sense of weakness, to exaggerate ourselves. While we are unconsciously feeling that there is something lacking in ourselves or that we are somehow imperfect, we try listening to this teisho in order to take something from it. But the koans change daily, and the more you try to learn from each new teisho, or the more you try to remember what has been said, the more confused you become. This applies not just to teisho, but to every talk you try to learn from. You can buy a variety of books, and you learn from those too. Hence your heads are rather like a child's toybox that has been overturned. The harder you try, the more difficult it becomes to understand what the practice is, what the essence of practice is.

Perhaps the monk who appears in today's koan, the one who came to visit Master Koyo, was in the same state. He thought of himself as imperfect and that somewhere there was a perfect Buddha. But the Buddha that he was looking for out there was a Buddha he himself had created, a figure of his imagination. Most likely he had travelled from monastery to monastery, encountered various masters, learnt many things on the way, had read the Sutras and learnt the sayings of old masters. In the *Lotus Sutra* he read that Daitsu Chisho Buddha had spent ten *kalpas* – that is an endless period of time – in meditation, but had not attained enlightenment. On reading this, he fell into confusion. The term *kalpa* is explained by the following comparison. There is this huge rock, a hundred miles square; a sage descends from heaven once in every five hundred years, and the gossamer sleeve of his kimono just brushes the rock; a *kalpa* has passed when the whole rock has thus been worn away. Reading this passage, the monk took it as having happened ages ago in some heavenly environment. He thought of Daitsu Chisho Buddha in the meditation hall as a perfect Buddha, engaged in zazen for an inconceivably long time. And yet, the sutra says that Daitsu Chisho Buddha did not attain enlightenment. The monk was confused by that.

But who is Daitsu Chisho Buddha? If you consider the Chinese characters for Daitsu, *dai* means great and *tsu* means to penetrate, so it means spreading through everything. Try to think of something that is as penetrating, as permeating as air or water. However small the space may be, air or water will find its way in. However, if water freezes, then it can no longer permeate anything. Likewise, it is with any of our conceptions, or any system of evaluation, or with our own ruler which we use to assign values, believing that there is some fixed benchmark. In doing so, we cease being able to permeate, and become inflexible. Able to permeate everything means not having any fixed values, having no conceptualisations, no particular standpoint, not being hung up between the opposites. Just as there is no fixed form for water, so in terms of the spiritual life it means not having fixed values. But having said that, this does not mean that there is no form, or no value, at all. Water does not have any form of its own, but changes form, according to the particular receptacle.

The basic force or energy of the universe cannot be described as physical or spiritual. It appears as it does throughout the universe because its form is not fixed, either physically or spiritually. With the advance of science, it was thought possible to discover the origin of existence through physical laws. Scientists today no longer try to do this; from the standpoint of physics or astronomy, looking at the infinitely small or the infinitely large, it seems that emptiness and physical existence merge and are the same. There is also the dawning realisation of there being no boundary between our existence and non-existence. This is stated by young scientists who describe themselves as the New Science Movement. I personally think it interesting that science is beginning to see the world in the terms in which the Buddha spoke. Daitsu, the 'Great Permeation', is spreading through everything, being part of everything. And for that reason, each one of us, each individual, is also Daitsu, and shares in this great permeation. Even though we are always caught within conceptualisations which we create for ourselves, tied up in the rigidity of judging and defining things as we see them through our eyes, yet our nature, our essence, intrinsically is this Daitsu, this permeability.

'Chisho' means Shining Wisdom. What do you think Shining Wisdom is? Is it remembering many things, or everything? No! This Shining Wisdom is not being carried away, in the sense of being captivated by what we see with our eyes, by what we hear with our ears, or by what we smell or taste, or perceive with our bodies, or feel with our heart/mind. Therefore, with Shining Wisdom one is always empty, and into this emptiness one is able to take, or to receive, everything around one. It is not that we cannot understand because we do not know, rather we always find that we do not understand because we know too much, or know other unnecessary things.

In my temple, the telephone may ring and one of the novices answers it. Through comes the voice of a charming young lady asking in an ever so friendly way, as if she knew him well, whether the Roshi happens to be in. If the novice wonders what the relationship is between this young woman and the Roshi, he will be unable to 'take in' her name and to tell the Roshi who called. I do not know whether that is the reason or not, but anyway, I am often given the wrong name.

This does of course not just apply to telephone messages. The message of the successive Patriarchs is transmitted in the same way to all of you. Daitsu Chisho Buddha is simply Daitsu Chisho, this free flowing, formless reality that permeates everything and is receptive to everything. So, this permeability and supreme wisdom and Buddha all have the same meaning and, therefore, we can say that this is the very root of the universe or the essence of being. We do not know when it may have begun or when it will end. It exists in all things, transforming itself, transforming from moment to moment everywhere. And this is what is meant by sitting for ten *kalpas* in meditation. If that is as it is, is there any need to supplement it, to add to it in any way? Or can you even add to it in any way? The meditation hall mentioned, that is reality as it is. Satori, enlightenment, is that condition, just as it is. If you believe that the Buddha has become the Buddha, often that means that Buddha has ceased to be, has died, and that cannot be! This process of dying and being born comes from within our conceptualisation. The reality is this Daitsu Chisho Buddha, the permeability that penetrates through everything, great wisdom, Buddhahood.

To repeat, all the suffering or pain that may beset us is just within our heads; in fact, we could not live for even an instant if we were separated from truth. Even if we do not consciously seek for truth or reality, we are every instant in the very midst of it. Whether you try to think of yourself as a fine human being or as a ne'er-do-well, you cannot escape from the reality that you are Daitsu Chisho Buddha. It is not a question of making a Buddha, or of making oneself Buddha by means of zazen. It is but recognising that intrinsically we are all Daitsu Chisho Buddha. What is important then in zazen is not attempting to remember what has been heard in a lecture or in teisho, but that by listening to teisho and lectures, and by sitting zazen, one liberates oneself from one's conceptions. There is no need to sit as if one were trying to become something. Trying to become a Buddha is just imitation. If you try to create a Buddha that corresponds to the image you have built up from listening to teisho or reading, this is merely a kind of play-acting rather than training. So, when you are sitting, quite simply just sit – this is fine as it is. Trust yourself. If you happen to be sad or alone, accept it, sit in loneliness. If you do not know anything, or feel foolish, just sit like that. Or if you have no particular ability, then sit without any ability. An outgoing, active person or an introvert, each should sit as they are. That is fine. When you realise that 'yes indeed, this is fine as it is,' then without realising it, a transformation will take place – you will be transformed into your true selves.

However, without realising it, you are all acting. By and large, extroverts tend to be over-enthusiastic; introverts are apt to feel that they are inadequate by comparison. But when you really return to your True Nature, then both the extrovert and the introvert will recognise that their respective levels of activity are quite appropriate; and the one who feels a lack of knowledge will be able to see things, and those who think they are without any ability, will quite easily and naturally, without much thinking be able to apply themselves. When you try to transform yourself according to some kind of blueprint or image that you have created for yourself, you do not really change. Why is that? Because when we are trying to act like that, we frequently tend to forget the role we are playing. We tell ourselves to be careful to do this, and not to do that, and we repeat it to ourselves, and then find that before very long we have forgotten to remind ourselves and we have fallen back into our old habits!

We are all makers of images, yet there is no need to create idealised images because the origin, the essence, is already ideal. For example, I like you as you are; therefore, I want you to like yourself or to love yourself as you are. That is all there is! A few days ago I said I am here speaking to you and you are there listening to me and so we are meeting again, and for me that is a great joy! People smiled at that, but I did not mean it as a joke. The trees are growing over there, and they say nothing. They do not laugh – and yet, though they do not beckon us with a laugh, we like to go into the woods. I have never heard woods or trees inviting us to come and visit them. In such advertising there is always some sort of ulterior motive, the intention to persuade somebody to do something. In your voice or in your body there is no need for any advertisements. Hence, there is no need for make-up or for adding extra eyelashes! You are splendid as you are! Because you are as you are; for that very reason, you are splendid. So, therefore there is no need to try to make a Buddha or to build a Buddha Hall.

'Daitsu Chisho meditated for ten *kalpas* in the meditation hall but could neither see into the Buddha-dharma, nor complete the Buddha Way.' That is why the *Lotus Sutra* expresses it in those terms. However, the monk was trying to make himself into some sort of a Buddha, and therefore he thought that some special training place and long zazen was necessary. In this world of opposites and discrimination, these words of the *Lotus Sutra* could not be understood by the monk. So, he asked Master Koyo why he didn't attain the Buddha Way. Koyo answered that it was obvious, self-explanatory.

And I have explained it to you now, so you should understand why it is obvious; there is no need for a Buddha to become a Buddha. There is no need for reality to seek reality. But the monk did not understand that answer, so in spite of sitting in a wonderful training hall, he asked again why was it that he did not become Buddha? He did not become Buddha because he did not become Buddha. This is very similar to the first reply, in the sense that this too is obvious, self-explanatory. But let us try to taste it, savour it, in a slightly different way.

The text says, 'Because he did not become Buddha.' Now who is the 'he'? Is it Daitsu Chisho Buddha who is the intrinsic truth or reality? But it has already been said that we are all Daitsu Chisho Buddha – we are not products created by Daitsu Chisho. Who would then seem to possess creative power! Not just ourselves, but trees, grasses, birds, flowers, all are manifestations of Daitsu Chisho. So, we are all Daitsu Chisho Buddha. When we do not believe that, I or we, who are Daitsu Chisho, are in fact Daitsu Chisho, can we then say that Daitsu Chisho has become Buddha? Can we say that the Buddha's teaching has manifested itself in the world?

Yesterday evening, I walked alone in the grounds, overflowing with happiness. Had there been someone sad nearby, what might they have thought? Perhaps that I say fine things in teisho, but really am sad, because somebody walking around alone may very well look sad. It is the same when parents are bringing up children. If the parents cannot see the Buddha-nature in the child, they think they have to instruct it in everything that it does, and so it is like working clay, moulding everything from head to toe into shape. It is not that one person raises or brings up another. It is that the Buddha-nature develops of itself. Very often when we extend our hands in love we are, in fact, getting in the way of the natural movement or function of the Buddha-nature. There is nothing more difficult than love, nor anything simpler. If it is natural, then very simply love will spread, permeate throughout the world. But when we think that we ourselves are creating love, then it is nothing but a source of great difficulty. When you come to be able to trust yourself, then you are able to trust others. When your heart overflows, then you can love others. But, for the most part, we try to trust others without trusting ourselves. Therefore trying to love others, while feeling inadequate ourselves, often courts trouble. Though we intrinsically are Buddha, if we cannot believe that, then we must train diligently. Which means not to stuff ourselves with knowledge, but to undertake a practice that is directed at releasing us, freeing us from mistaken notions.

In Mumon's comment, I suggest that you take the meaning of 'The Old Barbarian' as 'The Wisdom of the Buddha,' but avoid any discrimination about Buddha. In other words, it is fine to be relaxed in the consciousness of one's Buddhahood, it is fine just to be at ease and at peace within oneself. What is wrong is trying to analyse oneself, to understand oneself, to understand Buddha, or differentiate one's practice from the surroundings. When people can simply feel at ease with themselves, feel this relaxation within themselves, then they are already sages! But among those who are called sages, if they indulge in analytical and discriminating thoughts, they are no longer sages, but simply ordinary people.

As to Mumon's verse, we treat our bodies as important, and not just our bodies, but also other things that have form, but we very easily lose sight of things that have no form. Yet it is through the moment-to-moment transformations of these formless things that the world as we know it, the world around us, takes its life and shape. And therefore, these things that have no form and move freely are the most important! If we can also move freely along with these things, then there is no need for us to feel any sense of grief over our bodies, and there is no need to get excited, or to feel upset because at one moment we were well and at the next we are sick, and no need to become agitated because of losing our youth and growing old.

On a drive, with the car moving smoothly, it is natural that new scenery continuously presents itself before our eyes; if we keep seeing the same landscape, the car has broken down! While we are living, at times we are well and at times we are ill. There is a time for youth and a time for old age, and there are wonderful green fields and steep mountain views, vast horizons and narrow vistas. It is sufficient that, moment for moment, we melt into and enjoy them. The things without form are constantly moving; if we can move freely with them, then there will be nothing for us to grieve over or to lament in the world of forms that we see before our eyes. And those who are in that state are known as sages. Since we are sages of this kind, what need is there then to try to promote ourselves to nobility? If we have it already, why should we try to elevate ourselves to it? Or for somebody who is in that state, is there any need to attach the label Buddha? Or for somebody who is living that kind of life, is it necessary to sit again in that Buddha Hall? There is nothing that is wanted or needed. Not even thinking about oneself.

CASE 10 · SOZAN AND POOR SEIZEI

A monk asked Master Sozan, 'I am alone and poor. Please, Master, teach me.' Sozan called, 'Zei-jari!' Seizei responded, 'Yes.' Sozan said, 'Having drunk three cups of Haku of Seigen wine, yet you say that your lips still remain dry.'

MUMON'S COMMENT
Seizei pretends to be submissive, but what about his heart? Sozan with his single eye penetrates into the depth. But, however, that may be, just say how and where did Seizei drink the wine?

THE VERSE
貧似范丹
氣如項羽
活計雖無
敢與鬭富

Poor like Hantan,
Spirited like Kou,
Even though there is no means of livelihood,
Daring to compete with the richest.

SOKO ROSHI'S COMMENTS
Master Sozan lived between 840 and 901. Together with his Master, Tosan, he is regarded as the founder of the Soto Zen School. In fact, the first syllables of their names, So-zan and To-san make up the

combination 'Soto'. One day a monk came to Sozan and said, 'I have absolutely nothing; no home, no residence, no property, nothing. Please help me.' Not that he factually had nothing; what he was saying to Sozan was that through his training he had become nothing. It was a declaration of the extent of his training that he was tossing at Sozan.

There is an analogous incident of a monk who came to the famous Master Joshu and asked, 'I have nothing in my heart; what do you make of that?' Joshu immediately responded, 'Throw it away!' But the monk did not understand what he was told. He had come and said that he had nothing, and yet he was told to throw it away. So, he repeated, 'No, I have nothing.' Joshu said, 'If you cannot throw it away, then carry it away with you on your back.' At this the monk realised what Joshu had meant. The state of mind, or heart of this monk who came to see Joshu and that of Seizei who presents himself before Sozan in this koan are very similar; but the responses of Joshu and Sozan respectively are very different. Sozan immediately called out, 'Zei-jari!' 'Jari' is a form of address for a monk, and 'Zei' is the usual short form of Seizei; so 'Zei-jari!' is 'You!' And without thinking, instinctively, Seizei replied, 'Yes?' Sozan said to him, 'Can it be that having drunk three cups of the best possible wine in the world that your lips still remain dry?' Sozan's comment, directed at Seizei, is not a general comment. In other words, with a pocket stuffed with money could you truly say, 'I haven't got a penny on me'?

In his comment, Mumon says that Seizei presented himself to Sozan, as the text says, only seemingly humble. But what was really in his heart of hearts as he made this statement? Sozan, with the true Buddha-eye, the kind of eye that penetrates directly and clearly, saw immediately and straight into the very depths of Seizei's heart. Mumon also saw this clearly, but the question he is throwing at you is: to what extent does each of you understand, how it could be that

Seizei, although his purse is full of money, or although he has tasted the best wine, he says that he has nothing, that his lips are dry?

Above I referred to the encounter between Joshu and a monk. What Joshu shouted at that monk, and what Sozan shouts at Seizei – I want you to be very clear about this – is different. The monk said to Joshu, 'I have nothing,' and Joshu shouted at him because, by this statement, the monk was expressing pride, asserting that he was bearing something very great when he said, 'I have nothing.' Now, Sozan's case is different. When he came to Sozan, Seizei probably had the same kind of pride, asserting he had attained satori. But Sozan was not attacking that pride. What he was criticising was the shallowness of the assertion of satori as having nothing. Sozan was really striking at that shallowness. Do you truly understand the splendour of that nothingness? Do you really understand the gratitude you should feel at poverty? Do you understand the almost pleasure, the happiness that can be or is derived in unhappiness? Buddha-nature is expressed as voidness or emptiness – have you noticed and recognised the fullness, the richness contained in that? You seem to be listening as if you half grasp it and half do not, looking both illuminated and puzzled at the same time. So, I will tell you a story.

The story is, again, about an old lady who died ten years ago. She was about eighty when she died, so she was born about a hundred years ago, in a town high up in the mountains, in Takayama. Her father was a tatami mat maker, and they were so poor they could barely keep going, although the father worked hard all day long, every day. When she was three years old, she contracted a festering disease in her fingers, arms and toes. It was a kind of disease in which the blood ceases to flow to the fingertips and toes so they begin to rot. And because it was extremely painful, she cried night and day. But in such a poor household in the Japan of those days, if somebody was struck by disease, it was not easy to get medical attention. When at last she was seen and taken to hospital, her fingers had to be cut off. But the disease continued and before it was finally stopped, both her arms up to the elbow, and legs up to the knees had been amputated.

To make matters worse her father died soon after that. Her mother worried that even with the father alive and working ceaselessly, they had barely kept going; how could she manage now without him, and with a daughter to support who had lost her arms and legs? Thus, simply in order to survive and not particularly out of love, she married another tatami maker, a widower with children. When she and her daughter Isako moved to their new home, the neighbours, having heard the new wife was bringing with her a child without arms or legs, all came out to stare. In the tiny house, the ground floor was taken up by the workshop and kitchen. Isako was kept upstairs in an attic, out of sight. She took her meals with the rest of the family, but without hands she was not able to use chopsticks and had to put her face over the bowl to lap her food. The children in the new family, seeing her eating like this called her a dog or a cat. Moreover, at mealtimes her new father would grumble, 'It's hopeless! If she had arms and legs, she would be of use to the family when she grows up. But even if we feed her, there's no hope of that. The food she is eating is wasted.'

The mother had to leave home for three or four months at a time to work in a weaving factory to earn money to keep the family going. During such times, Isako stayed with her grandmother, who was also very hard up and made a bare living at sewing. She had no time for Isako, and no other children would play with this limbless child. So Isako sat or lay beside her grandmother, and getting hold of some odd pieces of cloth, somehow learned to stitch by putting a needle in her mouth, between her lips. I do not know how she did this, but somehow she persevered and managed to make a ball out of coloured fabric. Carrying it in her mouth, she crawled out to where the neighbourhood children were playing, and putting the ball down said, 'I'll give you this if you will play with me.' But the children said that the ball she had carried in her mouth was covered with her spittle and dirty and none would play with her.

When she reached school age, there was no school at that time that would accept such a handicapped child. Watching her stepsisters and brothers when they came home from school, working at their homework, she somehow taught herself to write, by picking up the pencil stubs that they left lying around to practise her characters. When she was nine, she began to suffer from an eye disease, and lost her sight. Her mother, who up until that time had done her best and felt that somehow they would get through, despaired. One night she tied Isako to her back and went off to a river, determined to commit suicide. She knew that even while she was alive and doing whatever she could, there was no hope for Isako; and if she killed herself, how could the child survive? So, they would die together, at the same time. Just as she was climbing the river bank the child asked, 'What are you doing?' Having been told this, Isako felt that however miserable her life might be, she wanted to live, and she pleaded with her mother, 'I will be a good child; please let me live.' At this, the mother could not go through with her intention. Luckily, Isako's eyes recovered, and she regained her full sight. But from that time on, her mother completely ceased to take care of her, telling her, 'If you want to live so much, you must do everything for yourself.' Now, Takayama is high up in the mountains with heavy snows in winter. In Japan, a century ago, houses were not heated. The only source of warmth in a room was a small smoky hearth with some glowing charcoal and a small table, covered with a quilt; to keep warm one put arms and legs under the quilt. In the cold winters, her amputation scars were particularly sensitive, but when Isako wanted to get under the quilt, her mother said, 'If you want it, make the fire yourself.' Now to do so you have to get twigs and perhaps paper, light that with a match, put some charcoal on it and then spread the quilt over it. Try to light a match without using your hands! Perhaps if you somehow manage to clamp the box in somewhere and push it open with your tongue, you may be able to get a match; or maybe if you sort of press the box somehow against a wall, and hold the match in your mouth, and work away at it, you may be able to light the match. But the flame from the short matchstick is burning just under your nose. If, startled, you gasp, the flame you have just managed to light will be blown out. I cannot imagine how Isako managed to light matches. Yet in order to live, she did. She also cleaned her room herself; nor would her mother do her laundry. With running water it might just be done; but in those days, if you wanted water, you had to draw it from a well, in a bucket. Again, it is inconceivable how somebody without arms or legs could do that; but in one way or another Isako managed to do her washing, and cleaning, and to light matches, and sew her own clothes.

But even though you can do everything for yourself, that does not yet provide any income. Isako had no money for her daily food. So she made a contract with a showman to be shown as a freak, and the money she earned she gave to her mother for food. Daily the limbless girl was on show, sewing, or engaged in some activity. Even a man, to some extent anyway, feels that he would like to look his best. And a girl of nineteen would naturally like to appear as attractive as possible. But she had to show her limbless body and clumsy actions.

After this had been going on for some years, Helen Keller came to Japan from America. She had been blind from birth, unable to hear or speak. But, unlike Isako, she had been born into a very wealthy family. Her parents had engaged the best nurses and educators from around the world, and although she remained blind, she had somehow learned to communicate and had become a wonderful person. She went on lecture tours addressing people who were equally unfortunate, and was called the 'Threefold Saint' – a saint who had suffered from a threefold handicap. She came to Japan to encourage people who suffered from serious handicaps.

At that time, Isako was chosen to represent Japan's handicapped, and to greet Helen Keller. So, Isako, shown as a freak by day and doing her own chores by night, made a doll as a welcome gift for Helen, complete with outer kimono, and all the underrobes and obi – the long sash. With it she was taken to the reception. On arrival she saw that there were already some splendidly dressed dolls in glass cases set on the stage which members of the press and the committee had presented. Moreover, all of these dolls had split-toed white socks on their feet. Isako's doll had no socks; having never worn them herself, she had forgotten them. So, though she thought that hers was a very poor gift, she had it presented. When the interpreter told Helen that this gift had been made by a woman without arms or legs, she felt Isako all over, then hugged her and said, 'People everywhere call me The Threefold Saint, but you are far greater than I; you are a masterpiece.'

How can one presume to imagine the joy and happiness Isako must have felt at that moment! Since she had been born, she had never had a birthday celebration, had never even heard 'Happy Birthday.' And though not expressed in words, in people's eyes she had always seen the condemnation, 'Why do you go on living?' She had lived with this, and now because of it she had actually been hugged by Helen, known world-wide for her strength in dealing with her handicaps. From then on, she ceased showing herself as a freak, and spent the rest of her life travelling throughout Japan, encouraging handicapped people. The second half of her life was a full one, also full of gratitude to her mother and stepfather, to the man who had agreed to exhibit her as a freak, and most of all to the Buddha. Can you think that she was poor?

In his accompanying poem, Mumon says that Seizei's poverty is like that of Hanshu. Hanshu is famous in Chinese history for his poverty. Mumon also likens his spirit to that of Kou, also famous in Chinese history for being very strong-hearted and having a tremendous fighting spirit. But Seizei could not compete with Sozan in riches – riches of the depth of understanding – because he did not understand that his poverty, having nothing, was his riches. So although he could not compete with Sozan in this sense, he still tried to get into some kind of competition, in terms of value or in comparing the greatness of what they had. Even though he was no match for Sozan, he still tried to compete with him.

I have put it in these terms for the koan – but just compare it with the situation of Helen Keller and Isako. Helen Keller came from a wealthy family and was recognised by everybody. But whoever looked at Isako would know that she came from a very poor family, and it was also known that in her childhood she had exhibited herself as a freak. The doll that she had made was not much to look at, and she had sewn it with her mouth. But when you compare the wealth accumulated in the disadvantages they both had, it is impossible to say who was the winner and who the loser, which achievement was greater and which less so. Isako simply did not have the time to grumble about what she had lost, nor the time to feel envy for people who had what she lacked, nor did she have the time to criticise anybody. However poor she was – not simply in the financial sense, but poor in the physical sense of lacking parts of her body – within the conditions she had been given, she had spent her life whole-heartedly realising each instant. Her poverty was just such a thoroughly experienced poverty, and she fully drank and savoured the three cups of the wine of Haku of Seigen.

Many of those people who come to see me have all kinds of problems and are unhappy. They have not yet realised to what extent the particular unhappiness they have encountered is a source of riches. Rather, they seem to think that as a result of bearing that burden of unhappiness, they somehow have the right to claim the sympathy of others. And if the expression of that sympathy somehow seems insufficient, they usually elaborate on their suffering.

To such people, as Sozan did to Seizei, one could certainly shout, 'How can you say that your lips still remain dry, when you have tasted three cups of the wine of Haku of Seigen?' That's all.

CASE 11 · JOSHU'S HERMITS

Joshu went to a hermit and said, 'Anyone there? Anyone there?' The hermit lifted up his fist. Joshu said, 'The water is too shallow to anchor here,' and went away. He went to another hermit and said, 'Anyone there? Anyone there?' The hermit lifted up his fist. Joshu said, 'Freely you give, freely you take away. Freely you bestow, freely you destroy,' and made a profound bow.

MUMON'S COMMENT

Both stuck up their fists; why is one accepted, the other rejected? Just say, where is the source of confusion between the two? If in regard to this you can speak a word of understanding, then you realise that Joshu's tongue has no bone in it. Now he rises up, now he dashes down, in perfect freedom. But though this is so, remember that the two hermits also saw through Joshu. Further, if you imagine that there is a comparison of superiority and inferiority to be made in regard to these two hermits, you have not an open eye. Neither have you an open eye if you suppose there is no difference of superiority and inferiority between the two hermits.

THE VERSE

眼流星
機掣電
殺人刀
活人劍

Eyes – like shooting stars,
Energy – quick as lightning
A sword that kills
A blade that gives life.

SOKO ROSHI'S COMMENTS

Having read the Case, clarify for yourself what points in the koan you do not understand, so that when reading these comments, you will see them clearly. The bigger the doubts are, the greater the chance that something will open for you.

When Joshu met his teacher, Nansen, at nineteen, he was already a monk and had penetrated deeply into Zen practice. He trained under Nansen for forty years, and a number of satoris opened to him. Some might think this strange, thinking that once satori is attained, that is sufficient. But that is a serious error.

After the death of Nansen, Joshu, now sixty, wandered around China for twenty years and finally, at eighty, started teaching. Think about this. Someone asked the Greek philosopher, Thales, 'What is the most difficult thing in this world?' Thales answered, 'To know yourself.' 'What is the simplest thing?' 'To correct other people.' But I believe that knowing oneself is easy, whereas having to correct others is difficult. So, I would like you to ponder this important point that although Joshu had many satoris, it was not until he was eighty that he took up a position where he had to correct others. For several decades now there has been a 'Zen Boom' in the West. But the problem is that those who propagate it may not have done so in the spirit in which Joshu lived.

I, having finished my training under Zuigan, stayed in the monastery for a further eight years; and after Zuigan's death I did not try to teach for another seven years. This was in order to truly understand myself. Two of the greatest Zen masters in Japan – Daito, the founder of Daitoku-ji, and Kanzan, the founder of Myoshin-ji – received transmissions from their teachers, but for many years continued to deepen their own understanding before attempting to lead others. Zen monks go into seclusion, not because they do not like people; and not because they love people, do they later begin to teach.

This koan tells of Joshu's encounter with two hermits. They had attained satori and were now deepening it, choosing remote temples where they could practise by themselves. This was during the Tang period, in the reign of Emperor Wu. He was a fervent believer in Daoism and a persecutor of Buddhism; he is said to have destroyed forty thousand temples and to have laicised over two hundred thousand monks and nuns. This is another reason why many monks would go off into the mountains and settle in remote temples and hermitages.

Joshu came upon such a hermit and greeted him with, 'Ariya, ariya.' This is translated in the text above as 'Anyone there?' But that does not quite fit a Zen koan. A better translation would be, 'Is there? Is there?'

If you were asked directly by Joshu, 'Is there? Is there?', how would you answer? If you were just asked, 'What is there?' it is so straightforward that if you had any doubts about it, you should not be doing zazen. Although everyone has different problems and reasons for following the Buddha's Way, in Zen there is only one single purpose – 'Is there?' You are not being asked if there is a lighter or some cigarettes. It is not zazen, it is not satori, it is not enlightenment, it is not love: it is the Buddha-nature showing itself, working ceaselessly within each of us, within all sentient beings.

However, there are even some monks who forget this. They boast that they do not sleep at night, but sit zazen instead, or try to show themselves greater than anyone else and make tremendous efforts to observe the rules. However, I say that this is beside the point; what is to be found in zazen is the Buddha-nature within us – and not just within us, but within everything. The Buddha-nature within each single one of us individually, is also at one with the universal Buddha-nature. That is what Joshu was asking and that is the question the hermits answered.

The first hermit raised his fist. If you ask what the meaning of raising the fist is, you are already lost. It need not have been a fist; it could have been a finger or a knee. The thing that moves everything, be it a fist, finger or knee, is not your own will, but the universal Buddha-nature. People think that by means of their own discernment, their own determination or their own mind, they can know how everything functions. But who can make their heart beat? Who can stop breathing when asleep? A baby about to be born cannot choose its parents, sex or nationality, when or where it will be born, nor its physical appearance. All our lives have started from the same point – unable to choose anything. I am sure you believe that you have made choices to be where you are now. Did you choose the face you have? Do you have your physical proportions because you like them? We have not been able to choose anything – all is given. An infant, of whom we clearly know that it has not chosen anything, can still live and function in its environment. The infant does not despair. If it cannot walk immediately, it does not feel frustrated. It may not understand words; it simply absorbs them. When you were in this position, did you create this power for yourself? Is this power to live, the infant's alone? No; it is flowing, brimming over, in everything.

So, the hermit, raising his fist, did not do so after deliberately thinking about it. The Buddha-nature may express itself at any time in any way. However, in a single instant, all the manifestations cannot be expressed at once; perhaps raising a fist is all that can be done at the moment. For Joshu that was sufficient. He recognised immediately that Buddha-nature was truly working in the monk. This is where Joshu shows his greatness. 'In this shallow water it is impossible for a great boat like me to enter and anchor.' When Joshu put the same question to the other hermit, he also raised his fist. Joshu bowed, showing great respect, saying how wonderful it was, this freedom to bestow or to take back, to kill or to give life.

Though both hermits acted in the same way, Joshu's responses were opposite. What was the difference between the first and the second hermit?

Perhaps you may think that if you explored things further, if you went into the background of the case more thoroughly, you would discover that, in fact, one hermit made a face different from the other. If you did, you would make a good historian, but you would not come to much in Zen training. What Joshu is looking at is not the hermit. What the monk was doing was responding to the question that Joshu asked. This point needs to be made very clear, but as it is not helpful to make things too clear, I will tell you a story to lead you astray!

About sixty years ago, some Buddha relics from India were sent to Japan. The priests and masters of the large monasteries in Kyoto put on their best robes and went to the station to meet these relics. However, Gassan, the master of Tenryu-ji, came in his everyday black robes with the straw sandals used for begging. One of the abbots, dressed in all his finery, said to Gassan, 'Today we are gathered to greet the relics of the Buddha, but you come in your workaday outfit.' Gassan replied, 'You say that we are awaiting Buddha relics, but you do not know what may be in the urn – it may be a piece of gravel or a tile, so what is the point of getting dolled up?' The story spread about and one person who heard it was furious. He went to Gassan and asked, 'I heard of this. Is it true?' Gassan said, 'Not at all. In the face of a Buddha relic, I would not say such a thing. But in this age of the decline of the Dharma, how could I as a monk don a gold-brocade robe to greet a relic of the Buddha?' Do you think that Gassan was a liar? If not, then which of his reactions was the true one?

This may still not be clear, but I cannot say more. Do not look at the form. If you concentrate only on the form, differences will inevitably appear; and you will begin to think that one is superior and one inferior, so the process of discrimination begins. What Joshu, the two monks, and Gassan saw was the Buddha-nature. None of them saw it as being external. Seeing it as operating externally, then inevitably one is bound by it. Seeing the Buddha-nature in this way, one thinks one is greater than other people. Thus, one becomes entangled in the external quality of the Buddha-nature, which is one's own internally.

When you say, 'I have really understood,' you feel that you have truly grasped something you have been studying or have experienced. But this feeling of 'I have got it' counts for very little; it is like comparing a glass of water to the Pacific Ocean. The feeling that you have captured the whole of the Pacific Ocean in a glass leads to a sense of superiority, but when you have really grasped the Buddha-nature working within, you realise that it is also working within others. This way of understanding does not belittle, nor lead to a kind of superiority; the problem of being bound by something within does not arise.

So, in the face of the same Buddha-nature, once Joshu bowed and once he dismissed it. The power to be able to freely bestow or to take, to give life or to kill, is a wonderful thing. If you were to bow hundreds of times, you could not venerate it sufficiently. It is not external. This power, the Buddha-nature, is working within the hermits, within Joshu, within us all. That is why understanding the Buddha-nature did not tie Joshu – the balance between external and internal was perfect. It does not stop a great boat like Joshu; it encourages him instant by instant to be himself, to work and act. If you have not understood, get on with your training!

Mumon says in his commentary that though each hermit raised his fist, Joshu accepted one and rejected the other. What is the root of this problem of understanding? If you can clearly answer, then you understand the freely moving state of Joshu's mind.

Mumon also says that Joshu's tongue has no bones. Actually, it is not just his tongue. In the whole of his body there are no bones. If something is badly upsetting you, does your tongue move freely? The legs even of an Olympic athlete will not move easily if he has a great problem on his mind if he is facing a real difficulty. So, having no bones means being able to move with complete freedom, to act absolutely freely. This is, of course, not freedom to do as you like, a licence to be selfish. To say that Joshu's tongue has no bones means that truth is expressed and at the same time he is not bound by it.

Why is Buddha-nature so precious? Because it is the power that allows the infant who could not choose its environment, to operate freely. This Buddha-nature of the child respects the Buddha-nature in others. If on meeting someone, the energy of the child is bound and tied up by the other expression of Buddha-nature, then it is not really the Buddha-nature. It cannot be, or this would not happen. So if you forget your own internal Buddha-nature and are drawn towards something external, then this very thing that should allow freedom of movement, becomes the rope that binds.

Mumon then says that Joshu saw into the bellies, into the hearts of the two hermits; and at the same time, the hermits saw clearly into the heart of Joshu. Do not think that these bellies or hearts differ from ours. Do not think that in their bellies are different things and these differences are important! Some people in Japan say my eyes look right into them. But what I am looking at is the Buddha-nature. Whatever the external form may be, however foolish the person may seem, however unprepossessing, what I am concerned with and what I see is the Buddha-nature. So, no one need be afraid of me.

Do you think there is a distinction – a superiority or an inferiority – between the two hermits? Naturally, you want to say, that because both see the Buddha-nature in this way, there is no distinction. But whether you say there is a difference between them or not, Mumon would say that as a Zen practitioner, if you take either position, you fail. Be careful! However strange you may be, or however bad, all I see is the Buddha-nature. I may also clearly see that you are in a bad situation or deteriorating in some way. If someone thinks that mountains are superior and valleys are inferior, he is a fool. But anybody who does not make any distinction at all, and says that mountains are not high and valleys are not low, he too is a fool. When the Buddha-nature is not bound or caught up by anything and is working absolutely freely, instant by instant, a myriad of things arises. To see the Buddha-nature clearly, instant by instant in this world of constant change, is what Mumon describes in his verse as 'His eye like a shooting star.' The responses are free; sometimes you receive, sometimes you are put out in some way.

It is because of this wonderful expression of action that Joshu is described as 'a sword that kills.' This, and terms like shooting star and lightning, suggest lightening action, and are used frequently. However, the meaning behind them is not just one of sheer speed. Some people think everything should be done quickly; but the true meaning is that there should be no hesitation, no wobbling, no loss of direction along the way. Not a clutter of pros and cons, no meandering, no diversions, but direct and straight purity of action. The working of the Buddha-nature is like a clear mirror reflecting instantly without any aid. Joshu's clear action can he described as the sword that kills and gives life; these are not two swords. When you cut through confusion, at that moment truth is born. In order to give birth to truth, you have to cut through complexity, confusion and error. A greater example might be the death of Christ which gives promise of life. Life and death are not separate; they are two aspects of one large Life.

The Buddha-nature is not only in us; it is in everything. But it is not something that is vast like a space. It is not just spatially large, but as it also runs through time, it is large in the temporal sense, eternal. Since it seems to have begun at some timeless point in the past, it is Life which had no birth. It is Life which has no death. So do not do zazen expecting that it will make you better or grander. Please know that without zazen, without doing anything, you are part of this eternal Life. If you do not grasp this, you cannot attain a true sense of peace. This is not saying that you are the receiver of the love of some distant God. What I want you to grasp is that *within yourself* there is this Great Life. Some may fear death or have worries about the future; the only thing that will relieve feelings of doubt and fear is this understanding.

Nor sit zazen thinking it will distance you from others or will contribute to moral virtue. Unless you have the firm understanding that this great Buddha-nature is operating within you instant by instant, zazen will come to nothing. That is all there is – that is the purpose, that is the end. It is not that through zazen you will create perfect beings. When eating scrambled eggs this morning, I coughed and it went all over the table. That's me! I make errors of that kind. Of course, the fewer errors or blunders one makes the better; but Zen is not to eliminate this kind of mistake. It is to grasp the tranquillity, the peace of the heart at rest, the understanding that lies within.

CASE 12 · ZUIGAN CALLS THE MASTER

THE CASE

Master Zuigan Shigen used to call out to himself every day, 'Master,' and himself answered, 'Yes.' 'Wake up!' he called out again, and again answered, 'Yes, yes.' 'From now on do not let yourself be deceived; do not take anything from others.' And answered himself, 'No, no.'

MUMON'S COMMENT

Master Zuigan himself sells and buys. He takes out and plays with many puppets of gods and devils. Which ones? Just look! One that calls and one that answers, one that says, 'Wake up,' and one that will not be deceived by people. But do not now mistakenly stick to them. Imitating others is the understanding of wild foxes.

THE VERSE

學道之人不識眞
只爲從前認識神
無量劫來生死本
癡人喚作本來人

If followers of the Way fail to see the truth,
This is because they acknowledge an understanding
Which is the source of innumerable births and deaths.
Only fools call such understanding the intrinsic self.

Before commenting on the koan itself, a few general remarks may be helpful. Look within and find what is there! Do not be misled by the paraphernalia I have on me or am carrying. Usually you see me carrying a Buddhist rosary and a *niyoi*. Symbolically, everything is made totally free by them – but putting it bluntly, beads and staff are just toys. I do not carry them because I am a monk, nor are they essential for giving teisho. They are simply my toys, and rather than that they make me free, I use them freely. It is the same with training. It has a variety of patterns or set forms, and in your practice you need to learn to use these forms, but to do so freely. They should not bind you.

Thus here in the meditation hall, the cushions are all laid out in straight lines. In Japanese training halls the greatest care is taken over just this. But seeing the cushions all lined up in such an exact manner does not mean that you in response should tighten yourselves up and get all tense. Though in good training centres the smallest things are rigorously enforced, the purpose is not to produce stereotyped or rigid human beings. If you see the cushions are out of line and you straighten them up again, this is a way of bringing your own practice, your own attitude and conduct, into accord with the form within the zendo, and by that deepening your own practice. So again, being exacting about the small things in daily life is not about making people more finicky or difficult in their dealings with others. Because even in Zen training, if you become over-zealous in small matters and then impose these demands upon others, you not only stir up trouble for yourself, but you cause trouble for others as well! So, the insistence on paying attention to small matters or to details is not to impose it on others, but to allow them opportunities for the deepening of their practice, for taking greater care with it.

To keep the form but not to be bound by it is important. In a Japanese monastery, everything is precisely ordered, but outside the meditation hall, if opportunity allows, the monks indulge in fun and games. The time for getting up is at three in the morning. The monk whose office it is to wake the others gets up half an hour earlier, and at the exact time he runs along the corridors, loudly ringing a bell and shouting, 'Rise, rise!'. But sometimes some joker the night before has filled the bell with soil so that it makes no sound! Many such instances would naturally become disruptive; but we must not become bound by the mere form of training either, must not be too serious in only keeping the form, instead of being liberated through the form of the training.

Pondering the previous koan about Joshu and the two hermits, Joshu made his prostrations, as you remember, to the Buddha-nature that bestows, takes back, kills and gives life. Certainly, he did not pay reverence to the hermits who raised their fists. And as to this Buddha-nature to which he had paid respect, Joshu said to one hermit he was too big a boat to anchor there. What he is indicating by this is that even the Buddha-nature is not great enough to bind Joshu. This is not trying to belittle the Buddha-nature or making fun of it – he only shows that the idea of the Buddha-nature does not bind him. And within me, too, this Buddha-nature is not just a concept, it is something that is alive and active. It is for this reason that Zen monks in the past have, on the one hand, prostrated themselves before the Buddha in veneration, and on the other, have struck a Buddha image or destroyed relics. So, if you see a monk bowing before a Buddha image, do not misunderstand Buddhism as a religion that worships Buddha as a god.

In Europe, all through the Middle Ages, the idea of God had a very powerful and regulating influence. But it was not God acting within people, rather the concept of God controlled and regulated them. There were Christians, even priests, who in the name of God or Christ acted contrary to the law. So people suffered in the name, that is in the concept, of God. And it seems to me that perhaps, as a consequence, a powerful undercurrent arose, which became known as the Renaissance movement, and many felt it liberated them from the concept of God. However, being thus liberated from one concept, they were now bound by another one, the ideal of the independent human being! And they became further bound and ensnared by the notions of science and its development, or the scientific revolution or industrialisation, or increased standards of living – all of them brought about by human agency and bound by emphasis on human progress.

In both Christianity and Buddhism, the worship of images is rejected. Of all the images that people create, the greatest is that of the human being. In the Old Testament, the worship of the golden calf was punished by God. However, the worst image in this sense, worse than any concept or image of Buddha, is the concept that human beings can act simply by virtue of their own human agency, and that nothing else is required. This 'worst' concept involves the recognition of a self that consists of only two components – emotional energy and rational energy. A self that operates only on the basis of feelings, emotions and intellect, such a self inevitably discriminates between I and others. Human beings today refer to this twofold character of emotional and rational powers as an individual; but in so doing, the spiritual dimension is not taken into account. Yet the power of the spiritual dimension transcends that of the human being.

So, the 'self' or intrinsic nature we are longing to discover by undergoing Zen practice is not simply the emotional and rational self, but is just this spiritual self (Not-I) that has always been accorded the attributes of the Divine. This self is not bound by anything; it is also called the Buddha-nature, and when activated, it functions freely, operates clearly and precisely, instant by instant.

The first sutra we chant in the morning service is the *Repentance Sutra*. What does the religious exercise of repentance involve? Is it feeling repentance for the wrong that has been done, like lying or stealing? That is only half the story; for, to an even greater degree, we also must do repentance for the good things we have done! The reason for this is that the experience that comes to us from our mistakes is not likely to bind us, but that which comes from doing good things, from our successes, that does tend to tie us up. Painters or potters, all artists have this experience. When the work they produce is such that they themselves admire it and that it is admired by others, then artists find it very hard to escape from their own creation, and so in a sense are bound by it. Likewise, if tied up in this way by either God or Buddha, this will cut out the Buddha-nature.

This 'I' that we think of as ourselves is but a solidification of our thoughts, emotions and experiences. Training to eradicate 'I' does not imply throwing away self, but means not being bound by one's experience or by one's knowledge. Hence the reason for starting the chanting with the *Repentance Sutra* is to use the sword that kills against oneself – which is also the sword that gives or restores life. Thus the experience acquired up to yesterday is cut off or killed and from that a new self is born.

Actually, we die and are reborn from second to second – and this dying is repentance. When chanting the *Repentance Sutra* in the morning, it is not just to feel sorry for our mistakes, but rather to incite us to throw away our present self, our successes and failures alike.

After the *Repentance Sutra*, the *Three Refuges*, the veneration of the Three Treasures, are chanted. What that means is simply that what is reborn, absolutely clear, pure and empty, is the Buddha-nature. This latter is not something forced, a drive of one's emotional or rational I, but is movement in accord with the spiritual self. For most of us, our lives are based on our emotional and intellectual experiences only; these shape and form us. But when we really think about it, they present the conditions of strife and war. Only the Buddha-nature makes it possible for people to live together easily in peace.

When we were born, what experience did we have? And what knowledge? Yet ordinary infants, easily and naturally learn to walk, to talk, to move around and so build up a store of experience. But then, growing up, we begin to pick and choose; this kind of life suits us, that one does not; or we would like to live here rather than there, do this rather than that! But the infant does not pick and choose like this, and so in a sense transcends these things. The power not to be swayed by one's preferences arises without experience and without rational knowledge. Though in our mind we cannot conceive what this power might be, cannot intellectually grasp it, yet there can be no doubt of its functioning.

We all constantly choose and judge – advantage and disadvantage, like or dislike, and thus seem to be constantly thinking. But the actual time we spend thinking in the course of a day is really limited. What is moving us for most of the day is not this discriminating intellectual activity but the non-differentiating Buddha-nature.

If this seems contrary to your experience, please try it out for yourselves. If somebody gets on your nerves and makes you angry, to maintain that anger throughout the day without a break – can you do that? And the same applies to a desire for something; with a really strong or overwhelming longing – try to hang on to it from morning till night, to keep it at a constant pitch!

So it is not just zazen, the giving into the count, into breathing, that is difficult. Getting angry or being angry, and feeling desire or greed is the same. If you try to concentrate the heart on doing only that, it is difficult. By 'heart' I mean the Buddha-nature, which is really free, always moving and functioning. However, its functioning is not in obedience to 'me'; though it may operate as directed, perhaps to our advantage, but it operates in harmony and in balance with all other things. We may not be aware of it, yet it is by that harmonious functioning of the Buddha-nature that we can enjoy harmony and tranquillity in our lives.

Therefore, in zazen, we must not attempt to become inflexible or unmoving. Though the body is indeed still, but the intrinsic nature, this heart, true face, is moving freely in harmony with all that is. Like a huge bird soaring seemingly without effort high in the sky – is your zazen like that? No? One result of being too tight, or of making too conscious an effort is that one becomes solitary and lonely, isolated. And is it not so that when doing zazen you at times become sad, and things seem to become dark? I notice that in the mornings after zazen some of you are hunched up when walking outside.

So, from your appearance, from your posture as you walk, I get the impression that you feel isolated, lonely or sad. If that is what zazen does for you, then it is better not to practise it!

What zazen is supposed to shatter is the self which is composed only of hardened rational and emotional elements. At that moment, the spiritual self then emerges, great and strong and in harmony with everything, and the eye of the Buddha-nature opens. At that, the very air around you becomes one with yourself, and you can fly in it like that great bird! That is the zazen that has to practised. But be careful now not to be hypnotised by these words, rather see to it that you actually, really want to do it and – accordingly sit zazen!

Now we can look at Master Zuigan's koan. The standard work of reference, the *Collection of Eminent Monks*, has little to say about

Zuigan. But for nearly a thousand years he has been renowned for this koan.

Every day, almost like a fool, he used to call to himself, 'Master!' The Japanese term for this is *shujinko* and is difficult to render into English, perhaps we can take it as meaning Master of 'I', in the sense as discussed above. Now, what does 'master' mean – someone very powerful? Or someone so collected in himself that he is indifferent to what is going on around him? Surely not, for somebody who is a master does not just hold to himself without responding to his surroundings, or to those with whom he comes into contact. He is rather like a man who comes home, where he can now feel at ease and comfortable. There, quite freely and naturally he relaxes.

One who can relax in this way can respond to whatever may occur. For instance, a woman may be a famous politician but at home she probably does not wear the face of a V.I.P.; if she did, she would likely have been divorced. Coming home and meeting her husband, she quite naturally, of her own accord, assumes the features of a wife. And when her child calls out to her, quite naturally and without effort she assumes the attitude of a mother. Nor is this a learned or acquired attitude based on knowledge, and it involves no planning. She instinctively responds to the situation as it is. That is the kind of master Zuigan called out to. That is what the koan is all about.

Someone once said to me, 'I have been doing zazen for five years. I would like to develop a heart that cannot be moved by anything, an immovable heart, but it seems impossible for me to attain it. I still feel angry and the like. How can I develop such a heart?' I told him, 'Your heart is already unmoving; since somebody kicked you on your way here and you got angry your heart has not changed! However, the heart that cannot be moved by anything is the heart that moves freely of itself. But someone stepped on your foot and you felt pain and with no apology forthcoming, you also felt angry. Yet when you arrived at your station and got out of the train, you saw all kinds of things on the way here – that is the empty heart. If you want a heart that is unyielding, rigid and does not move at all, then if between the station and here you were overwhelmed by anger, did not notice anything around you and had no other thought at all – if that is the immovable heart you are looking for, you have found it!'

So do not mistake the 'master' that Zuigan is calling to for the self that is made up of experience, emotion and intellectual knowledge. The object of zazen is not to consolidate this self, 'I,' still further and to make it into a kind of cement block, even strengthening it with iron rods into reinforced concrete – the purpose of zazen is the exact opposite.

Master Zuigan, when meditating, used to call out to himself, 'Master,' and would respond himself, 'Yes.' Though this 'master of I' has already been discussed, it needs careful examination. Expressed in one sentence, the purpose of training in Rinzai Zen is to become aware of the 'master,' of this intrinsic nature of self. Master Zuigan calls it the 'master of self,' and Rinzai refers to it as a 'man of no status.'

Indeed, the Greek philosophers also advocated getting to know ourselves. And so, from the earliest times, both in the East and West, one of the main drives of human beings has been to understand ourselves. However, again as I just said, most people try to grasp the 'self' in terms of emotional or rational faculties, in terms of I. And particularly today we seem to have forgotten that there is this spiritual dimension. The Japanese term for it is *reiseiteki* – and I do not know whether the connotation of 'spiritual' in English points deep enough. So perhaps an analogy may help.

As little children we were sent to school to start learning and acquired all kinds of knowledge. The more we studied, the more knowledge we accumulated. We also strengthened our bodies through sport, and likewise, the more we exercised, the stronger the body became. In the course of making all these efforts, we also make friends, and by our efforts we also attain to position in society, may start a family, etc. Thus at least for the first half of our lives, we are convinced that if only we make a sufficient effort, we will gain by it.

But at a certain point in our lives, we begin to realise that whatever effort we may exert, rather than gaining by it, we seem to lose in the process. So now we may begin to forget things we once made an effort to learn; the bodies we built up by means of physical exertion begin to weaken again. The children we reared with so much effort leave home. We hear of friends dying. Our eyes become dim and our ears hard of hearing, our teeth begin to drop out. This is now turning into a sad story – so enough of it! But one way or another, at some point in our lives all of us realise that the self, which we built up and developed with so much labour by our emotional, intellectual and physical efforts, is in reality a small, insignificant and sad little thing.

Now, in Zazen practice there are no physically strenuous movements as such, and even though it entails only sitting still, nonetheless everybody finds that it can be difficult as well as painful. Consequently there are some who consider Zen training to be only for young people – or perhaps believe that Zen practice will enliven or invigorate their lives, for they see life as consisting only of the emotional and the rational aspects. Now if the aim of Zen training were to strengthen these two aspects by means of putting tremendous effort into them, then this training would only be appropriate for the first half of life. But this is not so. Zen training is not limited to the fit and healthy or to a specific age group, but is a practice that is directed at the actual realisation of a wide, deep and lasting understanding.

It is the most vital and important practice, for old as well as young, men and women, for everybody.

Reiseiteki, the spiritual dimension, is this greater aspect coming into awareness. And another way of seeing it is as universal, not limited, not as restricted to just mine or yours, to man or woman. Nor is it limited to being just between birth and death; within this great life which is ever proceeding, we are simply a particular instant. Thus, birth, old age, sickness and death are but one condition within this larger life. The real experience of Zen, that comes through zazen, is therefore not simply in somehow finding or grasping 'self', but in transcending it. That is what soaring like a great bird is about – not just a relaxed flight, but entering a state in which bird, air and the whole world are perfectly blended and merged.

You may fall asleep in zazen, but then the *jikijitsu* will shout at you and you wake up; he is like an alarm clock! Then you may try to do zazen in such a way as not to be shouted at – thus putting yourself on the defensive and in doing so, into a relationship of opposition. Consequently, zazen becomes very painful.

At the Summer School, you go into the dining room where food is being served for you. Then there is time for zazen; and I am here to talk to you. It is like being in heaven – without doing anything all these riches are available, and even if you fall asleep in zazen, there is somebody to wake you up. So why do you feel you have to 'do' all this and struggle? Why do you get so tired that you even feel sick? Because there is opposition – you have not melted, cannot believe that everything around you is yourself. Yesterday someone was feeling tense and got a massage – that seems to have worked too well, for now they have gone into another bad direction and fallen asleep.

Having called out 'Master,' Zuigan then exhorted, 'Open your eyes, don't sleep.' And he himself answered simply, 'Yes, yes.' To sleep, is to lose oneself; it is a stopping of the functioning of Buddha-nature. I am asking whether the Buddha-nature is always working? Is it always active? At times one may feel it is and then one is soaring like that great bird – but that is deluding oneself. When I had talked of this great bird the other day, I noticed that afterwards everybody was erect and with a swing – and perhaps there was also then an awareness of the surroundings that had not been noticed before such as the sunlight, the woods, or the beauty of the grass. Is that not a wonderful feeling? But at such moments we must ask ourselves whether we have really melted into the scenery, or have we in some way been taken in by it?

On previous visits to London, I have stayed at Shobo-an, the Zen Centre which is located in a private residential area. But this time in Chelsea I saw another part of London, with many young people. Some had their hair dressed standing up like the horns of a rhinoceros, some had huge cockscombs on their heads, and I even saw some with a red horn in front of their head and a green one at the back of it! They looked just as if dressed in borrowed rags – all have been taken in by their horns and their cockscombs, have been stolen by the clothes they are wearing. And complete with their Walkman as they go along, they are not listening to the music – their self has been stolen, captured by the music.

This is only one illustration – human beings can be taken in like this in hundreds of ways, such as sport, sex, travel, etc. Walking in beautiful surroundings, we may be captured by the scenery. So Zuigan warned against being so captured and possessed, not to be cheated in such a way. And he himself replied simply with 'yes, yes'. For this way of being cheated or deceived is not a fraud or trickery played on us by another human being, but is being captured, tricked by one's surroundings. Experiment with this. From now on try to walk in a lively way yet in the regular kinhin manner. You should be used to this by now. Do not stoop or hunch yourself up, or flap about even if you feel like that bird soaring in the sky. Because you are yet immature, keep to this kinhin posture as a reminder that you still have a degree of reverence or respect!

In Japan nowadays, there is much talk about this being an age of rapid access to information. This does not mean that the Japanese are living with the experience of a high level of information. Though they may think so, the reality is different. All it means is that with information so profuse, humans cannot assimilate the lot themselves, so they have developed high-powered computers which can do it for them. I do not know how this is in England – but it seems that as soon as one needs and acquires a personal computer to use this information, two problems arise. In the midst of such an overpowering surge of information, human beings become dull. Doctors understand this, for our physical development is along the lines of self-protection.

In case of any excess, for example of food, we either vomit it or void it in some way. And if we are bombarded by an excess of information, then our nervous system is geared to protect us against this, to shield us and so we become dull. Because of this, many Japanese, especially the younger generation, are losing the awareness of their Buddha-nature. When you see someone who is sick or sad in some way, it is natural to cry; this is the action of Buddha-nature. Or seeing someone who is happy, the response of the Buddha-nature is to dance for joy. But people who suffer from an excess of information become dulled by it, their hearts deadened. This is one of the two problems referred to above.

The other is that all of this excess of information is man-made. Because of this, many young Japanese have become quite incapable of responding to a natural environment. All they can take in is the writings of academics or of journalists of some sort or other – this is all they can digest, and their ability to grasp what comes to them directly from their natural surroundings has diminished, atrophied. Thus young mothers no longer directly recognise the signals coming from their small children and rather read specialist books on child rearing and infant psychology or listen to the comments of the child's school teacher. On the basis of all this information they have gathered, they then try to bring up the child whom they do not actually see directly! I notice that some of you smile, so I suspect that the same applies here, too.

This may now give you some idea of what Master Zuigan meant when he admonished himself, 'Do not be deceived, do not be cheated.' A favourite Zen expression in Japanese is, *chika-tsuki,* to get in touch with or to contact something directly, with nothing intervening. And so, for this reason young monks go barefoot even in winter, not because they are poor; and in this world of high technology, they also still work with the simplest tools just to stress direct contact. People these days wear plastic gloves for washing and even have a machine to do the washing for them. Of those who still wash by hand and those who just press a button, which of them is the more likely to be cheated?

Zuigan lived over a thousand years ago, but his cautioning himself would seem to be even more appropriate today. So what kind of life is it then when we are not being cheated, when we come to realise this 'master of self'? Though it is possible to comment on the self, and on the question of not being cheated, yet to live such a life is up to each one individually. Zen is said to be severe – not because you may be hit with a stick, not because the *jikijitsu* may shout at you, or the teacher is very strict. Rather it is so because only you yourself can live such an 'uncheated' life. Nobody can help you to do that; and for that reason, Zen must be severe. But not only Zen – every religious discipline that is to help towards such a life must of necessity be severe. And so Zen is said to be severe just because it provides this feeling of direct contact.

Master Rinzai comments on this, saying that nobody can help us with this. And Master Mumon also offers just the same advice. What is it? What are we to do? Whether awake or asleep, thinking about the great doubt that arises from the koan causes us to go astray. I have spoken about this many times before. And seeing me here, you may think me a kind man. I am, but be careful because that type of kindness will lead you astray. The real kindness encourages you to develop an awareness of the problem. Thinking about this great life only during the Summer School and returning home and forgetting all about it is cheating yourself. And what I am trying to do is to somehow catch you on the raw, so that there will be a problem and when you are back home you will be hooked and so continue to work on it!

For example, if you were told by your doctor that you have cancer and as a consequence you now begin to be interested in that great life, that is leaving it a bit late. So it is better to start now while you are happy and strong and vigorous, while you feel joyful and are active, because you will need to put all that effort into realising that you have this great life. If you read Mumon's comment on this koan, you should now also understand what he is talking about – not necessarily his words but his meaning. If you chase after Mumon's words you will not get anywhere. And if you blindly copy Zuigan and call out to yourself, and respond yourself with 'yes', the mere imitation is not enough.

So what should you do? Work it out for yourselves!

As to the verse, it is the only one in the collection not written by Mumon himself. For this koan he used a poem by another Chinese Master, Chosa, which perfectly matches the koan. Chosa asks, why, of the many who undertook training, most of them did not find this master of the self? Because they only considered the rational and emotional self, only looked at themselves as distinct from their surroundings, split into 'I' and 'other'. And because they confused what they saw with the true master, a series of disasters emerged in the human world, with the concomitant suffering.

People who only look at the physical side tend to think that the suffering that humans experience can't be alleviated. But this master or intrinsic self has the realisation that whatever may happen – whether the body falls sick, or some disaster happens to them personally – there is this greater life. And this is not just knowing it intellectually, in the head, but directly. It is a question of training and going on training until one is confident and assured of it. And so it is up to you whether you choose to be satisfied with a mere intellectual understanding, or whether you decide to cultivate the deeply felt awareness of the greater life.

CASE 13 · TOKUSAN'S BOWL

One day Tokusan went down to the hall holding his bowl. Seppo saw him and asked, 'Old fellow, where are you going, the bell has not yet sounded and the gong has not been struck.' Tokusan then returned to the abbot's quarters. Seppo mentioned this to Ganto. Ganto said, 'The long and short of it is that Tokusan does not yet know the last word.'

When Tokusan heard of this he told his attendant to summon Ganto to come, and asked him, 'Do you not approve of this old monk?' Ganto confidentially explained his intention. Tokusan acquiesced and left.

The next day he ascended the high seat and actually was not the same as usual. Ganto went to the front of the monk's hall, clapped his hand and laughing said, 'How wonderful! The old fellow has succeeded in understanding the last word. After that there is nothing anyone in the world can do about him.'

MUMON'S COMMENT

As for the last word, both Ganto and Tokusan never actually even dreamt of it. Looking closely, you find it is very much like a group of marionettes.

THE VERSE

識得最初句
便會末後句
末後與最初
不是者一句

If you thoroughly understand the very first word,
Then you understand the last word.
The last word and the very first,
These are not one word.

The *Lotus Sutra* tells of a wealthy Indian merchant. His only son was still a child when he strayed too far from home and got lost. The merchant sent search parties everywhere, even into neighbouring countries, but in vain. Eventually he moved to another country and re-established himself there. His business soon flourished as before, and he found himself even better off than he had been. He lived in a splendid mansion with wonderful gardens and fountains and had many servants.

One day he noticed a ragged beggar at the gate, bedraggled and down-at-heel, but at one glance recognised him as his son. The beggar did not know that it was his father or his house; he had stopped at the gate because it was a great house and he thought he might get work there or in any case perhaps some food. But on looking through the gates at the great house and seeing all the well-dressed people, he became afraid and was just sidling away when one of the servants approached him and asked him to come inside. Seeing the beggar going away, the father had ordered the servant to bring him back. Scared of being imprisoned for loitering, he refused. But the servant, keen to obey his orders, tried to drag him in. Seeing them, the master intervened, deciding against using force.

Now, do you know who the master is and who the son? Many of you may feel that the Zen group is fierce and try to escape!

Anyway, the wealthy man had his son released, but ordered one of his servants to follow him and find out where he lived. On hearing that he stayed with the beggars in the poor quarter, the merchant sent another servant dressed in rags to stay there, make friends with him, and mention the opportunity of getting work at the rich man's estate. So, he went back and at his father's house, he was given the jobs he was accustomed to – cleaning the lavatories and sweeping the yards. After some time, the merchant changed into poor clothes, and himself approached his son, saying, 'I would like you to treat me as if I was your father. Speak quite freely.' But in the beggar's heart the fear he felt of this great house was not easily dispelled. Only gradually, being given different jobs and succeeding in doing them, did he become accustomed to the house and worked his way upwards. It took years, and the master was getting old. One day, feeling that he was approaching death, he told the young man that he was his father and that after his death, all the treasures would be his. Then he invited all the neighbours and introduced his son and heir. For the poverty-stricken youth, the life of a wealthy man now began.

So, this beautiful story tells of the son who was born to a rich merchant but lost his father and home and became poor. Nor was he able to take his place again as the son of a wealthy man until he had spent many years in training. Many people doubt that the Buddha-nature is inherent in everything, because if it is present in everything and in everybody from birth, why should it then be necessary to undergo practice? And why, in its presence, should there be so many problems in this world of ours? The above analogy answers that doubt.

The teachings of Buddhism may be divided into two general types: one is the course along which a person is brought to the great house and there gradually is introduced and trained in its ways; the other, from the outset tries to make the person immediately understand that he is the son of a wealthy man. The latter course of trying to force immediate understanding is called *ton-kyo* in Zen, which means 'at once', 'directly'; and the course of gradual training, of progression towards understanding, is called *zen-kyo*. But of course, from wherever you enter, the end is the same. I keep repeating that everyone has this Buddha-nature. However, on hearing this, like that son of the wealthy man, most try to escape from it. 'No, how could this be? The Buddha was so great, whereas I am a poor creature with many faults,' they say, and cannot believe that the Buddha-nature is within themselves. Therefore you must practise until your bones break with *ton-kyo*. And as for those who are following the course of gradual understanding, when they reach the end by this method, they also realise that they are children of the Buddha. Using words like Buddha-nature or child of the Buddha is only another way of expressing this Great Life I have mentioned before.

When he was young, Master Tokusan had been an ardent student of the Sutras. Later he settled in central China and specialised in lecturing on the *Diamond Sutra*. He believed every word of the sutra, and accordingly was convinced that Buddhist practice must take a very long time and must involve the accumulation of much effort over long periods or *kalpas*. Then he heard a rumour that in the south of China there were Buddhists, followers of the Zen School, who said that such long training was not necessary, and that it was possible to attain understanding here in this life. He was very agitated by this and taking it as a spurious teaching he set out for the South, determined to use all the learning he had acquired over many years of study, to refute these Buddhist outsiders.

Journeying down the Yangtse River he came upon a small village. Hungry and tired, he entered a dilapidated tea house and asked the old woman there, 'Give me some *tenjin*.' (Literally, to give just a little to the heart.) The old woman remarked, 'You are carrying a heavy satchel on your back; what is in it?' 'The commentary on the wonderful *Diamond Sutra*, an extremely difficult teaching, far beyond the understanding of an old crone like you.' But the woman retorted, 'I have heard that it is said in that Sutra, "The heart of the past is gone; the heart of the future is not yet here; where then can the heart of the present be grasped?" Is that so?' Tokusan was astonished. 'You really do know – that is exactly what the Sutra says.' She responded, 'Venerable master, you just asked me for some *tenjin*. Let me ask you – if it is impossible to grasp the heart of the past, the present or the future, then with what heart do you expect me to give you this *tenjin*?' Tokusan, dumbfounded, stared at the old lady, who scolded, 'If you cannot even answer my question, regardless of the pile of books you might be carrying on your back, I am not going to give you any *tenjin*.'

When my own teacher, Zuigan Roshi, gave teisho on this, he looked at me. 'Do you understand the greatness of Tokusan? Tokusan was challenged and so crushed by the old woman that he could not say a word. Yet a scholar of his learning could surely have got the better of the old crone, had he wanted to. But rather than trying to argue with and overpower her, Tokusan was honest and faithful to his own doubt. This was what later made him such a great Master.' Zuigan Roshi, pointing to where I was sitting said, 'When I try to get your head to bow, you escape with your tail, and when I try to get your tail, you escape with your head! All that you do is make rationalisations and prevaricate, and whatever I try to do, you do not open up – you cannot open!' So now, as a present, I am offering you what I have received from Zuigan Roshi.

When Tokusan was ousted by this old woman, he asked her, 'If you, an old crone in a dingy tea shop, can understand such things, there must be a Zen master hereabouts. Please tell me where.' On being told of Master Ryotan, he at once set off to his monastery, and there he attained satori – the account of which is the subject of Case 28 in our collection (*Mumonkan*).

So Tokusan, who had started as a scholar, later realised Great Satori. From of old, he has been considered to be of the same stature as Master Rinzai. The latter became famous for his shout or 'Katsu,' and Tokusan is remembered for using his stick. His favourite gambit with inquirers was, 'If you can answer, I will give you thirty blows, and if you cannot answer, I will give you thirty blows.' Do you understand – answering what? Tokusan, at the moment of meeting, would say, 'Go on, speak!', and then deliver his blows.

In the case of Joshu's visiting the hermits (Case 12), Joshu asked, 'Is there, is there?' He did not ask, 'What is there?' Wondering what it is that Joshu might be asking is not Zen training, which has no object other than concretely realising the Buddha-nature within ourselves. So Tokusan asks those he confronts about Buddha-nature; and with regard to Buddha-nature, whether you speak or not, he will strike. It is natural. In the case of someone who speaks, this is not the Buddha-nature, but simply the concept of Buddha-nature. And in the case of those not being able to reply, they have lost sight of the Buddha-nature. So what Tokusan wants to see is the Buddha-nature working at that instant, in a lively and vital manner. Thus in order not to be struck by Tokusan's stick, the working of the Buddha-nature must be demonstrated there and then, at that moment. Tokusan, with his stick at the ready, urges, 'Do, do!' He does not say, 'Tomorrow will be all right!' It is just as if someone held a sword to your throat, pointed a pistol at your head and demanded, 'Answer now!' But do not think that Tokusan is doing something violent. It's only that, however sloppy a person might be, in front of Tokusan they would shape up. That is the greatness of Tokusan, who accordingly became famous for the use of his stick. Throughout China, these two masters were well-known, Rinzai with his 'Katsu' and Tokusan with his stick; they were like lion and tiger.

When Tokusan was getting old, a young monk called Seppo was in his assembly. Even today Seppo is regarded as a model for monks in training. When he later went on pilgrimage, he always carried a large wooden cooking ladle. In the great monasteries with perhaps hundreds of monks, the hardest work was in the kitchens. Seppo would always help in the kitchens, or with cleaning the toilets, offering this work in the hope of eventually being able to break free from the faults he had committed in his early life.

Kosen was a famous Zen master from about a hundred years ago. When he was still in training at the Engaku-ji monastery in Kamakura, he would, on rainy nights while the other monks were sleeping, put buckets under the eaves and sit zazen until the buckets were full; then he used the water to clean the toilets. Thus he diligently tried to reduce the thick layer of unskilful habits he had accumulated.

Seppo practised thoroughly and with great care; yet the more he practised, the further away satori seemed to be. There he was, studying and practising in Tokusan's assembly, with the great Master growing old and feeble. One day, Tokusan came down well before the bell for the midday meal had been sounded. Seppo, working in the kitchen, said to him, 'Roshi, neither the bell nor the gong have yet been struck. Where are you going with your bowls?' Tokusan, without a word, went back to his quarters.

As we know, this same Tokusan is the master who said, 'If you can speak, I will give you thirty blows and if you are silent, I will give you thirty blows.' But at Seppo's words, he docilely went back. Seppo could not understand the wonderful quality of Tokusan's responses. Probably you do not understand either.

Anyway, Seppo prided himself in getting the better of his great Master. Disciples in general are delighted when they see their teacher make a mistake. Seppo could not keep this to himself and told Ganto, who was an elder brother disciple of his. Ganto saw the greatness of Tokusan's action, and also realised that Seppo was not enlightened. So he put on a little performance, and for it set up a wonderful scenario. We will look at it later.

Meanwhile, why was Tokusan's action, coming into the kitchen and then quietly going back to his quarters, so great? This splendid koan has been used for over a thousand years!

Though zazen, sitting meditation, is our main meditation practice, we also do *kinhin*, walking meditation. In walking meditation, we do not try to see things. Nor should we think about why we are walking. Our attention should not be captured by things we hear or see, but rather we should walk like a cloud drifting across the sky or a river flowing. Becoming one with nature, is not our deliberately going towards it, nor trying to see it from our point of view. Truly understanding something or somebody is not a matter of trying to do so, but of becoming empty oneself and so the other simply flows in. I frequently use the analogy of buying tumblers. Mostly we are concerned with their shape or make, but actually we use their empty space. In the same way, we tend to be concerned with the clothes we are wearing, or with our hairstyle, or how we walk, but forget that in terms of living, we use the empty part of ourselves. In zazen or *kinhin*, and ideally at every moment, we should strive to live from this empty part. That is perhaps the benefit from Zen – try to taste the grandeur of Tokusan.

At teisho, one of my disciples carries in the textbook. This is not merely ceremonial. The attendant carrying the book and bowing while placing it before me, symbolises that teisho is not given because I want to, but because I am asked to do so. It also shows that *shugyo*, practice, can only be done by our own effort or intention. Nowadays everything is organised and certain things are expected to be given. There are even people who mistakenly believe that if only they join some large organisation, they will somehow benefit from it. Yet religion is entirely individual, no matter how many people may gather together. If in the individual heart there is no great aspiration, the individual practice will come to nothing. But having said this, we must also recognise that there are limits to an individual's power.

Traditions are ways that have shown themselves to be of value over many generations and in diverse civilisations. Buddhism, with its 2,500 years of tradition, is worth attention; were it merely strange, it would have died out long ago. The patriarchs, who throughout this long time grasped and held the true meaning, are far superior to ourselves. So, from our side we need to accept that long tradition and to use it as a kind of gauge or test against which we can measure our own understanding. The most dangerous thing is to take one small bite of Buddhism and on the strength of that to imagine that one has consumed the full-course meal, and then to begin making one's own version of it!

Rinzai, the founder of the Rinzai School, spent three years in Obaku's assembly in intense practice. On the surface, his practice was perfect; he rigorously kept the rules and not for a second did he allow himself any unnecessary or wasteful action. But he did not go to Obaku for sanzen. The chief monk, having noticed this, eventually asked him, 'Since you have come here, have you ever had sanzen with Obaku?' 'No, I have not.' 'Why don't you go?' 'There is nothing to ask.' Perhaps Rinzai was satisfied with his practice and so felt no need. So, the head monk, Bokuju, advised, 'Go and ask Obaku what the fundamental truth of Buddhism is.' Rinzai, obeying naturally and easily, went for sanzen with Obaku, and there asked, 'What is the essence of Buddhism?' No sooner had he put the question than Obaku hit him.

Rinzai did not understand why, so he went back and reported what had happened to Bokuju. 'Why was I struck?' Bokuju told him to go once more and ask. Rinzai went again, but this time, with only half the question uttered, he was again beaten. He went and reported this to Bokuju, who told him to go yet again. This time, before he had even opened his mouth, he was hit hard. When you hear such stories, do you think that Zen is a very rough practice? Let us assume someone is sleeping here, and dreaming. In his dream of tumbling down a cliff, he is gripped by fear; suffering, he cries out in anguish. What would you do in that situation? Would you shake him, and if he still did not wake up, would you strike him?

Telling the sleeper that he is sleeping securely in his bed is useless. The only help is to wake him and make him recognise for himself that he is not in danger. In Zen practice, when somebody hits someone with a stick, it is generally seen as one person striking another person, and this seems to be inhuman; in fact, it is the opposite. You hit because you know that if the person but wakes, they will recognise the truth for themselves. In such a situation, it is much more 'inhuman' to try to explain things rather than hit, because this kind of 'inhumanity' arises from the feeling 'I understand;' but what *I do not understand* is that the person I am dealing with does not himself have the power to understand.

In Rinzai's case, too, though being struck three times by Obaku, his eyes were still not opened. But because of the pain from being beaten, it became a great problem for him, and he was made to face this problem. So instead of just rigidly following the forms of training as before, he was forced to confront situations directly. It was his acceptance of this problem that gave birth to the great Rinzai that we know.

Therefore, senior and experienced Zen teachers adopt such stern and fierce attitudes just because they believe in the person they are training. Without this conviction that there is something worthwhile in that person, such behaviour would simply be that of a tyrant; no Zen roshi or educator worthy of the name would be so misguided.

So Seppo was a diligent and devoted monk, but he had no great problem in his heart. Hence, though he was meticulous on keeping the form and the precepts, he still found he could not attain insight. He wandered from monastery to monastery, confronting different roshis, and committed to memory what they told him. But he understood it only with his head, and just believed that he had grasped it and was enlightened. Therefore he could not fathom the unprecedented quality of Tokusan emerging from his quarters like a floating cloud, and then when asked what he was doing, floating like a cloud, returning to his room again.

Seppo could see Tokusan only from the basic view of winning or losing the encounter. Then, full of himself and feeling that he had scored a point, he told Ganto, who at once recognised the greatness of Tokusan's behaviour and Seppo's immaturity, and he realised that the reason for it was that Seppo had no great problem. Accordingly, rather than striking him with a stick, he presented Seppo with a great doubt. This is what is usually referred to as 'the last word of Zen.'

Ganto does not say that Seppo does not understand this last word of Zen, but phrased it as if Tokusan, famous throughout China, did not understand the last word of Zen. Thus, like a fisherman, Ganto puts out bait that even the most wily fish could not resist. Seppo was at once drawn by this bait. He promptly rushed off to tell the other monks what Ganto had said. The rumour that Ganto had said Tokusan did not understand the last word of Zen swept through the monastery and soon reached Tokusan himself. He sent for Ganto and said, 'I have heard what you are saying about me. Is there something you do not approve of, that you do not accept?' Ganto whispered something to Tokusan, who nodded. Next day, Tokusan's teisho was quite different from his usual style, and very powerful. For Seppo it was probably the first teisho he had really heard because the hook of Ganto's bait went ever deeper into him. But Ganto, when it was over and the monks had left, began to dance and clap his hands. 'At last our Roshi Tokusan has understood the last word of Zen! Everyone throughout the world will think there is nothing Tokusan can do – he is hopeless. Not just people in the world – everybody, dying, being sick or whatever, will see that there is nothing Tokusan can do!' Hearing this, the hook inside Seppo stuck fast. What was this wonderful 'last word of Zen'?

Unless this baited hook is swallowed by you too, Ganto's kindness will be for nothing. And in his own commentary, Mumon, too, vaults onto the horse that Ganto is riding, and says that if you ponder this last word of Zen, not only Tokusan failed to understand it, but Ganto could not imagine it even in his dreams.

What is this last word? Looking at it as far as Mumon or I have investigated it, it is nothing but a play, with verses added. If you understand the first word, you understand the last word. However, having said this, nevertheless, the first and the last words are not the same. Ganto placed Seppo on a revolving chair and spun him round. Mumon then, moving in the same direction, whirls the chair even faster. If from the beginning there is something that you cannot fathom, when whirled round you become even more confused. Just this is the kindness of Zen, is the purpose of a koan. Reading the signposts that indicate north, south, east and west is not all that important, but it is essential for each one individually to discover where he is. Seppo, though he had received all this kindness from Ganto, still had not attained insight at the time of Tokusan's death.

Thereafter, Seppo and Ganto together set out, wandering from monastery to monastery all over China. One day, in a raging snowstorm, they had to put up at a village. There Ganto promptly fell asleep while Seppo sat in zazen far into the night. Ganto enjoined, 'Seppo, go to sleep! At this time of night you should rest. Stop doing zazen with a serious face, deceiving all around you! As if Seppo was great!' Seppo objected, 'Elder brother, I am not sitting with that intention. I cannot help doing zazen because I have a problem and my heart is not at rest.' Hearing this, Ganto got up from his bed. 'Well, then, I will join you. But do tell me what experience you have had up to now.'

Seppo then told Ganto that when he was with Tokusan, he had had this or that experience, had been struck and so on. At that, Ganto scolded him, 'Are you not simply recounting what is common experience? A proverb says that what comes in by the front door is not a treasure of the house. All you have told me is what you have heard from others, or things which have come in from outside. But it is useless unless it comes from within and spreads over heaven and earth.'

At these words, all his experience, all that he had built up over long years, splintered and cracked, and Seppo's eyes were opened to the wonderful thing that he had within himself. Dancing round in joy, he exclaimed, 'Today, just now and here in this very village, the eyes opened!'

When Zuigan Roshi gave teisho on this koan, he too seemed to be delighted. Those of us who were listening always felt that even if one had not had satori yet there was some power flowing from this. So put your faith in what is within, and do not look for what is outside! Master Rinzai also repeatedly exhorts us to do just that. And I, and others who give teisho, also constantly repeat it. But people understand it with their heads only, or they may remember the words; but when it comes down to daily life, they lose sight of themselves and turn to what is external.

However, we must not misunderstand this, and so I stress again and again that having trust in what is within, in the real self, does *not* mean trusting one's habits, one's experience or one's knowledge; it means following the intrinsic nature we were born with. This wonderful power is not derived from practice, it is there from birth, only it has become submerged and forgotten under acquired notions, or obscured by emotions. Thus what in itself is empty has become filled to the brim with all kinds of -isms. The Buddha says it is filled with illusions – like a someone who is securely in their bed and yet dreams that they are rushing about and shouting.

The kindness Ganto shows is not unique to him; all patriarchs display it; rather than letting it go to waste, we should learn from Seppo.

CASE 14 · NANSEN KILLS A CAT

When the monks of the East Hall and West Hall were quarrelling about a cat, Nansen took the cat and, holding it up, said, 'If you can say (a word) I will spare the cat; if not, I will kill it.' All remained silent; Nansen killed it. In the evening Joshu came back from somewhere. Nansen told him what had happened. Joshu took off his sandals, put them on his head, and walked out. Nansen said, 'If only you had been there, I could have saved the cat.'

MUMON'S COMMENT

Just say, what is the meaning of Joshu's putting the sandals on his head? If you can say a word about the meaning, you will see that Nansen's deed was not in vain. If not, DANGER!

THE VERSE

趙州若在
倒行此令
奪却刀子
南泉乞命

If Joshu had been there,
He would have turned the action;
He would have snatched away the knife,
And Nansen now begs for his life.

In dealing with this koan, it is as if you were walking barefoot on the edge of an upturned sword. In general, events presented in a koan, as well as in teisho comments, are utterly different from a learned lecture. The present koan is a particularly good example. The protagonists are two outstanding masters of the late Tang dynasty when Zen was at its most vigorous. Joshu became renowned in his own time and has been revered ever since. He had trained under Nansen whose assembly of monks filled two Zen Halls, an eastern and a western one.

One day, the monks of these two halls were quarrelling over a cat. The koan does not say why; perhaps the cat was cited as an example in a discussion about Buddhism, or while they were joking some argument flared up. It is, however, likely that the monks were serious and that the subject of their dispute was not a trivial one.

But from Nansen's point of view, whether they argued about the nature of Buddhism using the cat as an example, or were seeking some religious insight intellectually, all was empty discussion. And further, all attempts to convince an antagonist by argument are beside the point. Nansen therefore demanded that they stop bandying words about and instead express precisely and in a single word their religious understanding. To illustrate that he grabbed the cat that had become the bone of contention and, holding it up, threatened, 'If you can say a single word, I will spare the cat. If not, I will kill it.' Thus challenged by Nansen, the monks suddenly fell silent and no one could say a single word – which proved the futility of their arguments. This is the first point. Even if you can eloquently discuss Buddhism, or Zen, or religion, but when challenged by Nansen who has grasped the very core of the argument, you cannot reply. It is a mistake to think that Nansen has grasped a cat; what he has grasped is the essence of what each and every one of his monks was seeking. No doubt each one thought he was seeking Buddha or satori. However, what they should truly have been seeking was not Buddha or enlightenment but the essence of their own being. This essence Nansen grasped and held up to them.

The first reaction to this koan most likely is, 'Didn't Nansen break the first precept of Buddhism, not to take life?' Those who have even the tiniest hint of such a reaction should not work on this koan. It cannot be stressed too often that even if a koan refers to somebody or something that happened in China a thousand years ago, when actually working on the koan it must be taken not as an ancient story but grappled with as the experience of this moment, here and now. If you look at Nansen, the cat and Joshu from the outside, evaluating or criticising, you are not working on it as a koan.

So what Nansen is grasping then is not a cat, but Nansen himself. And what the monks were shown by Nansen was not a cat but their very own lives. It was against this that Nansen put his knife. There is then no escape, there is no way of sliding off into some other problem. And Nansen is putting the knife not to other people's problems but to himself, directly. What Nansen cut was not the kitten, but Nansen himself – and that Nansen is I. It is the same as if each of the assembled monks was putting a knife to himself. And so, over time, transcending time, we ourselves must do as Nansen did, put the knife against ourselves.

But as none of the monks could respond, Nansen killed the cat. To repeat: Nansen did not kill a cat; he killed himself. This is as much as can be said and having put everything into it, more cannot be said.

To repeat again, this koan is frequently criticised as offending against the first precept of Buddhism, not to take life. How then can Nansen's action possibly be justified?

Once again, should there be the slightest flicker of an ethical judgement with regard to the koan, you had better stop, for then you are putting that koan and that experience at a distance and, separated from it, pass sentence. From the Zen point of view, this is the most remote approach; our practice consists of taking whatever happened, wherever it happened, as our experience here and now.

As to Joshu, he had not been there. When he returned in the evening Nansen told him what had happened. Without a word, Joshu took off his sandals, placed them on his head, and walked out.

Mumon's Comment: If you can really understand what Joshu did, you will understand that Nansen's action of killing the cat was not meaningless. If you can't understand Joshu's action then for you to go on with this koan is extremely dangerous. For again, what Nansen cut was not the kitten but Nansen himself – and that Nansen is me! And the Joshu who put his sandals on his head and left is not Joshu, but is the revitalised form of myself who has taken a sword and thrust it into my very being. So, if you cannot approach this koan and work on it in this way, then please do not even begin, for nothing will come out of it but fruitless, time-consuming disputations which become a barrier to your training.

The terrible atrocities perpetrated in Japan during the persecution of Christianity some three hundred years ago serve as reminder of what man can do to man. Their converts were tortured and the missionaries forced to witness their agonies which were prolonged until they apostatised and were made to trample on what to them was most dear and holy – pictures of Christ or the Virgin Mary. At the moment of doing so, I believe some must have entered another dimension of experience. For they trod on their highest value only on being forced to see the terrible pains afflicted on their converts, of excruciating suffering piled up wave after wave.

But a picture that can be trodden on is not a representative symbol of God. What is most fundamental to our lives, to our existence, is that which cannot be trodden upon, cannot be wounded and is not sullied, however much it is spat upon or pierced with a knife. Among those apostatising missionaries surely there must have been some who recognised this.

You have to understand exactly, fully, the meaning of Joshu's putting his sandals on his head. If you can present a wonderful word or expression in response to this working of Joshu, then you will understand that what Nansen did was not a meaningless act. But then, as Mumon comments, there is danger!

The Verse: If Joshu had been there when Nansen took his sword to kill the kitten, and if Joshu had taken hold of the sword, even the great Nansen would have been at a loss. But even Joshu taking Nansen's sword is not enough, you yourself must take hold of it.

The verse thus shows that although Nansen and Joshu are two separate bodies, they are not two separate beings. And so at the same time are we – I and you and the cat. What, then, is to be killed?

CASE 15 · TOZAN'S SIXTY BLOWS

Because Tozan came to Ummon for instruction, the master asked, 'From what place have you just come?' 'From Sato,' replied Tozan. Ummon asked, 'What place were you at in the summer?' Tozan replied, 'At Hozu Temple south of the lake.' Ummon asked, 'When did you leave there?' 'On the 25th of the eighth month,' replied Tozan. Ummon said, 'I spare you sixty blows of the stick.'

The next day Tozan came again and respectfully asked about what had happened the day before, saying, 'Yesterday, Master, you spared me sixty blows of the stick. I do not know where I was at fault?' Ummon said 'You rice-bag, wandering about like that, west of the river, south of the lake.' At this Tozan experienced great enlightenment.

MUMON'S COMMENT

If at that time Ummon had given the original fodder, then Tozan would have had another way of living activity, and the gates of the school would not have become silent and desolate. Tozan spent all night in the sea of right and wrong until dawn arrived. He again went to Unmon, who helped him push through. Tozan was enlightened directly, but his nature was not yet refined.

Now I ask all you, should Tozan have suffered sixty blows of the stick or should he not have suffered them. If you say he should have been beaten, then all grasses, trees and thickets should be beaten. If you say he should not have been subject to blows, then Ummon becomes a liar. If you are able to clearly see into this, then at that moment you and Tozan will exhale with the same breath.

獅子教兒迷子訣
擬前跳躑早翻身
無端再敘當頭著
前箭猶輕後箭深

The lion teaches her cubs in a bewildering way,
Intending to vigorously jump forward, turning around again.
Perplexed he tentatively speaks, but is dumbfounded
The first arrow was still light, but the second arrow went deep.

SOKO ROSHI'S COMMENTS

All of us wish for inner peace. Yet, hardly having attained it, we again become anxious, and begin to wonder whether it can last, or worry that something might be wrong in our lives. Thus, we may discover that though life is superficially peaceful and tranquil, there is still a sadness deep down in our hearts. Even though we ourselves have set up the pattern of our life, yet at the same time we find sadness within ourselves, and begin to wonder where that sadness or loneliness or suffering is coming from. If we feel such sadness, pain or loneliness, should we then not somehow change our way of life? So we try to create a life without any sadness or loneliness or suffering. Accordingly, some marry, while others divorce or live singly. Still others take a long holiday, travel abroad, or attach themselves to a large organisation – seeking new experiences, or activities. For a time, such pursuits may be successful, but once the new routine has settled in, they somehow begin to feel a lack of interest, and sadness, suffering or loneliness once more emerge.

So although people seek change, they will accept only the kind of change they themselves instigate, and are quite unable to accept changes that happen to them. The fact is that though people do not want to be sad or lonely or to suffer, a peaceful life soon becomes boring. Most people believe that there really can be a life free from suffering, sadness and hardship. Perhaps you believe that at least for me, a Roshi, all is tranquil and there is no sadness. Yet I, too, feel sadness and suffering daily; and there are many things that I cannot do, that I have to bypass rather than pass through.

Once a disciple asked Confucius, 'Does a sage find anything difficult to deal with?' He probably expected to hear that a true sage never finds himself in such a situation. But Confucius replied that a sage, too, may find himself in a difficult situation which he cannot overcome. The disciple was surprised and asked, 'In that case, what is the difference between a sage and one who has not attained the Way?' Confucius said that a person who has not yet attained, when confronted by a difficulty, is shattered; but the sage, when confronting a difficulty, changes his pattern of behaviour. If one changes, or transforms oneself, then one can pass through or find another path. Confucius suggests that when confronted with a difficulty, we should change our pattern of behaviour. When coming across a wall most people adapt themselves and find a way around it. In daily life, however, when people are confronted with some barrier however small they are often thrown into confusion instead of adapting to the situation.

But why do I (Soko Morinaga) personally accept the sadness, loneliness or suffering that is part of daily life? Because I do not believe that it is something I have to eliminate. Rather, I gladly savour it, and take sadness, loneliness and suffering as the spice of human life. Dogs, cats and all animals live by their instincts. Accordingly, they do not do anything specifically good, nor anything particularly bad. Human beings, however, live almost entirely by their head-knowledge, and confidently base their judgements on it and accordingly make their decisions. All the same, we instinctively know that decisions made with the mind only raise difficulties or are weak and feeble. We can send rockets to the moon or the planets and we can incorporate in them means of changing course. Likewise, having made certain judgements and lived with them for a while, when loneliness or sadness overcomes us again, we can change direction.

However, the loneliness or sadness we feel is actually a wonderful intimation of the Buddha-nature, is an opening out that leads to understanding. Those who feel this sadness most strongly are quite literally able to approach the gate of heaven. The Buddha taught that suffering is one of the signs of being. We should realise that feelings of sadness or loneliness are not something to be eliminated or denied, but rather something to be experienced and understood. We do not sit zazen in order to eradicate suffering or sadness, but to taste this sadness deeply. There are those who find it difficult to savour this feeling deeply; but when sitting zazen, they do feel this sadness and some feel sadness deepening further still during zazen. This does not mean they are being misled, only that a power we all are born with, an instinctual power, is working.

'I am an upright person, living correctly, not doing anything wrong; within my family there are no problems.' Somebody who can feel this way is deluded! Truly, sadness and suffering are a kind of spice to heighten the taste of human life. Those who can use this spice properly have no need to go abroad on holiday, no need to transform the tranquillity of everyday life, and no need to search outside themselves when anxious. In the most humdrum, ordinary everyday life we can taste everything – there are hundreds of opportunities.

As for myself, although on the surface I appear peaceful, nearly every day there are opportunities to taste life in this way. Every day there is joy, loneliness, surprise, astonishment – that is the kind of life I live. Basho, a famous poet, expressed it thus, 'Looking closely, the pimpernels along the fence are all in bloom.' The fence is always there for us to see, yet we do not see it, still less the small flowers. One day Basho happened to look at the fence in a way he had never looked at it before and so saw it now for the first time, with the tiny flowers, and it had the impact of a whole world. Something welled up in Basho's heart, a sense of awe and wonder which so overpowered him that he trembled all over. His *haiku*, 'Looking closely, the pimpernels along the fence are all in bloom,' refers to this experience. *Haiku* is a unique Japanese form of poem, and no translation can really do it justice or convey the true taste of it. But not only *haiku*, all true forms of art – poetry, painting, music, literature, drama – arise from this sense of awe and wonder. It is this feeling of awe and wonder that has given rise to, has actually enabled human beings to create great cultures and civilisations – and in that we differ from the world of the animals. Therefore when we make mistakes, we shed tears over these mistakes; when we feel sadness or suffer, out of this a new self can emerge, and out of such moments poetry and painting and music are born! So on the one hand, while we are seeking peace and tranquillity, on the other we are looking for moments or impacts that deeply move us. This power to be so moved is inherent in all human beings. Nor are suffering and sickness our individual possessions, although most people believe them to be their very own dis-ease.

When people talk to me – and many do – they talk about 'their' illness or difficulty. But it is not! Far from being an illness, it is rather a jewel that we all hold in common. Suffer more fully! Be sad thoroughly, be wholly sad. Do not just occasionally feel sad, or get excited when you discover something new – but rather give it life, open up to this sense of awe and wonder and let it enter into all aspects of your daily life. People seeking a life that is entirely tranquil, or that is devoid of any sadness, are like children looking for sweets. If they cannot constantly have sweets, or have peace and quiet, life seems insufferable to them. And yet, surely, in addition to the sweetness, a person's life is enriched by the experience of sadness, the spice of bitterness.

In Japanese, the word for 'sweet' may be used for tasty or good to eat, as well as for anything that goes well or is good. The word 'bitter' is also used for what is hard and difficult, and 'pungent' also has similar connotation. So the same Chinese ideogram is used for specific tastes of food and life. Whoever devised them millennia ago must have had a very deep perception of the essence of life to be able to associate tastes in this way.

Yet in our practice we generally strive to create a life devoid of sadness. We learn enthusiastically how to bow, how to walk in *kinhin*, sit zazen and so on, but though we may strive diligently to master all this, we still fail to make it our concern to let the Buddha-nature well up in us and operate freely. With that as an introduction, we may now look at the koan of 'Tozan's Blows.'

From the above introduction, it should be possible to see into this koan. Tozan presented himself before the great Master Ummon. Ummon asked, 'Where have you come from?' 'From Sato.' 'Where did you spend your summer retreat?' 'In the Hoji Monastery in Konan province.' 'When did you leave there?' 'On the 25th of August.' The answers are straight and clear, no mistake anywhere, no disrespect expressed toward Ummon, yet Ummon said, 'Really I should beat you, but today I spare you the blows!'

Do you understand? Why should he have been beaten? Tozan did not understand either. All through the night, he kept asking himself where he had made a mistake. In the morning, he again went to Ummon and bowing politely asked, 'Yesterday, Roshi, you said you would spare me your blows. I do not understand. What was my mistake?' Ummon shouted, 'You empty rice-bag! Is that how you have wandered from monastery to monastery?' At these words, Tozan had satori.

What is *shugyo* (training)? What is within oneself? Is *shugyo* a training for getting rid of things and for acquiring things? Or is it something in which there is nothing at all to dispose of? No rice-bags to get rid of, only a fuller way understanding! Then Mumon's commentary and verse to this koan are no longer necessary.

I would like to add that you all have a jewel. The heart you think of as bad in some way, that heart is a jewel. Please recognise this and accept it as within yourselves. Do not blame the heart that gets angry – what is bad and what is to be blamed is that in your deepest self you fail to savour that anger, or that in the face of anger you create all kinds of pretences. Everything passes, constantly changes. An honest, accepted anger has gone within an instant; and the same applies to suffering and sadness when it is without any pretence.

If we learn to accept the sadness or suffering that wells up of itself, and respond to it, then it will transform itself into something else. But when we grab at it, attach to it, love or hate it, then we are re-creating it within ourselves. So when bound by sadness, this kind of sadness will, for example, not express itself as art, it rather destroys one. And because of that, we do not see sadness as a treasure, but in truth, sadness is a jewel. So use it as a jewel. Whatever is within you and constantly emerges, just let it well up and naturally respond to it; this natural changing and transforming is the wonderful taste of human life. Even if we ourselves do not struggle to bring about a change in life, the Buddha-nature inherent in all of us changes from instant to instant. That is why being born, dying, being born, dying, being born, dying, is true human life.

Tozan had lived an ideal life as a monk, but only on encountering Ummon's shout were his eyes truly opened. Commenting on Keichu's Wheel (Case 8) I told you about the old woman who looked after Zuigan Roshi. Though she lived an almost perfect life, her heart was not at peace because she did not fully savour the taste of life. But just before her death she was able to transform this into something quite wonderful; though approaching her end, instant by instant the Buddha-nature in her provided her with wonderful food, so that she could give up trying to mould herself into some ideal image, and left this world feeling she was going out to play ball on the lawn. So please savour your own life; then you will discover that it is a food seasoned with all manner of spices and prodigiously diverse in its tastes.

CASE 16 · UMMON'S SEVEN-FOLD ROBE

Ummon said, 'The world is vast and wide, why do you put on the seven-fold robe when the bell sounds?'

MUMON'S COMMENT
In general, training in Zen and studying the Way means refraining from following sound and chasing after forms. Though on hearing sound there may be realisation, or by seeing form the heart may be enlightened, nevertheless this is the general way. What Zen monks especially do not understand is how to guide sound, use form, see each thing clearly and know clearly each wonderful activity of the heart. But be that as it may, just say, does the sound come to the ear, or does the ear go to the sound? And what can you say when sound and silence are both forgotten? It is difficult to hear when listening with the ear, but listen with the eye and you begin to hear clearly.

THE VERSE
會則事同一家
不會萬別千差
不會事同一家
會則萬別千差

To the one enlightened, things are as of one family;
To the one not enlightened, the ten thousand things seem to be
    separate and to differ.
To the one not enlightened, things are as of one family;

To one enlightened, the ten thousand things seem to be separate
and to differ.

SOKO ROSHI'S COMMENTS

The text of this koan, however carefully we may read it, is extremely
difficult to understand. Actually, there may be many koan cases which
on reading seem beyond understanding, but that does not mean that
we should not read the text before hearing teisho on it. Just when the
text seems intractable, wrestle with it, ponder what it is trying to say
and then listen to teisho.

In the present case the difficulty is not that the translation of the
koan is wrong, but that the original text itself is extremely difficult to
understand. Books written by Zen monks are not necessarily logical;
the connecting links between one sentence and another are very often
dropped, leaving it to the reader to supply them. But in making these
connections, do not try to understand the sentences rationally, or
you will fail to make the links. Instead ponder what it was that the
person was trying to say, what they were pointing at? And then you
have to see it the same way. Listening to teisho after having read the
text, you may often have wondered how I came to seeing it this way,
because you think in terms of interpretation. But I, having read a
short sentence and seen into the reality that lies behind it, can then
from my own insight into reality present it to you.

Buddhism is not trying to teach something that can be defined,
designated or specified as Buddhism; Zen is not something that can
be labelled as Zen – it is here and around us. What exists, what is, is
the only reality, is the very reality in which we live. Therefore when
reading koan texts you have to read them in relation to that reality.
Peace does not come about because we talk about it, nor does a war
start because we talk about fighting. In what we call peace or war,

irrespective of how we label or define them, reality is running through them. We should not be deceived by the conceptualisations of human language, rather see into reality. In order to help us to do that, the patriarchs presented us with a variety of such problems. A koan is not an end in itself, it is merely a means or a trigger to encourage us to see reality as it is.

Ummon was very skilled in presenting such triggers by means of which we can see reality, and he used to present them in simple and straightforward words. So we can picture the 'scene.' One day Ummon, addressing the monks training under him, said, 'Now look around you. Isn't the world vast? And this vast world and yourselves are one.' The purpose of Zen training is deliverance, liberation from all the constraints that hold us in, or bind us in our daily lives. The newly born Buddha stepped out freely, to the north, south, east and west, and pointing with one arm at the sky and with the other to earth, proclaimed, 'In this vast world I alone am the World-honoured One.' But in saying this he was not asserting that he was more precious than the rest of us, but that every being, everything, is in itself, 'vast and wide.' Ummon then continued, 'All of you in training here, with the world so vast and wide around you, why do you put on your robes at the sound of the bell and all go to the Buddha Hall?'

This highlights a vital problem. Putting myself in Ummon's place, let me ask you, why is it that in this wide and free world you spend your money and give up your summer vacations to come here to the Summer School where you know that your legs are going to hurt every day? Perhaps you can answer this question; but let us put it another way. In this vast world we live in, why is it that you are human beings? Why is it that you do not sleep on the floor but in a bed? Why is it that when one meal a day would be sufficient, you have three meals daily? Why is it that you marry or why is it that you remain single? If you get married, your partner may become difficult or troublesome; if you stay on your own, you may become lonely. If you have to prepare three meals a day, it becomes a chore; but if you do not eat, you will be hungry. If you come to the Summer School, your legs hurt; if you do not come, you think you might be missing something. WHY, in spite of the fact that the world is vast and wide, are you living this kind of life?

As to Mumon's commentary, generally in practising Zen or studying Buddhism, you should not chase after forms or sounds, and you should not think of them as outside of yourself. This does not, however, mean that you should ignore, or be indifferent to forms and sounds, to external objects. Master Reiun attained enlightenment on seeing the peach blossoms. Kyogen became enlightened on hearing a pebble strike a bamboo stem. Such things do happen.

However, most Zen trainees, though trying to look like diligent students of Zen, are only chasing after external sounds, or things that they see with their eyes. They do not know that they can use everything freely from moment to moment, or that they can live their lives freely from moment to moment. As I just said, we should not chase sounds or sights, but rather use them freely. With respect to that, let me ask you, can you hear because you have ears? If, for example, we could somehow transcend both sounds and ears, how would you explain such a state? One who only hears sounds with the ears probably would not be able to offer an explanation. Only when you can hear sounds with the eyes for the first time, will you be able to explain it. Although you may not understand the full meaning of this, at least you can understand the words. You may think that 'hearing with the eyes' is a very Zen-like, paradoxical way of talking. But this is not so; it is fact, reality.

For example, in a Japanese primary school a teacher was

explaining the protective camouflage of some plants and animals. A chameleon, he said, adjusts itself to blend in with the surrounding colour; the students nodded their heads. And he went on, so also do tiny shellfish (used for soup). The students were surprised, and one asked, 'But they have no eyes, how can they know and adjust?' The teacher could not answer; he saw things through the eyes and was not able to see through the ears. Why do these tiny shrimps have to see colours? Why should they need to look at colours? Trying to find this out by reading books on biology will not help.

We constantly have a sense of freedom on the one hand, and a lack of freedom on the other. Is this not because we see things with our eyes, hear things with our ears, feel with our hearts, and then feel that we are tied up, that we are constricted and bound by them? And consequently we have the situation where we look at things, and things are being looked at. We try to find freedom in this oppositional relationship, but the kind of freedom we should truly be looking for is a freedom in which we are not disturbed, influenced or affected by what is around us. Nonetheless the kind of freedom which we try to exercise aims at making use of the things around us. Thinking in this way has encouraged the development of science, but we are not simply surrounded by physical objects, for there are laws governing physical objects and matter as such; perhaps the most fundamental among these is cause and effect.

Both the physical and the human sciences have developed through clarifying what cause produces what effect. So those people who have a strong desire to live freely and happily have studied these laws and make use of them for their own purposes, and these people usually have a strong sense of self. Though they may achieve limited success, they will inevitably find that however much they study these laws and make use of material objects, there comes a stage where there are things that cannot be attained unless the activities they have been engaged in are transcended. Perhaps the most obvious of these is the process of ageing. However much we may study the laws of medicine or take care of our health, there is no way that we can avoid occasional illness, and in the end we all die. However much we try to strengthen our independent self, the range of activity in which we can really operate freely is and remains extremely limited.

Some continue to try and strengthen this self by study, practice and effort. And it is true that if only they persevere, they will in time achieve great results. Thus they gain confidence, become proud, and then by their own efforts, will and drive, they attempt to lead others and control their environment. But when they realise that they are getting old, they become afraid of ageing and dying, and this fear tends to grow in them and becomes obsessive. This kind of freedom is not the freedom pointed at in Buddhism, for in this vast world in which we live, the kind of freedom they are pursuing is not continuous, doesn't last.

What then is the freedom that Buddhism offers? Is it the freedom to get rid of or eliminate self? If there is a limit to the freedom that we can achieve by strengthening our sense of self, then if we eliminate all sense of self and just sway in the wind as the breeze blows, or be like an insect which on the surface of water is just carried with the current, is that the freedom presented by Buddhism? Try it; all that will come of it is a sense of sadness or emptiness. Even if one makes oneself empty, 'MU', or recognises one's environment as empty, or makes oneself large and tries to control one's environment, none of these is reality.

Whether you have an ear or not, whether there is sound or not, what Mumon is pointing at in his commentary is not just the relationship between ear and sounds, but the relationship between self and object. However much we may ponder this, we cannot go beyond the two possibilities of either taking self or object in terms of freedom; we either make the self stronger and more grand, or we make the object, the environment, dominant. But if we eliminate eyes and ears and nose and all thoughts, or eliminate the world of objects around us, and look anew at reality, then there is only harmony. It looks as if I am here, but it is only that I am in harmony with you. When walking in the woods it is not that I am and the trees are, what is there is the harmony between the trees and myself. Why is it that when we walk in the woods, we feel peaceful? Or when, for example, we lie down in the grass and look up at the sun or the sky, we somehow feel a great sense of relief? Why is it, having tea together or chatting, that you are drawn into things? Because we exist in a world of harmony that is fundamentally given. When we lie in the grass and look up at the clouds, or walk in the woods, or happily talk with our friends, we return to the reality of our lives. But when sitting in our room we cease to achieve and maintain the harmony between ourselves and that room, or when we cease to maintain harmony where we are working, we are then in the situation where self is self, where the wall is the stone wall, the floor is the floor, and the ceiling is the ceiling. Then, at the office, our work, our position, is separate from that of everybody else. Yet these are just the same as the trees or the grass or the relationships with friends; we do not live apart from this harmony. Do not make the mistake of thinking there is a special you and a special object. Now you may perhaps think that humans and trees and stones are all the same; but what it amounts to is a stone in harmony, or a tree in harmony. Think of it in these terms.

If the relationship between a husband and wife is really good, then in that relationship the man can become more of a man and the wife can become more of a woman. When we forget ourselves in this harmony and when we forget the partner, the object, then the harmony that is created becomes its defining characteristic.

This is what Mumon is referring to and expressing in his verse. If you do not understand reality, then everything seems to be the same. If you understand reality, then you see that within this harmony everything has its unique characteristics. That is the meaning of the latter part of Mumon's verse. The earlier couplet is the opposite to this – however individual things may seem, when you look at them they are in harmony; but if you do not understand, then they seem to be, or you see them as separate and opposed. Well, having read this koan and found it difficult to understand, do you now understand that what is being offered in it is not random, meaningless or without any connection? Nor are my comments an explanation of the koan; what has been said refers to reality.

CASE 17 · NATIONAL TEACHER ECHU CALLS THREE TIMES

The National Teacher called out three times to his attendant, and the attendant responded three times. The National Teacher said, 'I thought I had wronged you, but it is you who have wronged me.'

MUMON'S COMMENT

The National Teacher called three times – his tongue dropped out. The attendant answered three times, responding brilliantly. The National Teacher was getting old and lonely, and pushed down the head of the buffalo to make it eat grass. The attendant would have none of it. Even delicious food does not tempt a full stomach. But tell me, what is the meaning of this betrayal by Echu? When the country is at peace, talent is esteemed; in a well-to-do family, the children are brought up well.

THE VERSE

鉄枷無孔要人擔
累及兒孫不等閒
欲得撑門并拄戶
更須赤脚上刀山

He is made to wear a yoke with no hole in it,
And not even his descendants can find peace or rest.
If you wish to hold up the gate and the house,
You must climb the sword mountain barefoot.

SOKO ROSHI'S COMMENTS

In China and Japan, the title, 'National Teacher' was granted only to outstanding masters. However, the National Teacher here without name refers to Echu, the first master who was granted the title. No doubt there are similar cases of illustrious persons whose names come to mind immediately when the title is mentioned.

Echu was a disciple of one of the Sixth Patriarch's successors. For over forty years he lived as a recluse in the mountains, but in time reports of his power and strength spread until eventually it reached the Tang emperor. He was then called to the capital and reluctantly obeyed the summons. There he taught two successive emperors and is said to have died at the age of 134.

Approaching death, Echu said farewell to the emperor. The latter knew Echu was close to death, and so asked, 'Is there anything I can do for you after your death, any favour that I can grant you?' Echu replied, 'I would like a seamless tomb, a tomb without joints in it.' The emperor asked, 'What kind of tomb is that?' Echu was quiet for a while and then said, 'Do you understand?' But the emperor had not grasped the point. So Echu then suggested, 'After I have died, ask my disciple, Oshin, about the seamless tomb.' Echu died, and the emperor asked Oshin, 'What is a seamless tomb?' Oshin answered, 'Master Echu is one with the universe. There is no need for you to do anything because this seamless tomb has existed from before time. If you really want to do something for the National Teacher Echu, then realise it yourself.' This is part of a koan in the *Hekiganroku*, but there it is different from how it is presented here. I have pointed at the special meaning of this koan, which is not accessible by just reading it. Part of the point is that there was a deep harmony and understanding between the National Teacher Echu and his disciple Oshin.

'The National Teacher called out to his attendant three times' – that attendant was Oshin. But it may be difficult to understand why this interplay of call and response between Echu and Oshin should have been used as a koan for hundreds of years. If you feel that it is natural and obvious that this simple sequence of call and response should have been preserved, there is no need to read on. If you have not understood, then please continue reading with an open mind.

Late on a winter's evening it has become very quiet. In his familiar chair by the fireside an elderly man sits reading. Opposite him his wife sits knitting. He lowers his book and looks across at his wife. Somehow sensing this she also stops knitting and glances towards her husband. Just as if on a still lake a few ripples were breaking the surface gently, they smile. Then he turns back to his reading and she continues her knitting. Now, if young people brim full of energy, or having just fallen in love and therefore highly emotional, or a youth intent on great deeds, saw this exchange between the old couple, they might easily miss the point of it; or else see only two old fogies nodding at each other.

But seen by someone who in their own life has gone through a variety of experiences, joyful and sad, or seen by a married couple who together have lived through all the usual problems that are part and parcel of life and so have accumulated joint experiences, to them it might seem like dry leaves rustling in the wind that blows through them, and when the wind has passed, the leaves are still again.

Oshin, the disciple and attendant, must have undergone many trials and difficulties to win Echu's approval and Echu, before being recognised by the emperor, cultivated and forged his spiritual insight by working through and overcoming many problems and difficulties. And Oshin, too, in order to later be able to train his own disciples and to bring them to an understanding, must have gone through many further hardships. Thus the difficulties or strivings of both Echu and Oshin must have been so great that they cannot be compared with those of, say, an ordinary husband and wife. For theirs was not just the suffering that accompanies ordinary life, but that of the striving and struggling towards an existence that transcends birth and death. So after having crossed the sea of birth and death, after the long journey that both of them had made of also crossing the sea of understanding and of doubt – such a simple call and response is just like a mirror that accurately reflects the marvels of a palace or of a palace garden, with nothing added and nothing left out. Or as if at night with the moon shining, you hear the sound of a temple bell on a distant mountain and from the dark valley comes a response. Do not be deceived by calling three times – once only would have been all right, or even five times, it does not matter how often; the real issue is that it is a selfless call from an empty heart (*mushin*) and an equally selfless response. So the important point is the state of the empty heart, that state of understanding and matching between these two.

A simple example may help. I call out, 'Hey!', and my disciple answers 'Yes' – but however long I wait, he does not come; he just answered, but does not do anything further. Do not confuse these two! Or again I may call out, 'Hey!', and the disciple answers, 'Yes', his head already spinning with a thousand thoughts of 'Why is he calling? What am I going to be blamed for this time?' Thus both his understanding and his response are blocked, and we do not 'match'!

So we need to be aware and to realise that there are different levels in the simple exchange of 'Hey!' and 'Yes.' When you are sitting zazen together and you hear noises outside, or music upstairs, or your neighbour's coughing, how do you react? Many responses are possible. Some may react to the music, or perhaps get angry and tighten up at children shouting, resenting the noise. Still others might feel pride, thinking, 'I am different from them, thank goodness!' Or one might try to make oneself into a kind of fortress in which one is completely impervious to any sound, etc.

And the question is, are you sitting zazen like that dark valley that simply accepts, that responds in its way to the sound of the mountain bell? Are you feeling at peace, tranquil, with a sense of sitting not as an independent fortress, but have blended in and are effortlessly mingling with what is? Within the family, too, we do not constantly repeat 'I love you,' and expect others to respond with 'I love you too'! Or when in the kitchen, though your husband or the children are not constantly helping you, yet you know that, though engaged in different activities, you are all under the same roof, is that not in itself a source of tranquillity and comfort? On a walk, though we do not constantly talk to the trees, or may not be conscious of every gust of wind, yet we harmonise with the trees and the wind and the grass, and we take comfort and find joy in doing so.

It is our original, intrinsic nature to perfectly accept and take everything in. But we try to make ourselves conscious of things because, unless we can verbalise things in some way, we find it difficult to come to terms with them. And although in fact nobody is putting obstacles in the way of our own heart, we ourselves create our problems.

In this koan there was no special need for National Teacher Echu to call, nor for Oshin to respond, because both of them were the truth of the universe itself. This was not only so because their own spiritual condition was such that it was the universe, but reality is of a suchness. Even though we may not realise this, everything, the universe around us, is also in us. Echu called 'Hey!' and Oshin responded 'Yes' three times. Echu said, 'I thought I had wronged you, but it is you who have wronged me.' Another way of saying it might be 'I haven't been of much use to you', or even, 'I've been a hindrance to you' – with the meaning of foolishly doing what is not needed. Not just between Echu and Oshin, it applies to me too; to come all the way from Japan to give a foolish teisho, and all of you listening. The National Teacher Echu implies, 'I am a fool; you are a fool too; fool and fool, both great fools.' Is this not a good match?

Mumon's comment is, 'The National Teacher called three times – his tongue dropped out. The attendant answered three times, responding brilliantly.' Mumon's meaning is that the National Teacher Echu talked too much, explained too much, so his tongue dropped out. But in fact, Mumon is not talking about Echu or Oshin, he is talking to trainees confronting this koan, and in whose heads thoughts are spinning round. What are you missing? What is it that you are trying to grasp from Echu or from this comment? 'I'm troubled, I'm no good, I'm lacking in something' – for such people, intent on grasping, talking is a waste of time. Why? Because everybody is intrinsically, originally, perfect. Oshin knows that, he has attained enlightenment. Yet Echu calls out to that enlightened Oshin three times. Do you understand the foolish kindness of Echu? That is what Mumon is saying. In contrast, Oshin the attendant, did not say to Echu, 'You fool!' and leave him, or merely say, 'No, thank you', he just replied, 'Yes' each time. Was this not a splendid response? In perfect mutual understanding, where speech is unnecessary, one called and the other responded. Such responses may be friendly or may seem quarrelsome. Although he wanted to praise this exchange, Mumon could not find ordinary words in which to do so. So he resorted to an adverse approach, seemingly denigrating it: 'That fool Echu is getting old and lonely. If he was younger and more vigorous, he would let things be, but being old and foolish, he is overdoing it with excessive kindness, like forcing a buffalo's head down into the grass to make it eat.' Oshin does not eat of the grass because he is already full. However wonderful the feast you have set out, it will not tempt one who is already replete. Or expressed in reverse, hunger is the best cook. The translated text reads, 'The National Teacher was getting old and lonely, and pushed down the head of a buffalo to make it eat grass. The attendant would have none of it. Even delicious food does not tempt a full stomach.'

Up to this point it is all right. But then Mumon adds a nuance, 'Well, what I have said is by the by; but tell me, what is the meaning of this betrayal by Echu?' Do you now understand what I said above that a fool and a fool make one great fool? Mumon asks whether we understand this, and then continues, 'In the past it was said that when a country is at peace, talent is esteemed,' and that 'In a well-to-do family the children are brought up well.' But if you just take these words as they are written, literally, it can be dangerous. There is always a front and a back to such expressions.

Oshin understood this; he was enlightened, aware of the original nature. From there, the words can be taken as they are. However, in our case they may take on an opposite meaning, such as that in order to achieve peace, people sometimes become foolish; in order to achieve prosperity or wealth, people become greedy. Or, in order to gain freedom, people sometimes become nervous and troubled. Or that in the pursuit of equality, inequality increases. So let us try to taste both sides of this expression, 'When the country is at peace, talent is esteemed; in a well-to-do family, children are brought up well.'

Few people these days can instinctively accept and truly appreciate and cherish the most common everyday activities and exchanges. In our everyday lives, we tend to chase after the unusual, the extraordinary. Recognising this tendency within us, we might come to feel almost jealous of the elderly couple, of that kind of relationship in which they can exchange their feelings so simply and naturally.

Mumon also composed a poem. The translation reads 'He is made to wear a yoke', but actually it means that everybody wears such a yoke with no hole in it. By yoke is meant the wooden board that prisoners in China were made to carry around their necks. Yet this board, Mumon says, has no hole in it! You can understand this in terms of somebody undergoing Zen training, for whom, on being confronted with this exchange between Echu and Oshin, this calling and response becomes a koan with no hole in it. Thus Mumon is saying that not just for Echu's and Oshin's generation, but for all subsequent ones, and for both monks and lay practitioners who are seeking the Way, this answer and response has become a koan with no hole in it. However, instead of continuing to present the koan as a burden, here is another way of pondering it.

We sentient human beings all wear such a yoke with no hole in it. We ourselves, our parents, our children, and grandchildren, all bear this burden which cannot be thrown off. The Buddha himself carried the burden of such a yoke when he set out to seek enlightenment. And when he broke out of it, he taught others how to find release from this yoke. 'Come in at this gate!' The word 'gate' used in the sense of supporting or holding up the teachings. So even though 'gate' has the same meaning as 'teachings', it is also that which allows us to escape and break away from the yoke around our necks. Mumon made his comment on Echu's Koan around the 13th century when the Song dynasty was collapsing and the Mongols were pressing in from the north. It was a time when not only the political and military strength of the Song dynasty but also the teachings of the Buddha were declining, hence Mumon, addressing his monks, put a great deal of energy and effort into his comment. A teaching about the natural and commonplace is the most difficult to grasp. For it not to be lost from the world, each one of us must resolve to climb barefoot up the sword mountain.

So please, in your training, climb barefoot up this sword mountain. However, this does not mean that your feet are streaming with blood; it means from second to second only doing whatever it is, simply not allowing doubts to interfere, and thus enjoying yourselves. Do you enjoy zazen? Even with music blaring next door? Even if you hear children shouting outside? With your legs aching? Or even if you have planned a good walk and it is now pouring with rain?

CASE 18 · TOZAN'S THREE POUNDS OF FLAX

THE CASE

A monk asked Master Tozan, 'What is the Buddha?' Tozan replied, 'Three Pounds of Flax.'

MUMON'S COMMENT

Old man Tozan was trained in the Zen of a clam; opening the shell ever so little, it reveals liver and bowels. Be this as it may, say, how do you see Tozan?

THE VERSE

突出麻三斤
言親意更親
來說是非者
便是是非人

'Three Pounds of Flax,' the response flies out;
The words are intimate, and so is the meaning.
He who explains 'Yes' and 'No'
Is himself a Yes-and-No man.

SOKO ROSHI'S COMMENTS

Tozan has already been mentioned in Koan 15 where he entered satori under Master Ummon. Masters often took their name from the place or mountain or monastery where they taught. Through the generations Tozan Monastery on Mount Tozan had many abbots, but only two 'Tozans' stand out. One of them is Tozan Ryokai, venerated founder of the Soto tradition of Zen. The other, Tozan Shusho, was a disciple of Ummon, and he appears in this koan.

Tozan Shusho is considered one of the great early Masters. A monk asked Tozan, 'What is Buddha?' The question of 'What is Buddha?' has always been one of the central concerns in Zen training. This question is raised in four of the forty-eight koans in the *Mumonkan*, in Cases 18, 21, 30 and 33. It seems that in the history of the Zen School, this query is continuous. I once asked an audience whether anyone had actually met the Buddha? A third of them laughed. They could not imagine themselves meeting the Buddha. How could one? Somewhere up in heaven, or down below on earth?

The word 'Buddha' literally means one who has awakened, or is enlightened, who has come to the great realisation. It is a generic term, but Shakyamuni's enlightenment was so great that the term 'Buddha' automatically became associated with Gautama Buddha. While some still hold to that understanding, after his death the term 'Buddha' was also used with a doctrinal and philosophical meaning, not only in India, Burma, Sri Lanka and Thailand, but also in China, Tibet, Korea and Japan. Thus with time and diverse cultural backgrounds, the word 'Buddha' acquired a variety of different meanings. Moreover, the concept of Buddha as studied by scholars or commentators became so complex and intricate, that it no longer could be explained simply, or in a few words. The Buddha of the sutras permeates everything and is revealed in all places and at all times.

The monk who asked Tozan about the Buddha certainly had some such concept in mind, but the transmission that Bodhidharma brought from India had no such concept of Buddha. In his teaching Buddha is not venerated as vastly distant, but can be experienced directly and immediately at this moment, and cannot be found outside it. Neither books nor lectures can reach him. The Second Patriarch

Eka (Case 41) cut off his arm in order to be accepted by Bodhidharma and to find this kind of Buddha by training under him.

As for Tozan himself, he had wandered about far and wide before attaining enlightenment when Ummon shouted at him, 'What are you running after and what are you looking for?' Later he settled on Mount Tozan, hence his name. When the monk asked Tozan, 'What is Buddha?', it might have been when flax was harvested, and was being weighed. Or it might not – it does not matter. Asked 'What is Buddha?', Tozan replied, 'Three Pounds of Flax.' In this reply there was nothing lacking, nor any attempt to urge the monk to attain enlightenment, simply a pure response, 'Three Pounds of Flax.' Without troubling himself to make an effective reply, quite instinctively and naturally, Tozan replied as if the best Buddha at that moment was 'Three Pounds of Flax!' And at that instant the function of these words ended. So if you concentrate on the words and puzzle over them and try to squeeze some meaning out of them, however much you labour at it, you will not find Buddha within the words. If a horse has run past and you grab at its hoofprints, have you thereby grabbed the horse? It cannot be done.

Yet ever since this koan came into use, and even up to the present day, whenever it is given, most focus on the 'Three Pounds of Flax.' In our daily lives, too, we frequently try to grab at the footprints of the horse. A visitor once said to me, 'Ten years ago I was told by Roshi....'; I even forget what I said yesterday. Trying to understand what is in my heart now by taking hold of and cherishing what I said ten years ago is not just difficult, it is impossible! If you hold on to what your spouse said twenty years ago, or how your wife looked yesterday, or your newborn baby, clinging to it as it was then, we create a situation in which we speak to the memory and not to the person in front of us. Do we not frequently do just this – holding on to old impressions while talking to the actual person?

So Tozan said, 'Three Pounds of Flax', but the monk failed to get it. He left and next went to Master Chimon. There he related, 'When I asked Tozan, "What is Buddha?," he said, "Three Pounds of Flax," and I just did not understand. Will you please tell me?' Chimon replied, 'Flowers are blooming gloriously; the silken sheen of brocade!' At this, the poor monk was even more confused. So Chimon added, 'Bamboos in the south, pines in the north.'

When I was once asked, 'What is Buddha?', I said, 'A cat is climbing the tree.' Anyway, the monk did not understand what Chimon said and went back to Tozan. Because of people like him, shoemakers remain in business!

The monk told Tozan what had happened and again asked him to please explain. Tozan said, 'I will not explain it to you alone, but expound it at the assembly.' Next day at teisho, he said, 'Words cannot express the Dharma; enlightenment cannot be attained by words.'

Yet there are people who cling to words; they will become ever more confused and move further and further away from understanding and truth. The words 'Three Pounds of Flax' were not just Tozan's reply to 'What is Buddha?'. As in the 'Three Pounds of Flax', so in all his daily life, instant by instant, Buddha emerged through his breathing, from his eyes and nose, and ears and mouth, emerged and entered. Regardless of whether life was regular and steady, or even unsettling and disturbed, on days when the sky was clear or when cloudy, in his daily life, Buddha was expressed as it was when asked 'What is Buddha?' and he replied, 'Three Pounds of Flax!' This totality of Buddhahood, expressed in every moment of daily life, emerged and came out from his genuine insight, satori. If one ignores the emergence of the 'Satori of Daily Life' in his responses and only concentrates on the words, then 'Three Pounds of Flax' makes no sense.

Mumon's Comment: 'Old man Tozan had achieved the Zen of a clam.' This seems to denigrate Tozan or make fun of him; but after reading many comments to koan cases, we realise that Zen masters frequently seem to belittle or make fun of what they are praising. As for the Zen of a clam – not only clams, but with any shellfish, opening their shells however little, what is inside can be seen. From that it might appear that Mumon belittles Tozan's explanation, saying that he had opened so that everything inside could be seen. So from one point of view, Mumon's comment could suggest that Tozan was rather shallow and that by just saying a little, he had exposed himself fully. However, the comment may also be seen as praise that Tozan in just a few words expressed himself completely. In this latter sense, can you express yourself fully and perfectly? Bearing in mind that it is not a question of whether the person you are talking to understands or not? The number of those able to understand Tozan's response, 'Three Pounds of Flax', will be rather small; however, if you look at things with the eyes of Tozan's direct experience, then in his brief reply lies the wealth of direct insight.

Now referring to Tozan in this way does not mean distinction from others. Tozan had reduced or eliminated any distinction between himself and others; when he replied, 'Three Pounds of Flax', that was Tozan and 'Three Pounds of Flax' was, or is, Buddha. So Mumon asks us, where in this koan do we see Tozan?

The Verse: 'Three Pounds of Flax' – instant-by-instant perfect response. In reply to 'What is Buddha?', the words 'Three Pounds of Flax' are the perfect response. The translation reads, 'The words are intimate' – that conveys the sense of perfect appropriateness. And the way of life, the heart that is expressed by the 'Three Pounds of Flax', is also perfect to the situation. Yet, somebody merely trying to grasp the words 'Three Pounds of Flax' or trying to distinguish whether this response to 'What is Buddha?' was appropriate or inappropriate, such a person can only see a world of discriminations and comparisons, and does not understand this complete way of life in which we see person by person, or thing by thing, or moment by moment.

Let me stress again, the Zen training that we are engaged in is not a training for conceptual understanding, it is not a philosophy, nor is it aimed at an abstraction of the divine, but is a direct, immediate understanding of our everyday experiences. If we become aware of this direct understanding or this 'taking in' – for all are capable of it – then we can never feel lonely or isolated anymore. Thousands of people, though inherently part of humankind, nonetheless, feel cut off and lonely even if given words of consolation by those around them. Because they live in the midst of conceptualisations, or amidst discriminations and comparisons, they have never experienced this our world as direct, immediate, absolute reality.

I give teisho in a gentle voice so that hearers will not get upset and run off! But Tozan's 'Three Pounds of Flax' cannot be expressed in that way. If you put aside your Zen experience, or your life experience, you cannot give teisho on it. It does not matter whether or not you understand 'Three Pounds of Flax', happiness can only be fully realised by direct experience of the world.

CASE 19 · THE ORDINARY HEART IS THE WAY

THE CASE

Joshu asked Nansen, 'What is the Way?' Nansen answered, 'The ordinary heart – that is the Way.' Joshu said, 'How does one strive for it?' Nansen replied, 'The more you strive for it, the more it recedes.' Joshu said, 'Then how can one know the Way?' Nansen replied 'The Way does not belong to knowing or to not knowing. Knowing is deluded seeing; not knowing is without discrimination. When you reach the Way beyond doubt, it is wide and vast like the great void – and also beyond yes and no.' At these words Joshu was suddenly enlightened.

MUMON'S COMMENT

When Joshu shot out his question, Nansen explained; the tile worked loose, the ice dissolved, no further communication was possible. But even though Joshu broke into satori, he needed a further thirty years of training to understand completely.

THE VERSE

春有百花秋有月
夏有涼風冬有雪
若無閑事挂心頭
更是人間好時節

Flowers in spring and moon in autumn,
The cool breeze in summer and snow in winter –
If the heart is not upset with useless fancies,
This is a happy time for human beings.

SOKO ROSHI'S COMMENTS

The benefit of reading such a koan-text – and the comments on it – is that we set our own understanding against it, and then can correct and transform our own understanding. In our training, there is no need to search for the truth, only the need to become aware of and look at our mistakes. The moment we perceive or understand them, the coloured spectacles drop away, and the blocked passages in our ears are opened.

As for truth or reality, there is no need to hear it extolled or to learn it from somebody else – it can be perceived with our own eyes and through our own ears. We need to remind ourselves of this fact when reading teisho texts or when listening to Dharma talks. There is no need to be taught the truth, important is only that within ourselves we eradicate and get rid of what is mistaken.

Case 19 tells of an encounter between Master Nansen and Joshu. In the previous koan, a monk asked Tozan, 'What is Buddha?' In this koan, Joshu asks Nansen, 'What is the Way?' Though the questions use different words, 'Buddha' and 'Way,' the underlying content is the same. A 'way' is something that appears when animals or humans pass to and from over the same ground. In time, the word 'way' took on deeper meanings, no longer as simply a track along which people or animals walk, but a way along which it is fit that humans should walk, that is, it gradually came to embrace ethical connotations. And finally, it was not only conceived of as a way along which people should walk, but also as the way of the universe. Thus in the natural course of events, the way along which humans should move meets the way of the universe, of nature. In China, even before the arrival of Buddhism, 'Way' was understood in this universal sense as the Way (Dao) of the universe, and as such, the Way (Dao) is the central teaching of the Daoism advocated by Laozi and other Daoist philosophers.

This 'Great Way' includes a practical, experiential factor, and accordingly expresses both truth and direct human perception. In India, the equivalent expressions for 'Way' or 'Truth' tended to be more conceptual and philosophical. Truth or ultimate reality was conceived of in terms of Emptiness, of insight-wisdom, or Nirvana. So, when these somewhat metaphysical concepts and their texts were transmitted from India to China, the difficulty was how to translate these rather abstract Indian terms. Eventually they were rendered more concretely as the 'Way'.

The Buddhism that the Indian, Bodhidharma, transmitted to China was a tangible and practical teaching. Chinese monks, when confronted with questions such as, 'What is Buddha?' or 'What is Truth?' understood this in terms of a search for the Way. In the comments to the previous koan it was explained how, in China, with developing practice, the term 'Buddha' was gradually transformed from a rather abstract concept into something much more concrete, so that talking about Buddha was speaking of direct experience.

Though in time specific teaching styles and schools developed, giving rise to the various religious traditions, ultimately they are all the same. In the Zen transmission, the aim of the training is experiential, direct understanding.

When Zen was transmitted to Japan, the term 'Way' came with it, and through Zen it came to permeate Japanese culture. In the Japanese martial arts as well as in the performing arts, the ideogram for skill or for ability is frequently replaced by or simply understood as increasing development along the Way. In modern Japan, 'Way' is used for almost any aspect of life, as in the Way of Flowers, the Way of Judo, the Way of Tea, or the Way of Swordsmanship.

Now back to the koan. The 'Way' that Joshu is asking about is the Great Way. This is not the fragmented way of human experience but the single, universal Great Way that underlies all the manifold individual manifestations of the Way, beneath all the various manifestations we see around us.

At the time of their meeting, Nansen was probably in his fifties and Joshu about twenty. Master Joshu has already appeared in our text. Until he was nineteen, he studied in North China, devoting himself to Buddhism, but then gave up his search for abstract, intellectual knowledge of Buddhism and, seeking a more direct and tangible understanding, came to Nansen. In his search for truth, he had already become acquainted with suffering, and had certainly encountered the difficulties of breaking through to satori. So Joshu asked Nansen, 'What is the Way?', and Nansen answered, 'The ordinary heart – that is the Way.' Joshu asked, 'How can it be attained, how does one strive for it?' Nansen replied, 'The more you strive for it, the more it recedes.'

Looking at this exchange from the word-level only, it seems an intellectual approach, even an immature wordplay of Joshu's. But Joshu had already been in training up north and had spent time intensively searching for truth; he understood what Nansen said. Nansen's words, however, reflect a problem that Joshu had long worried about but could not resolve. Thus, contrary to a surface understanding, the simplicity in Joshu's simple question and Nansen's simple answer reveals the great depth of training that Joshu had already attained to. In zazen, those who search and practise have already experienced what is expressed in these phrases. Joshu then pursues the issue still further, and Nansen replies, 'The more you strive for the Way, the further you get away from it.' The more you try to grasp it, the further it seems to recede; but if you do not try to grasp the Way, how can you attain it? So this is not a merely intellectual exchange, the question is how to grasp reality by direct experience. Nansen kindly replies that the Way is not something that is to be understood or not to be understood. If you say that you have understood the Way, then all that you have done is to conceptualise, in your own terms, the small segment of the Way that is within your range of experience and thus only consists of your individual discrimination. But if you feel no need to understand, you remain in a state of unawareness and will never attain to realisation but will just go on walking rather foolishly down a pitch-black road. So the Way, rather than being understood or not, is easy and comfortable without logical reasoning, without feeling any doubt or uncertainty – just as water flows or as clouds float. If you can attain to that insight and direct realisation, then you are completely free like the clear blue sky. In that state, there is no room for even the slightest discriminating thought such as whether something is good or bad – such thinking has simply become irrelevant.

On hearing Nansen's reply, Joshu burst through into satori.

In the preceding koan (Case 18) a monk asked Tozan, 'What is Buddha?' and Tozan answered, 'Three pounds of flax.' That monk still did not understand and went on to Master Chimon, who replied to the same query, 'Bamboos in the South, pine trees in the North.' The monk still did not understand and trotted back to Tozan and heard him addressing the assembly, 'Truth cannot be expressed in words, Satori cannot be entered by words.' Running around and chasing words and phrases will only add to confusion and separate one still further from insight.

In this present koan, Joshu also asks, 'What is Buddha?' and Nansen kindly answers in very simple words, and on hearing these Joshu breaks through into satori. This may seem contradictory – the same question being answered differently. Yet, at still another time, Nansen was asked, 'What is Nansen's Way?' What is the Great Way on which Nansen walks in his enlightened state? Nansen seems to have been cutting grass at that time, for he held up his sickle and said, 'I bought this for thirty pennies.' The monk explained, 'I am not asking you about the sickle but about your Way.' But Nansen persisted, 'It's sharp and cuts well, it's handy.' So after all, Tozan's 'Three Pounds of Flax' tallies with this reply. Nansen's style, his approach, was not to explain things, when dealing with questions. On the one hand he might use an indirect means, the sickle, to make his point; or as we see here in this koan, he could also express it quite simply.

Thus, if trainees are conscious of a problem, and becoming more and more confused are unable to break out, then the function of a Zen Master is to try to help them by getting them even more confused – rather like putting someone who has lost direction on a swivelling chair and whirling them around swiftly, and then saying, 'It doesn't matter. Just get off!' Joshu had already been swirling on such a whirly-gig; when he first presented himself to Master Nansen, the Master happened to be lying down. Seeing the young monk approach, he asked, 'Where have you come from?' Joshu had been training in the North, in a temple known as that of the Shining Buddha and related this. Nansen asked, 'Have you seen the Shining Buddha?' Since that temple was famous and thousands of pilgrims visited it from all over China, it was inconceivable that Joshu should not have seen the image. There was thus a thorn in Nansen's question, but Joshu, completely unruffled, said, 'I have not seen the Shining Buddha. I see a Reclining Buddha!' Hearing that, Nansen sat up! Presumably, he recognised that this young monk should not be confronted lying down. Then he asked young Joshu, 'Do you have a Master or not?' Joshu answered, 'It is still early spring and rather cold; I am glad to see the Master so well.' Thus Joshu had attached himself to Nansen.

Even at this first meeting, Joshu already had sufficient insight to engage with a Zen Master at such a profound level of understanding. He had already seen into 'the ordinary heart' which is the Way, but not completely yet, and consequently had been suffering from this lack. You, too, are in just the same condition – suffering from this lack; only, in Joshu's case both the depth of his confusion and the strength of his determination were exceptional. Nansen was well aware of the depth of Joshu's understanding and of the intensity of his search, and so his response was on the same level. Joshu broke through to satori not because of any logical exposition of Nansen's, but because there was no more than a gossamer veil between him and full insight. The fruit of Joshu's satori had become ripe, and all that was necessary for it to fall was the merest ghost of a breeze.

Neither in the preceding nor in this present koan was satori entered by means of explanation; in this sense, the two koans are the same. But although truth cannot be expressed by words, it is also a fact that inherent in Nansen's words was the full weight of his, Nansen's, own insight. So Nansen and Joshu, one of shining insight and one who had gone to the very depths of shining suffering, met – and Joshu entered satori.

Mumon's Comment: Not in the text but in my explanation, Mumon says that when this fool Nansen was asked questions, he was unable to parry and smash them, and had no answers. Asked, 'What is the Way?' he held up his sickle and said, 'It cuts well!' By doing so, he could be proud of himself. But in explaining kindly and further, Nansen was reduced to rubble.

Such seemingly derogatory expressions of Zen masters are really praise of the highest order, and thus Mumon is extolling the understanding and perception of Nansen. The translation of this Comment is somewhat vague, but anyway, Mumon then turns to Nansen for a comment on Joshu. Under Nansen's response, Joshu certainly had broken into satori; yet Mumon says that without a further thirty years of training this will not fully mature. The number of thirty does not matter, it stands for limitless, infinite. Why were another thirty years of endless practice necessary for Joshu? What had come into experience in satori was not something special, just the ordinary heart; but in order to let this ordinary heart always prevail, it has to be used constantly, endlessly.

People are keen to climb mountains, especially unassailable ones that have not yet been climbed; it is something special, it may be very difficult, but nevertheless to the summit they strive, and even the most difficult mountain has a summit. Training also heads for a summit – satori. As in mountain climbing, the venture can be called successful only when the peak has been reached and the climber has come down again. So after attaining to the summit of training, of satori, it is necessary to come down again. This descent into ordinary life is the practice or training that continues limitlessly.

Joshu, thus enlightened in his twenties, continued practising under Nansen until the age of fifty-seven. When Nansen died Joshu remained for another three years and conducted the proper memorial services for his Master. Only then, at the age of sixty and until he was eighty, did he wander all over China. He always said that if he should meet an eight-year-old child who had something to teach, he would learn from it; and if there was an eighty-year-old who asked to be taught, he would teach him. At eighty he settled at the Temple Kannon-in, and until his death at the age of one hundred and twenty, his life was the fullest expression of this 'The ordinary heart is the Way.' It is said that Joshu had 'gold on his lips,' his words shone as if light was reflected from them, for though expressed in the simplest of words, everything he said showed his deep insight. Mumon, knowing the vitality and depth of Joshu, presented him thus to his monks. Though he seems to talk critically about Joshu, his words are aimed at his disciples – and at us!

The Verse:
'Flowers in spring, moon in autumn,
The cool breeze in summer –'

This is beautifully expressed, but do not be fooled; even the most beautiful flower withers and falls, and clouds obscure the moon that is shining in the sky. You exclaim, 'Ah! What a nice, cool breeze!', because it is hot; and when bright, white snow falls, your fingers get blue with cold. Behind a beautiful death may lie a very painful life; there is always this side and that side. There is transformation, everything changes, as from spring to summer, then autumn comes and winter follows; if we do not lose sight of this 'ordinary heart', do not lose it through clinging to some foolish illusion, then there is not one out of three hundred and sixty-five days of the year that is not wonderful. As to that, training for another thirty years!

CASE 20 · SHOGEN'S MAN OF GREAT STRENGTH

THE CASE

Master Shogen said, 'Why is it that a man of great strength does not lift his legs?' And continued, 'It is not with his tongue that he speaks.' (Lit.: 'Opening the mouth, there is no tongue.')

MUMON'S COMMENT

It must be said of Shogen that he shows stomach and bowels, but nobody can take it in. However, should there be one, let him come to me and I will beat him up. Why the many blows? If you want to assay pure gold, you must test it in fire.

THE VERSE

擡脚踏翻香水海
低頭俯視四禪天
一箇渾身無處著
請　續一句

Lifting his leg, he kicks up the scented ocean,
And bending his head he looks down on the Fourth Dhyana Heaven.
There is no place large enough to put his body.
Please compose the last line yourself!

SOKO ROSHI'S COMMENTS

The Master Shogen of this koan is in the line of transmission that is chanted every morning in monasteries of the Rinzai school. This line was brought to Japan by Nampo Jomyo who went to China and studied there under Master Kido. Master Shogen was three generations before Master Kido. Shogen practised Zen as a layman for many years and was over thirty when he took ordination. He died in 1208 at the age of seventy-one. At that time, Mumon, the compiler of the *Mumonkan*, was in his twenties; though there were fifty years between them, Shogen may be said to have been of the same generation as Mumon.

Of the Zen masters who appear in the forty-eight cases of the *Mumonkan*, the only contemporary of Mumon is Shogen. The fact that Mumon included him in his collection is an indication of Mumon's high esteem for Master Shogen's Zen. The *Mumonkan* collection was completed some twenty years after Shogen's death.

These particulars of Master Shogen are not just informative but are meant to assist in establishing a sense of closeness and familiarity with Shogen. Nor does this apply to koans only, but also in our training, the ability to relate with familiarity to everything is of utmost importance. It is therefore a real sign of poverty if we just see this as a koan by some Chinese monk who lived eight hundred years ago and therefore having no connection with us today. Zen training consists in re-establishing a relationship or familiarity with persons or things, irrespective of their historical period or place. Being receptive is just this ability to open up and to take in living information.

This koan differs from the usual ones by not being an exchange or dialogue, but was recorded by Shogen's disciples from one of his talks. The question is why someone, who through Zen practice has come to great understanding and power, should be unable to lift his legs? And Shogen added, 'It is not with his tongue that he speaks.' The translation does not fully convey the meaning and so as to make it clearer, the question might be rendered as, 'Why is it that a man of great strength, when speaking, does not use his tongue?' This question was originally raised by Master Mokuan, and it is likely that Shogen had had great difficulties grappling with it, and had attained his great power or strength by resolving these. The deep understanding he had come to by means of this koan he then passed on to his disciples.

So actually we have two koans of Shogen's here; usually, in this connection a third one is then also raised: If by assiduous Zen training clear insight into the way all things are – satori – has opened for someone, why can't they then throw away discrimination in everyday experience?

Two generations later Master Kido put these three koans together and called them Shogen's Three Turning Words. By 'Turning Words' is meant a turning away from confusion and misunderstanding towards satori. These three 'cases' are used in contemporary Zen training, and working with them demands much energy and entails great struggle.

There are some Zen Masters who interpret these three koans morally, as Shogen giving his disciples moral advice. The moral interpretation of 'Why is it that a man of great strength does not lift his legs?' would be 'Why does somebody who has done zazen for a long period and has entered satori, not then get up from his cushion and help the people of the world?' This interpretation is in accord with the Mahayana tradition of Buddhism, that all training should be undertaken for the benefit of others; it is of no use to just sit constantly, like a stone or a withered tree. In this ethical interpretation, the second koan, 'Why does a man of great strength, when speaking, not use his tongue?', the essence of Zen training is shown to involve practical experience, so that the teachings of the Buddha are not interpreted in metaphysical or intellectual terms. And with regard to the third koan, the interpretation would be: Why, after practising Zen for many years, and having achieved profound insight, should one then be unable to cast off the sense of discrimination, and be unable to let go of the heart that picks and chooses? So much for the moral interpretation which on a shallow level seems to be appropriate enough, yet is off the mark. Anybody in need of this kind of interpretation or admonition would not yet have attained to great strength, whereas a man of great strength would not need this kind of caution.

Real insight into these three koans might be expressed in very simple and direct terms as 'Walk without using your legs; talk without using your tongue; freely live your life without casting off discrimination; and instead, wholeheartedly and fully accept discrimination, or delusions.' In that case, how do you respond to these koans as presented above? Without any kind of explanation or running commentary, actually walking without legs, talking without using your tongue, and being free, without rejection or throwing off any worldly discrimination and at the same time without being bound by that discrimination. That is all that can be said about these three koans. Unless already in training under a teacher and working on a koan, try to ponder not all but just one of these, keep working at it. The Mumonkan collection presents forty-eight cases, commented on by me. Do not think that yesterday you read about that problem, today of this problem, and tomorrow there will be still another problem – that is very harmful. Rather, with utmost effort, putting all your strength into it, strive to actually resolve a single problem. If you take the different teisho texts and comments into your life and harness and direct them towards a single problem, then they can become a source of great strength and be a real help. When grappling with a problem in this way, you arrive at a wall that you cannot get over or break through, then suddenly out of seemingly nowhere something you have read in these texts and comments comes back to you and provides the energy to break through the barrier or obstacle that confronts you. As a pointer, how does a violinist play the violin without using it? Try working with that.

In old Japan, the lay Zen Master Tesshu, who had deep insight, told a famous storyteller, 'I do not want to listen to a story that you tell with your tongue; please talk to me without using it!' The storyteller did not know what to say, but eventually he did talk to Tesshu without using his tongue; Tesshu then gave him the name 'The Tongueless Lay Practitioner.' That is by way of explanation.

Mumon's Comment: 'Shogen showed stomach and bowels, revealing everything!' This translation of Mumon's comment is not as clear as it might be, and so we shall have recourse to the Chinese original to render it more explicit. Thus, Mumon's comment is, 'In spite of the fact that Shogen literally opened up his belly and revealed everything, there was nobody to take it, nobody to learn from him.' Had there been, and had he then come to Mumon, Mumon would have beaten him up. Why? 'Gold is tested in fire.' No further comments are needed.

There is yet another patriarchal anecdote that might be helpful, Case 23. Eno, the Sixth Patriarch, had received transmission from the Fifth Patriarch, Gunin, and was told to leave because the other monks might resent his being made the successor. However, they became aware of Eno's flight and pursued him. Most of them soon gave up their chase, and eventually only one, Myo Choza (Elder Myo), caught up with him on the Daiyu-rei mountain. The Sixth Patriarch and Myo Choza faced each other, alone; there the difference in spiritual power between these two became evident. For though the Sixth Patriarch was rather small in stature, and Myo Choza, who had been a soldier, was a burly, powerful man, the power of satori shone from Eno, and Choza was suddenly like a child before him and asked for guidance. The Sixth Patriarch then said, 'Without thinking of good and bad, at this moment, what is the True Face?' On hearing that Myo had satori.

Some time afterwards Myo Choza again visited the Sixth Patriarch, and said, 'Besides what you taught me, are there any other secret words?' 'Secret words' here, of course, stand for 'Truth,' or 'words of truth.' These are concealed within the confusion in which we may be. So, too, with Myo Choza, who thought that perhaps there was something more or better. The Sixth Patriarch told him, 'The secret is within yourself, it is not hidden outside.' Confucius once told his followers, 'Do not think that I am hiding a secret from you. I hold nothing back, there is no secret that I have not revealed to you. Do we not live always together?' But no one could accept this.

'Secret words' are there in the trees, the birds are expressing them; so do we, each and all of us. However, in spite of the fact that these secrets are apparent everywhere around us, we always rely on information somebody else has cooked up and processed for us. We do not try to look for the secret words that are manifest before our eyes, nor do we seek out the secret heart that penetrates everything. Yet each of us speaks without using our tongue, and we all walk without using our legs, but we are not aware of it. What remains in our memory as the self that speaks, walks, etc., is our own will or discrimination. Our recollection then is the form of our self as disturbed by suffering, sadness, etc. Most of us, therefore, tend to think of ourselves as not sufficient because we do not see the splendid self that is there; yet at the same time, turning towards others, we hope that they will see us in the best light. We want others to see us as good, to believe in us, and yet at the same time, looking at ourselves, we do not trust ourselves or think well of ourselves. Thus rather than looking into Shogen's entrails, it is important to look within at that self which walks without legs, or which talks without using the tongue. At that moment we will become 'this man of great strength.'

Mumon's Verse: This man of great strength, 'lifting his leg he kicks up the vast, scented ocean' and he is so tall that he can 'look down on the heavenly realms at the top of Mount Sumeru.' This giant body of great strength 'cannot be contained by the universe.'

Chinese poems of this type usually have four lines; here, Mumon has composed three lines and says that he leaves the fourth one for us to complete the verse.

This is where we stop. Any more to be said might weaken the urgency of application!

CASE 21 • UMMON'S SHIT-STICK

THE CASE
A monk asked Ummon, 'What is Buddha?' Ummon said, 'A shit-stick.'

MUMON'S COMMENT
Ummon is so poor he cannot even prepare simple food, and is so busy he cannot even write properly. He takes up a shit-stick to support the teachings of our school. Just look at the decline of the Buddha-dharma!

THE VERSE
閃電光
擊石火
貶得眼
已蹉過

A flash of lightning,
Sparks struck from flint;
In the twinkling of an eye
It is gone forever.

SOKO ROSHI'S COMMENTS
During a recent stay in the U.S.A. I met a young Japanese student who was just about to return to Japan. He had for a time helped carpenters and had been much liked by them for his willingness and eagerness to help. So they gave him a great farewell party, and the boss repeatedly told him, 'You still have life before you; whatever you do, please

do not commit suicide.' He told me of this incident, and asked rather bewildered, 'I cannot understand it – surely I do not look suicidal? Why should he caution me thus?' I told him, 'It does not matter whether you understand why he told you; just remember his words.' I then tried to explain to him that, although he might not recognise it, those cautioning words conveyed deep affection, and were an expression of love. As I see it, the master-carpenter, in his mid-thirties, already had a deep understanding of human life. He knew that for a nineteen-year-old there are always emotional problems and tensions, and that there is choice, whether to engage in a variety of activities, or not. For example, he can decide not to let himself be sucked into the whirlpool of life, whether at home or while abroad in a foreign country for his education; and he can also choose to go skiing if he wants to.

For all of us, when young, there is great flexibility and leeway for activities. But as we grow older, although that broad sky remains, we will gradually cease to see it. Inevitably problems and psychological tensions will arise when we neglect to see mountains, sky, and nature around us, and instead are only concerned with egocentric relations, or with our own psychological problems. If we really want to uproot this anguish and these psychological problems, we must first realise that this root is within us, and that it is deep and large and strong. Zen practice aims at realising that root. Thus from Zen practice, from sitting zazen, we get a sense of ease and realisation, but that ease and realisation must be without any trace of logical reasoning or conceptualisation.

Now to the koan. 'Cases' involving Ummon appear several times in the *Mumonkan*. However, it will also be helpful to repeat a few details, about Rinzai, the founder of the tradition to which we belong. Repeating descriptions of the lives of Ummon or Rinzai, or other Masters, will increase your sense of familiarity with them.

Rinzai's Zen practice was outstanding; while in Obaku's monastery, he was careful and thorough in everything he did. Though by now a man of real insight, he never went to Obaku for sanzen-interviews. It seems that he had possibly fallen into a conceptual hole, thinking that because Zen is practical, and involves practical realisation, there was no point in going for sanzen. The head monk, feeling that Rinzai needed help, suggested he should go to Master Obaku for a sanzen-interview. Rinzai said he did not know what to ask. Written down in a book, Rinzai's answer to the head monk may seem very naive, the kind of answer a raw beginner would give. But behind that answer was perhaps the preconception that there was no point in asking anything. So Bokuju, the head monk, gently suggested he could ask, 'What is Buddha?' or 'What is the Buddha-dharma?' Rinzai obediently went and put the question to Obaku. But barely had he got his question out when Obaku struck him thirty blows. Rinzai reported this to Bokuju who told him to go again! Rinzai went and this time, before he had finished speaking, was again beaten. Once more he told Bokuju, and once more was told to go again. But before he had opened his mouth he was again beaten.

At this point, the dust of Rinzai's rather shallow conceptual understanding was probably wiped away. But he also seems to have felt that he could not attain to satori under Obaku, and told Bokuju that he would leave and search elsewhere. Bokuju said, 'That is as you wish, but before you go you must pay your respects to Obaku.' Then Bokuju hurried to Obaku and said, 'That young monk who came several times and you beat, he is really a very fine monk. In the future he will grow into a vast tree spreading huge branches and will provide shade for many.' In northern climates the heat of the sun in summer does not scorch and blight, and rather than looking for shade, one would seek sunshine; but in India, China or Japan, summer is really fierce, so a great tree provides shade and shelter for people in the heat. In Japanese, this great tree is also conceived of in the sense of the Master's room, hence 'Inryo-ju' (*inryo* meaning the room and *ju* this tree). My own teacher, Goto Zuigan Roshi, called his room *inryo-ju*.

So Bokuju then entreated Obaku, 'When this monk comes to take his leave of you, please find some beneficial means of helping him.' I like this story very much. In Zen training, the treatment of monks is sometimes rather rough, and blows or the *katsu* shout are frequently used. But the other side of that rough treatment is the kind, gentle, thoughtful treatment by Bokuju. This is an aspect of Zen that we should not overlook; unbeknownst to Rinzai, Bokuju was quietly and kindly working on his behalf. So when Rinzai then was before him, Obaku said, 'There is no need to go far away, just go to Daigu of Koandan and there you will find what you seek.' Rinzai did as he was told and under Daigu entered satori. Rinzai then went back to Obaku, and eventually received transmission from him; but Bokuju may be considered as being instrumental for his attainment of satori.

Ummon also came to satori under Bokuju. Having left Obaku, Bokuju wandered around and eventually set up his own training temple. His method was extremely severe; monks were rarely able to get through the door for sanzen with him. When Ummon went for sanzen, he called at the closed door, 'I have not yet attained satori; please find some way of helping me.' Bokuju opened the door a crack, looked out, saw Ummon and slammed it shut again. Next day Ummon came again, but the same happened – he could not get inside. Ummon went yet a third time, determined that even if he should die in the attempt, he was getting in.

Can we imagine Ummon in this state? At that moment he was probably not even thinking of satori; all he had in mind was getting through that door, and to do so he had become like a ball of fire. In this state Ummon had come a step or two closer to satori. And as for us, do we not all tend to look here or there, up or down, around and about, but rarely ever become the concentrated ball of fire that Ummon was in his tremendous determination to get through? And Bokuju's kindness – which was apparent in his going to Obaku on Rinzai's behalf, and which made him close the door repeatedly in Ummon's face so as to force him to become a ball of fire – both these actions are prompted by the same kindness.

Anyway, Ummon, having become this ball of fire, thrust himself into Bokuju's room; Bokuju grabbed him, and shaking him, said, 'Speak, speak!' Ummon naturally did not know what to say; it was rather like water being poured on that ball of fire – suddenly he found himself thrown into the water of confusion. Racing around in his head was the question, 'What do I say, what do I say?' So the ball of fire had become confused and fumbling at Bokuju's order to speak he could not reply. At that, Bokuju flung him out and slammed the door on him. Ummon screamed with pain as one of his legs was caught and broken. In this complete scream was not the slightest space for any thought or delusion to enter. At that instant, Ummon entered satori – but limped for the rest of his life. Losing the use of one leg is a cheap price to pay for the opening of Great Satori. For such a tremendous, total insight the loss of both arms or legs would be nothing at all. Accordingly, Ummon's Zen, attained in such a powerfully concentrated way, was very simple and direct. Ummon appears in many koans, and often the key, or turning point, is just one single word. In later times it was said that Ummon's Zen was like a far-off wood above which is hoisted a royal standard. This brilliant flag can be seen flashing in the distance, but it is impossible to know how many others there might be, or what kind of a palace or palaces, or gardens, or how many troops there may be deployed. Just so was Ummon's Zen, very lofty, very deep, very straightforward and simple.

The National Teacher Daito, founder of Daitoku-ji, entered into satori by means of Ummon's Barrier Koan, and subsequently was thought to be a reincarnation of Ummon. After his death, the memorial temple in which he was buried became known as Ummon's Hermitage.

I am the incumbent of a temple that belongs to the Myoshin-ji lineage, which was founded by Kanzan Egen who had inherited the Dharma from Daito. He, too, had entered satori when working with Ummon's 'Kan' (Barrier) Koan. The name 'Kanzan' contains the ideogramme 'barrier' and was the name given him by Daito on resolving Ummon's 'Kan' Koan.

This seems a very roundabout introduction to the koan under review, but it serves to emphasise the fact that Ummon and Rinzai were contemporaries and had both practised under Bokuju. It also shows that some of the great patriarchs of Rinzai Zen attained satori while working on Ummon's Barrier Koan. It is important for trainees to feel a familiarity with, and have a sense of being part of the lineage of these patriarchs. And it indicates the direct realisation, or satori, of these Zen Masters – in contrast to a merely bookish understanding of Buddhism.

As to the koan itself, a monk asked Ummon, 'What is Buddha?' In the comment to Case 18, 'Tozan's Three Pounds of Flax', it was emphasised that this Buddha is not a conceptual idea, is not referring to the historical Buddha, but is a direct, tangible grasp of 'Buddha'. In response to this question, Ummon replied, 'A shit-stick.' It is, however, quite wrong to interpret this 'What is Buddha?' as a significant question which Ummon counters with such a dirty image in order to overturn the idealised version of Buddha. Ummon's 'Shit-stick' is a pure, direct expression, and as put forth with 'Three Pounds of Flax,' there is nothing further to add to it.

Lectures on Buddhism or Buddhist books extol a fundamental reality or truth called 'Buddha' which is revealed by all phenomena, manifested at one moment and then disappears. Therefore, this Buddha is fully manifest even in a single hair, and there is nothing that is not Buddha. This is as far as the conceptual understanding of Buddha goes. A whole dimension separates this kind of intellectual understanding of Buddha from, for instance, a single finger being held up, and the full, complete, instantaneous realisation of that as Buddha.

Human beings should love everything. But there is a world of difference between knowing that intellectually and actually loving somebody who is beside us at any particular moment. Truly aware of this direct and full perception is called Zen.

Mumon's Comment: 'Ummon is so poor that he could not even prepare simple food; and he is so busy that he cannot even write a proper composition.' As usual, Mumon adopts a seemingly critical and denigrating attitude but, in fact, greatly praises Ummon. The words 'poor' and 'being busy' are Mumon's way of expressing the very moment Ummon had his foot caught in the door of Bokuju's interview-room and of his scream of pain; at that moment there was not the slightest room or space for anything other than pure perception. Mumon's words reflect just that. But if trainees who work on this koan in sanzen grab hold of and cling on to the word 'Shit-stick,' and take this as Zen or the Buddha-dharma, and if they go about brandishing this stinking stick, shouting, 'This is Zen,' or 'This is satori,' then obviously Buddhism will decline and collapse.

The Verse: 'A flash of lightning, sparks struck from flint; in the twinkling of an eye, it is gone forever.' This may be misunderstood as referring to speed. But what is important here is not the speed of lightning, or of the twinkling of an eye, but rather the purity of action, and that the degree of purity of action is a very great one. So the phrase 'in the twinkling of an eye' refers to one who, when confronted with Ummon's Shit-stick, does or does not allow one single shred of illusion to enter. If even the tiniest sliver or a fraction of a moment of conceptual rationalisation is allowed to enter into the reaction, then it is just as if a rocket had passed – you have missed the moment, it has already gone and is miles away.

As in the example of 'What is Buddha?', 'Buddha is loving people,' and there is no need to conceptualise or explain 'loving'. Looking at Buddha, is an exposition or rationalisation necessary? There is no need even for putting out a single leg in this search!

CASE 22 • KASHO'S FLAGPOLE

Ananda asked Kasyapa, 'The World-honoured One transmitted the robe of gold-brocade to you; did he transmit anything else?' Kasyapa called out, 'Ananda!' Ananda responded, 'Yes?' 'Knock over the flagpole at the gate,' said Kasyapa.

MUMON'S COMMENT

If you can say a turning word, you will see the assembly on the Vulture Peak still in solemn session. If you cannot do so, pay heed to Vipasyin Buddha – right up to now the subtle essence has not been attained.

THE VERSE

問處何如答處親
幾人於此眼生筋
兄呼弟應揚家醜
不屬陰陽別是春

The question is something like it, the answer more familiar.
How many people have their eyes glued with dough!
The elder brother calling, the younger brother answering – the family
    secret is revealed.
This spring does not depend on Yin and Yang.

SOKO ROSHI'S COMMENTS

In Case 6, the Buddha holds up a flower and Kasyapa smiles, which illustrates the first transmission of the Dharma. The present koan tells of the transmission from Kasyapa to Ananda. Neither of these two cases is meant to present a historical fact, and it is well-known that these stories originated in China. Whether they are historical or not is irrelevant for contemplating them; rather, they are an expression of the way in which the early patriarchs viewed the transmission of the Dharma.

The Buddha is believed to have died around 486 BCE; Kasyapa was one of his great disciples and is said to have lived to a ripe old age. He was deeply devoted and carefully and minutely practised all the regulations of the Vinaya. The word *zuda*, which I have translated here as 'concern to keep the Vinaya', has perhaps the sense of 'throwing away' in its Pali origins. Thus the practice of maintaining this *zuda* is keeping the precepts for the purpose of eliminating or throwing away all our attachments, all our desires, all our cravings.

Looking at Kasyapa as an outsider, one might think he exhausted himself in so minutely observing the Vinaya, and that his was a harsh and hard life. The Buddha, having himself grown old, saw old Kasyapa religiously keeping the precepts, his very carefully regulated life, always wearing an old, coarse robe that surely must have chafed his body. Moved by compassion, he asked Kasyapa, 'At this stage there is no more back-sliding, so why do you not take it just a little easy?' But Kasyapa replied, 'Please do not worry! Fashioned by many years of practice, this life as I now live it, like this robe, fits me very comfortably. I meticulously observe the precepts not for the sake of discipline, but because I enjoy it.'

It seems Kasyapa became known for his care in keeping the precepts not only because he meticulously observed them, but because he enjoyed their observance. He is said to have been rather ugly and a man of few words, shunning the light of acclaim. In the monastery of Myoshin-ji a carving is venerated with the Buddha in the middle and Kasyapa and Ananda at each side. Kasyapa's face is dark and he is presented as an ugly man. However, this very Kasyapa inherited the Buddha-dharma.

After the Buddha's passing, his grieving disciples debated as to what to do with the Buddha's ashes. Kasyapa said, 'As to the ashes, let us leave them to others. What we should be concerned with is the Buddha's Teaching leading to enlightenment. For that we had better gather in an assembly and make sure that the true Dharma will be preserved and transmitted.' Five hundred of the Buddha's enlightened disciples assembled, and at this first council the Buddha's Teaching and the Sangha was developed and consolidated.

Ananda is the other disciple who appears in this koan. In contrast to the severe Kasyapa, his very name means 'joy'. It is said that he was given this name because he was born on the night of the Buddha's enlightenment. Said to have been a cousin of the Buddha, he took the robe while still quite young and remained beside the Buddha as his constant attendant. He is thought to have been very good-looking, and the Myoshin-ji sculpture reflects this. As a disciple of the Buddha and close to him for twenty-three years, he was undoubtedly thoughtful, considerate, and very loving. Being for so long attendant on the Buddha, he had more opportunity than any of the others to hear all the sermons, and he is said to have had a powerful memory. So, if Kasyapa is remembered as the primary keeper and exponent of the Vinaya, Ananda is remembered as the one who heard most, or the one who kept and preserved most.

Ananda, then, so very fair of face, attractive and perfect in deportment, had all advantages; but perhaps because of these, because of his attractiveness and beauty, he sometimes became involved in affairs with women or got himself into other difficulties which created problems within the early Sangha. On one occasion, when he was asked by a community of nuns to address them, he asked Kasyapa, his senior, to go with him. The nuns tried to get Ananda to take the lecturer's seat, but Ananda deferred and wanted Kasyapa to give the sermon. However, when the nuns insisted on Ananda's doing so, Kasyapa gave a smile as much as to say, 'Well, it cannot be helped,' and let Ananda speak.

It has been related from of old that Ananda did not become enlightened during the Buddha's lifetime. This statement points to the fundamental question of what is truly important in a person's training. Ananda, who for so long had been close to the Buddha and had been striving towards enlightenment, was in grief and sorrow at the Master's approaching death. Unable to bear the prospect of his departure, he left in order to hide his grief. The Buddha, seeing that Ananda was missing, asked, 'Where is Ananda?' When told he had gone off towards the gate and in his grief was supporting himself on the gatepost, weeping bitterly, he had Ananda called back to his side. Ananda then told him that, with the Buddha's imminent departure, and not yet come to be enlightened himself, he felt like being left on a dark road, with the last flicker of light going out. At that, the Buddha told him, 'Although I am dying, make yourself into a lamp and transmit and illuminate the teachings that I have been giving you.'

It would be a great mistake to take what is implicit in these words as two different activities, Ananda making himself into a light, and Ananda as a recipient of the teachings of the Buddha. The truth that the Buddha expressed is inherent in each individual – oneself and the Dharma are not two separate things. But even at this stage, Ananda still could not see this.

After the Buddha's decease, as mentioned already, Kasyapa gathered the disciples in a council to ensure that the true Dharma would be preserved and transmitted. In that council led by Kasyapa, Ananda should have played a central role because of his remarkable recall of what the Buddha had taught. But as not yet enlightened, he could not be included in the group of the five hundred closest disciples gathered to establish the Teachings. Kasyapa probably was himself unhappy about this, and Ananda must also have felt that in some way he had missed an opportunity and he was sad. We can also imagine that Ananda made every effort with his practice and with all his energy approached this new leader, Kasyapa, who had inherited the transmission from the Buddha. We might liken it to the energy with which Ummon tried to get his foot in the door of Bokuju's room (Comments to Case 21).

So, Ananda then asked Kasyapa, 'The Buddha transmitted the robe of gold-brocade to you; did he transmit anything else?' This of course is not historical; it is unthinkable that at that time the Buddha would have had such a robe. Instead of being concerned about the golden robe, picture it in terms of Ananda having become a ball of fire and asking Kasyapa, 'The Buddha transmitted his Dharma to you – what was that Dharma?' Kasyapa, responding, called out, 'Ananda!' Ananda instinctively answered with 'Yes?' between call and response, what was it that intervened? We try to evoke all kinds of conceptions, but there is no conceptual element here at all. The sentence simply states that Kasyapa called out and Ananda responded. However, who is it that really called? Who is it that really answered? Any further explanation, rather than being helpful, would only confound the issue still more. But compare the comments to Case 17, the National Teacher Echu calling Oshin three times. When Ananda answered, 'Yes?' Kasyapa told Ananda, 'Knock over the flagpole at the gate.' The flag is to indicate that a Dharma teaching is in progress. Even today in Japanese temples a flag is put up at the gate when a large ceremony is being held. So the lowering of the flag, or knocking down the flagpole, has the meaning that everything is ended, everything is over. 'Hey!' 'Yes?' – that is all; I need not interpret that for you. There is nothing other than that.

Remember the circumstances in which Kasyapa inherited the Dharma. The Buddha held up a flower, and instantly, on seeing the flower, Kasyapa smiled gently. Nothing else. But the others in that assembly probably expected the Buddha to start talking about the flower.

Ananda asked Kasyapa, 'What is the Dharma that has been transmitted?', and when Kasyapa called out, 'Ananda!' and Ananda responded, 'Yes?', perhaps he thought Kasyapa was to expound the Dharma to him. But Kasyapa just said, 'Knock down the flagpole at the gate.' Everything is done with and finished; just that, and that alone. Though not mentioned here, but at that moment Ananda had full and genuine insight.

Mumon's Comment: The main point in the first line, 'If you can say a turning word,' is Mumon's emphasis on that moment – Kasyapa calling and Ananda responding. What is in that exchange? What is working there? If you can see it and seize it within that single instant, then the assembly, the Buddha with his disciples on the Vulture Peak millennia ago, has not yet dispersed. Expressed differently, if you yourself can see, perceive and grasp the functioning of this instant in which Kasyapa calls and Ananda answers, and can express it appropriately and perfectly, then, Mumon says, you too, all of you, can transcend this particular place and time and are at that assembly, and equally present at the encounter between Kasyapa and Ananda.

Kasyapa became the first pillar of the Dharma by truly enjoying his minute and careful observance of the precepts. His wearing a coarse old robe was not for the purpose of gaining something; he was simply wearing it. His very careful observance of the precepts was also just that. Hence his words to the Buddha, 'I have now become so used to this careful observance of the precepts that it fits me most comfortably.'

Ananda, who was very gifted and intelligent, who had heard so much, and remembered it, probably indulged in logical reasoning, in intellectual speculations such as, 'This exists because of that, and that as a result of this,' or 'If I practise with this in mind, or in this way, then enlightenment will follow like that.' But what simply did not exist in Ananda's life was this perfect moment, the perfect action. If you follow and practise the training Ananda had done so far, there will be no deliverance. The Transmission from Teacher to Teacher which is chanted every morning, starts with the name of Vipasyin Buddha (Bibashi Butsu). He is the first of the Buddhas, aeons ago. Even if continuously training since the time of Bibashi Butsu right up to the present, but training the way Ananda did before becoming enlightened, there would be no insight, nor the resulting functioning of the Dharma.

The other day at the end of a lecture, I asked if the barbed wire I had seen around an oak tree might be removed. If, on hearing me ask this, it had been treated as some kind of koan and as that had been tossed around in the mind, then the barbed wire would still enmesh the tree. Fortunately, somebody simply went and removed the wire, and I am pleased. In order to remove the wire, you must go to the tree, must use your body and hands. That much for the barbed wire around the oak tree. But to remove the chain that binds us, does not call for any movement of hands or feet; it takes no time, it is done in an instant. And just like the oak tree, from which the wire has now been removed, can return to its natural self and grow and spread, so we too can recover our original functioning, if we give ourselves into this realisation of each single instant.

The Verse: To help you with it, I will try to express it in different words. Ananda asked Kasyapa about the Dharma, and when Kasyapa called him, he answered, 'Yes?'. But when called, he and the Dharma were separate, for he was entangled in concepts. Yet at the moment he responded, 'Yes?', he had become one. How many people, trying to find this state of realisation, have looked for it so closely that their eyes have become bloodshot! Yet very few people have found it. As Nansen said to Joshu, 'The more you look for it, the further away it recedes!'

Here in our Case, the Elder Kasyapa called, and the younger brother Ananda responded, 'Yes?' In that simple exchange they expressed the depths of the Dharma. The text says that they exposed to the world the secret of their hearts, meaning that what to others may seem mysterious, the Dharma for example, they have fully exposed for later generations. Mumon then adds that what so brilliantly emerged between them continues to shine, like a glorious spring that permanently pervades over and above the changes of the four seasons. In ancient China, the seasons were seen as originating from the interaction of Yin and Yang; hence, as translated here, 'This spring does not depend on Yin and Yang.'

As Mumon expresses it in his Verse to Case 19, 'Flowers in spring, the moon in autumn, a cool breeze in summer, and shining snow in winter' – here, too, we have the same feeling. If there are no unnecessary concepts or notions in your heart, and if you are able in that instant to take in the flower as it is, or the wind as it is, or the snow as it is, then, as said in Case 19, 'If you can do that, you are enjoying a permanent and perfect spring.'

A relationship is from both sides. If there is just one side, you cannot have a relationship. If you have a bell and nobody strikes it, then no sound comes out. No need to worry who is the bell and who the clapper; just ring!

CASE 23 • ENO'S WITHOUT THINKING OF GOOD AND BAD

The Elder Myo pursued the Sixth Patriarch all the way up to Daiyu-rei Mountain. Overtaken, the Patriarch put down robe and bowl on the rock and said, 'Take it – if you can!' Myo took hold of it but it was as heavy as the mountain and he could not lift it. Trembling with fear and awe he said, 'Elder Brother, please teach me. I have not come for robe and bowl, I have come for the Dharma.' The Patriarch said, 'Without thinking of good and bad, what at this moment, is the True Face of Elder Myo?' At that, Myo had satori – lathered in sweat and with tears in his eyes, he said, 'Besides the secret words and the mystic meaning, is there some other hidden meaning as well?' The Patriarch replied, 'What I have just told you is no secret. When the True Face lights up, the mystery is seen to be in yourself.' Myo said, 'While at (Master) Obai's, I did not realise the True Face. Now that you have pointed it out to me, I am like a man who on having drunk the water, himself knows how cold it is. You, Elder Brother, are my Master.' The Patriarch said, 'If that is so with you, both you and I have Obai as our Master; just guard it and keep it well!'

MUMON'S COMMENT

It has to be said of the Sixth Patriarch that this is an emergency requiring grandmotherly kindness. It is like peeling a fresh lychee, taking out the pip and popping it into your mouth. All you need to do is to swallow it.

THE VERSE

描不成兮畫不就
贊不及兮休生受
本來面目沒處藏
世界壞時渠不朽

It cannot be described, cannot be portrayed,
It cannot possibly be praised enough; so stop questing after it.
There is nowhere for the True Face to hide;
When the whole world has perished, only this remains.

SOKO ROSHI'S COMMENTS

Before commenting on the koan, a few general remarks about zazen may be useful. The first is to feel a sense of thanks for being able to sit zazen on our cushions, gratitude for the joy and peace that arise from it. While sitting zazen, do not try to achieve anything, least of all satori. Important is only that we sit on the cushion as if melting away. Originally, we are nothing, we are empty; when sitting on our cushions, we melt back into this original emptiness. Without this melting back into emptiness, the sense of I and of self-assertiveness become ever more powerful and strong while sitting. The more this sense of I is allowed to develop the more it will crush you, so that you begin to feel ill. Therefore sit relaxed, easy; ideally in a frame of mind that, 'If I die on the cushion, it would not matter.'

Now to introducing the koan. Before Bodhidharma's arrival in China, Buddhism there was based on the sutras and treatises, with rules, rituals and observances. After Bodhidharma, Chinese Buddhism became oriented towards religious experience, and by the time of the Sixth Patriarch, the development of Chinese Buddhism had lost the Indian flavour that up until then had clung to it, and had become free, natural, and direct in its practice. Hence the Sixth Patriarch is traditionally regarded as one of the greatest of the patriarchs.

He is said to have lived for about seventy-four years, born in 634, some 1,350 years ago. His father had been an official in the capital, but for some reason had lost his position and was exiled to southern China, and died while Eno, the later Sixth Patriarch, was still young. To help his mother, Eno would go and gather firewood in the mountains, and sell it in the town.

In his time, north of the Yangtse River was regarded the centre of civilisation, and northerners described the provinces south of the Yangtse as backward and barbarian. Tradition stresses that Eno, being poor, had no education and was illiterate. Here I would like to add a comment. Although it is said that he had no formal education in the usual sense, it was perhaps just because of this, that being less influenced by people's ideas he grew up more naturally and instinctively. He was a very good son to his mother. In China, it is said that respect for the parents is the source of a hundred virtues, of a hundred good actions. Perhaps the first object of the free and natural expression of our feelings is towards the parents. So Eno, direct and natural, was also devoted to his mother. This is very important to bear in mind.

One day Eno was in the town to sell his wood as usual, when somebody bought the lot. Eno carried the load to the customer's home and on being paid, was about to leave when from inside he heard sutra chanting. When chanting or listening to sutras, you probably do not understand them; but Eno was Chinese, and the chant was in Chinese, so he could understand what he heard. He listened with his heart completely open, and thus immediately and directly received a powerful impact. This was Eno's first real religious insight. Unable to pull himself away, he inquired what sutra this was and where it came from, and was told that it was the *Diamond Sutra*, and the chanting had been learned at Master Gunin's, the Fifth Patriarch's monastery.

From that moment, Eno was filled with longing to place himself under Master Gunin for instruction, but also knew he had to stay and look after his old mother. Then one of his customers offered to take care of her and so Eno could set out to Obai, the monastery of the Fifth Patriarch, Gunin Daiman. It took him perhaps a month to reach there, and one cannot but be impressed by the determination of monks like Eno to really seek the Dharma. Public transport was non-existent, and what roads there were, were poorly maintained and the going often arduous, through wilderness and mountain fastness, with one's life being endangered by wild animals or bandits. But Eno had the strength and determination to seek the Way, and so he persevered.

Eventually he arrived at Gunin's, who asked Eno, 'Where have you come from?' 'I've come from Shinshu in the south.' 'What are you seeking?' 'To become a Buddha. I have no other purpose.' The Fifth Patriarch remarked ruthlessly, 'Aren't those southern provinces from which you've come the home of barbarians? It is not possible for somebody from there to become a Buddha.' Eno responded very calmly, 'Among people you can make distinctions of north or south, but with regard to the Buddha-nature, there is neither north nor south.' What a magnificent response! Of course, we must make efforts to avoid discrimination or ill-treatment of people; but is it not more important that the person who has been discriminated against, or who has been victimised, has the determination to coolly respond that although there may be distinctions of north and south among people, there is no north and south in the Buddha-nature!

The Fifth Patriarch made this devastating judgement to test Eno, and Eno passed with flying colours. What the Fifth Patriarch saw from this encounter was that this young man had already come to a considerable depth of insight.

Though Gunin's assembly was a large one, with many well-advanced monks, yet they all held the prejudice of their time that southerners were ignorant, stupid barbarians. The Fifth Patriarch knew that his monks would feel jealous if he were to single out young Eno, and might try to expel or even harm him. Therefore he told Eno to make himself useful in the monastery and so, still a layman, Eno worked for eight months hulling rice.

The Fifth Patriarch was getting old and one day told his monks, 'It is not enough to just remember what I tell you; you must come to your own insight. Each of you compose a poem, and he whose insight is genuine will inherit the Dharma from me.' Most of the monks thought that since the head monk, Jinshu, was bound to become the successor, it was a mere waste of time to compose a poem.

Jinshu, the head monk, was well aware that all expectations were focussed on him. Thus compelled, but unsure of himself, and in agony and anguish, he composed a poem; but he did not have the confidence to show it to Gunin.

In the course of my own training, I remember when I had just started sanzen, how I agonised about some response to the koan! At the core of my anguish was, 'If I give this response and it is accepted, then there cannot be much depth in Zen. Where, then, would I go?' But I can assure you, please put your minds at rest – such a response was never accepted. Because in fact, going for sanzen, we ourselves know very well whether we have full confidence in the response we are going to make.

So Jinshu composed a verse which, though good, did not go all the way. Realising this himself, and not daring to present it to the Fifth Patriarch, he brushed it on a wall in the middle of the night.

'This body is the tree of enlightenment;
The heart is like a bright mirror on a stand.
Carefully and constantly wipe this mirror
So that no dust does settle on it.'

Next morning, the Fifth Patriarch, on seeing the poem, knew whose it was and that, although very good, it did not go all the way. So he told the monks who had crowded around to read the poem, 'This is really good. If you memorise it and always observe it you will not go astray.' Then he summoned Jinshu, the head monk, to his room and told him, 'Your poem is not yet perfect. Go and amend it.' At that time Jinshu was unable to transcend the verse he had composed, only years later did he become a great Master.

Anyway, the monks did as they were told, and went about reciting the poem in order to memorise it. One of the young novices, thus engaged, happened to come into the shed where Eno was hulling rice. On hearing the poem, Eno at once realised that it was not complete, asked to be taken to where it was, and, since he himself could not write, asked to have his own poem brushed next to it.

'Originally there is no tree of enlightenment
The clear mirror has no stand.
Fundamentally, there is nothing.
So where can dust settle?'

Few of the monks had full insight, yet on seeing the two poems side by side, all could feel which of them expressed greater profundity. Astonished, they again crowded round, babbling with excitement. The Fifth Patriarch, hearing the commotion, emerged from his quarters and after a glance at the verse took off one of his sandals and wiped it out, commenting, 'This verse is not expressing enlightenment.' Most of the monks felt relief – of course, they were right, had been right from the beginning; how could one expect a poem expressing enlightenment from a barbarian!

The intention of the Fifth Patriarch is clear. In Eno he recognised the unexcelled disciple, but he also had to prevent jealousy and resentment on the part of his monks. After all the excitement had died down, he went to the rice shed where Eno was working. In old China the device used for hulling rice was a kind of mortar, the pestle released by lever action from a foot treadle. Stepping on it with full force with the foot would raise the heavy pestle which then, when released, fell down on the rice. Now, Eno was rather small and light so his weight alone could not lift the heavy pestle and he used to tie a rock to his waist for increased weight.

The Fifth Patriarch, seeing Eno working hard like this, was pleased. This, too, is an important point; those on the Way must throw themselves wholeheartedly into the practice. One of the things that I always heard in the monastery was 'Become a fool!' If you try to use your head or to reason things out, your training will not prosper. And not only with the training, but whatever you engage in, there are no shortcuts. Constantly using the brain to think out shortcuts does not further.

The Fifth Patriarch asked Eno, 'Have you finished the rice?' It is obvious what he really referred to and hence Eno's reply, 'The rice is done, but rice and husks are not yet separated.' The Fifth Patriarch returned to his room, but in the night summoned Eno to see him.

Eno's reply, 'Rice and husks are not yet separated,' refers to the state of Eno's insight: he had not yet had this personal insight checked against the cumulative insight as set out in the Sutras and the Teachings of the Patriarchs. This, too, is one of the important points. Without personal insight, Zen training is pointless, has no meaning. Yet by itself alone it is extremely dangerous, for however profound the individual insight might be, by just clinging to it and depending on it alone, one is literally bound and tied by one's own insight. It is therefore essential that one constantly keeps checking one's insight and so, in a sense one raises it by comparing it with the transmission of Buddhism and of Zen and using that as one's framework.

I myself know people, even leaders of Zen groups, who have had very deep insight, but because they did not go through with this checking process, they went widely astray. There is a saying, 'Throw light on and illuminate your insight by checking it against the old texts.'

So when Eno said, 'The rice is hulled, but it and the husks are not yet separated,' this checking is what he was asking the Fifth Patriarch for. So in his room that night, the Fifth Patriarch at length expounded on the *Diamond Sutra*. On hearing, 'Cultivate the heart that does not settle on anything,' Eno had another profound insight. This saying from the *Diamond Sutra* is still in use as a koan.

After this check by the Fifth Patriarch, Eno received the robe of the Dharma transmission from him, but was told to leave before daybreak and to go south. The Fifth Patriarch himself guided him part of the way. In Zen training, the relationship between the Master and disciple is very formal indeed, and the Fifth Patriarch's gesture shows how important an acknowledged disciple is to a Master. It is not just affection, but arises from the awareness of the need for the continuing transmission of the Dharma.

Thus, Eno, the barbarian from the south, had become the Sixth Patriarch. Since, from then on, the Fifth Patriarch ceased to give teisho, his monks realised that a transmission must have taken place. Noticing also that robe and bowl had gone, they began to suspect that it was that rather beggarly individual from the south who had been working in the rice shed who had gone off with them. Furious and feeling deprived by what had happened, many set out to chase after

Eno to recover the robe. Foremost among them was Myo, a stalwart, powerful monk who had once been a soldier. Most of the monks soon got tired and returned to the monastery, but Myo persevered and caught up with Eno on Daiyurei mountain.

Our koan starts at this point. Imagine this meeting between the big, burly monk Myo, and the rather frail, slight Eno. In a physical contest, there was no way in which Eno could win. Anyway, when Eno saw Myo bearing down on him, he put the robe and bowl down on a rock. But make no mistake here – he did not put it down because he was afraid. Even though this robe stood for the transmission from the Buddha and Bodhidharma, for him it was only a robe. He said to Myo, 'This robe symbolises faith, and is not something that should be fought over. Take it if you really want it. For somebody taking it without true faith, it is only an object.'

Myo tried to take the robe, but found he could not lift it. This, however, does not indicate that the robe had become miraculously heavy! Imagine a situation when many people are present and you have an encounter of this kind; then you present yourself in the best possible light, deck yourself out one way or another. But with just two people meeting in the loneliness of the mountains, the decisive factor there is the direct power of insight by one or the other. So here are the burly Myo, not sure what he was looking for, who saw the robe only as a thing; and Eno who had full and deep enlightenment. The difference in power of insight between them is self-evident. Thus Myo, face to face with Eno, lost his strength and could not lift the robe. Trembling with terror, he said, 'I did not come for the robe, but for the teaching; please teach me the Dharma.'

Imagine this encounter again. Myo is not only big and strong, but wears the robe of the fully ordained monk. Eno is just the puny rice-pounder, not even a monk. Yet the big powerful monk humbly asks this frail youth, 'Please teach me the Dharma.' From this you may get an inkling of what the Dharma actually is!

But equally you need not think that all Eno ever did was to hull rice and never sat zazen and that therefore zazen is of no use. That would merely be foolish. From his infancy, a deep understanding had been growing in Eno quite naturally by itself, and so he is sometimes referred to as religiously exceptional. But if Eno is considered exceptional, then this means someone whose heart is always open, empty, naked. We, all of us wear too many masks, always tend to put many robes over the naked heart and so have accumulated a lot of unnecessary claptrap. Therefore we have to sit zazen to again lay bare that natural and naked heart. So please sit on your cushion relaxed and peacefully, without any striving, simply melting away. The cushion is not a place for building up a self. We spend most of our time elaborating ourselves, or artificially presenting ourselves one way or another, making ourselves into this or that. But when sitting zazen, that is the last thing to do.

So, the monk, Myo, overcome by the Sixth Patriarch's spiritual power, asked to be taught the Dharma. Eno said, 'Without thinking of good and bad, what at this moment is the True Face of the Elder Myo?' This reply of Eno has been handed down over the centuries and is still used in sanzen, causing much suffering!

When people hear these words, they at once think that without thinking of good and bad, society will collapse and break down. But is there such a thing as an absolute good, or an absolute bad in this world of ours? Inevitably and unconsciously we always set up a standard of good and bad. Thinking of good and bad from a relative point of view, we inevitably do so in terms of I and other – and just this relative I must firmly be thrown away. The Sixth Patriarch's 'Without thinking of good and bad,' implies just that. When you throw away the self that has only been grasping after the distinction between good and bad – then, for the first time, the true self, the True Face, emerges. So at the Sixth Patriarch's 'Without thinking of good and bad, what is the True Face of the Elder Myo?', Myo had satori.

Reading this, do you ask yourselves what kind of an insight that was? If so, it is no good. Myo was not enlightened by something. Rather, that which had bound him until then broke, and he was released.

Good and bad, thinking oneself distinct from others – to this extent Myo was not only bound by such discriminations, but was also tied up in ideas and concepts about Zen practice itself. The Sixth Patriarch's 'Without thinking of good and bad', in one stroke cut the rope that had bound him.

If you have a bandage over your eyes, you only need to take it off and without bothering to see, you see. Without knowing it, we wear such a blindfold all the time, and with it covering our eyes, we try to see or try to attain satori!

Anyway, for Myo, the bandage was removed and he saw clearly. The text says that cold sweat covered his body and he shed tears of joy. Prostrating himself before the Sixth Patriarch, he said, 'Is there yet some other hidden teaching?' The Sixth Patriarch answered, 'What I said is no secret. If the True Face lights up, the secret is seen to be in yourself.'

In my training, I also suffered from this koan of the True Face. Mornings and evenings, I went to my teacher Zuigan, but for a long time he would not accept my responses. To begin with I tried to explain it in words; words and words, a bellyful of them. 'Show me, here! Display before my eyes your True Face!' Finally, unable to think of any other way, I just stuck my face out; Master Zuigan looked rather strangely and said, 'You really look like that, but your face is too dirty,' and rang his bell to end the interview. So, you also need to struggle for yourselves.

Myo then said to the Sixth Patriarch, 'I have practised at Obai under the Fifth Patriarch for a long time, but could not see my True Face. Now you have pointed it out to me, I am like a man who on having drunk water, himself knows how cold it is.' Since then, 'Knowing the true taste of water' has become a well-known Zen saying, expressing realisation. Myo then concluded, 'So now you are my teacher.' However, the Sixth Patriarch told him, 'If this is how you feel, we both are disciples of the Fifth Patriarch. Keep and cherish this insight and understanding.' Myo then went to Mozan, and in that region worked hard to propagate Zen.

Mumon's Comment: The Sixth Patriarch, when cornered, kindly offered the wonderful workings of the Dharma. Thus, Mumon seems to criticise Eno, who, in the emergency, had to make some response. But of course, Mumon is really praising the Sixth Patriarch, who, in confronting Myo, did not use his head, did not reply in concepts but responded directly out of his deep insight. However, as Mumon says, 'Though his response was wonderful, it seems too grandmotherly', too indulgent as to a grandchild. Mumon says it is like peeling a lychee, taking out the pip, and then popping it into the child's mouth, so all he needs to do is to swallow it. Again, Mumon here seems to criticise, but the Sixth Patriarch is not alone in peeling the lychee, taking out the pip, and offering the fruit! Look! Everything has been peeled and laid bare, and all you have to do is to accept. There is no cover anywhere. The peel that must be peeled, or the pip that must be taken out, all of those have been added by your hearts; they do not exist in reality!

The Verse: 'It cannot be described or portrayed, it cannot possibly be praised enough.' Do not try to grasp it with your consciousness or your standards or judgements. If you try, then in that moment of grasping it ceases to be the True Face and has become but its traces. Yet there is nowhere you can shut away or hide this True Face because it wells up and overflows always, everywhere, eternally throughout the universe. Even if this world of ours were destroyed, it would not in the slightest affect this True Face.

CASE 24 · FUKETSU'S SPEECH AND SILENCE

THE CASE

A monk asked Master Fuketsu, 'Both speech and silence concern *ri* and *bi* (the principle itself and its manifestion in the 10,000 things). How can we transcend?' Fuketsu remarked, 'How I remember Konan in March – the twitter of partridges among the sweet-smelling blossoms.'

MUMON'S COMMENT

Fuketsu's natural spontaneity functions like lightning. He can walk his way; so why does he rely on the words of the sage and does not get rid of them? If you can clearly see into this, the way out opens. Cease from being at one with words and speaking, and say a word.

THE VERSE

不露風骨句
未語先分付
進步口喃喃
知君大罔措

Fuketsu did not use special words,
But with them he keeps pointing.
If, however, you just go on talking and chattering,
You will fail to understand – so having it pointed out to you was
    of no use.

SOKO ROSHI'S COMMENTS

Master Fuketsu is in the fourth generation after Rinzai, the founder of our school. In Fuketsu's time, Rinzai Zen had already spread widely. Fuketsu inherited the 'house style' of Rinzai Zen, and was strict and severe in training his monks. In this koan we see a different, less severe aspect of Fuketsu, but his Zen insight shines like a bright, clear spring day.

The monk who appears in this koan seems to be steeped in Buddhist philosophy, and also rather intellectual and argumentative. He asked Fuketsu, 'Whether you are silent or whether you speak, you run afoul of *ri* and *bi*. Is there any way that, without depending on one or the other of them, you can find the Way?'

This was his question. The *ri* and *bi* need explanation. In the transmission of Buddhism to China, Kurmarajiva was one of the greatest and most productive translators of Indian texts into Chinese. Among his many illustrious disciples was the monk Sojo, who, while still a young man, was condemned to death, for unknown reasons. His appeal for one week's reprieve was granted, during which he wrote a major treatise on Buddhism, known as the *Hozo-ron*. In it, *ri* is the Great Way of the Universe, its essence or principle as distinct from *bi*, its functioning in the universe, in its various manifestations in daily life and in nature around us.

So, the monk confronting Master Fuketsu is referring to this treatise and presenting *ri* and *bi* as a challenge to Fuketsu. For the koan, however, the intricacies of the *Hozo Treatise* are quite irrelevant. I prefer to talk about *ri* and *bi* in terms of our everyday lives and daily practice. When sitting zazen and entering samadhi, that state is *honrai mu-ichi butsu* – the state of 'originally there is no-thing.' There is no distinction between man and woman, between old and young. In that state, perfect emptiness is entered, separate from all forms and all conceptualisations. However, on getting up from zazen and again beginning to engage in all the activities and pursuits of daily life, from that moment on a man is a man, a woman is a woman, somebody old is old, and a youngster is young.

If you meet your child, then you are a parent; if you meet your parent, you are a child; meeting your husband you are a wife; meeting your wife, you are a husband. When it is time to eat, you eat, and at night you sleep. So it is clear that there is a very subtle yet constant transition from moment to moment.

Now, the common state of things is not like that, is it? When in zazen, you are in zazen, but when you engage in other activities, you separate yourself from or forget zazen. When, after having been doing something, you then return to sit zazen, you sit zazen, but the activities somehow are not incorporated into it, and so you do not come to a true *honrai mu-ichi butsu*. For when there is a separation or dislocation between the two, then what happens in terms of *ri* and *bi* is that in whatever you are doing, you move in the direction of either the one or the other of them.

How is it then – and this is the core of the problem – that the state you are in in zazen informs and is part and parcel of the everyday activities? How does sitting zazen easily and naturally give rise to all of the activities of your life?

Well, the monk's question was extremely conceptual, logic-chopping. I now put that question back to you, not in conceptual terms, but in relation to your actual lives. Then, if in response to this question you are simply silent and enter samadhi, you are grasping the essence, the underlying reality, but have moved away from the manifestations, the functions. But if, when that question is thrown at you, you try to answer it verbally, though you may show wonderful resourcefulness in response to the question, yet you will nonetheless have moved away from the essence, from the original universal reality. So, then what do you do?

Master Fuketsu was asked just this question. And in the most natural, fluent and easy way, he replied with a poem, 'How I remember Konan in March; the twitter of partridges among the sweet-smelling blossoms.' The region of Konan is on the southern bank along the middle reaches of the Yangtse river, and is renowned for its beauty. Especially in spring, everything bursts into bloom, and though hidden, birds sing everywhere, quail, partridges and sparrows, etc. In all of China, Konan has the reputation of being scenically the most beautiful and so also of being one of the most desirable places to live. Therefore people who were born and brought up there and then moved away, would never forget the spring in Konan. The poem is not by Fuketsu, but by the famous Tang poet, Du Fu.

Another poet says about Konan that in the presence of a man from Konan one must not talk about partridges. The mere mention of partridges would recall to his mind spring in Konan with all its wonders, but they would be tinged with the sadness of separation, and bring tears to his eyes. So as for Konan, the place and its beauty were deeply embedded in the Chinese mind.

Among the things I first heard about England was that the English abroad like to have their remains returned to the green pastures of England, when they die. So I think you can gauge that not only for the Chinese or for the English, but for anybody who is separated from home, there is always a nostalgic longing, a desire to return. Of course, today there are many people who do not have this feeling for place or home; and there are also those who, whether close to their native place or far from it, do not think highly of it anyway. However, as they get older, they tend to look more fondly or longingly back to their home, wherever it was.

So, Master Fuketsu, responding to the question about the distinction between *ri* and *bi*, quoted, 'How I remember Konan in March – the twitter of the partridges among the sweet-smelling blossoms.' Although the verse may have been written by Du Fu, from the moment that Fuketsu quoted it, it became the expression of his state of Zen. Fuketsu was not born in Konan. The 'native place' that Fuketsu was pointing at with the word 'Konan' – where was it? He was not talking about a native place in which there were trees, mountains, grass and partridges, was not referring to a place either attractive or ugly. His 'Konan' is a metaphor for the state of spiritual awareness that is much broader and deeper, more universal than Konan, and refers to a native place that has existed from before one's birth, before the birth of one's parents, from the very origins. He is saying that wherever one may live, or whatever one may do, at any time, in any place, one cannot be separate from that native place. There is no need to recall that place to mind. Why? Because not for an instant has it ever been forgotten; and with that thought one lives in all kinds of places, at all kinds of times, involved in all kinds of activities.

If I try to explain further, the flavour will begin to diminish. In our daily lives, are we not always trying to establish the connection between that native place and the place we are in at any particular moment? Are we not consciously trying to establish a link between the various manifestations of 'our daily activities' and the state of *honrai mu-ichi butsu*, of originally there is no-thing? Whether we are conscious of it or not, not even for a moment can we separate ourselves from that original place. Whether you call the state of *honrai mu-ichi butsu* our original state or you call it Buddha or God, not for an instant do we live apart from it.

To express it in my own words, what are you afraid of? What are you worrying about? You are not apart from this spring in Konan, even for an instant. In this spring in Konan you can play at leisure and enjoy yourselves morning, noon and night, even when sleeping.

Perhaps my interpretation of this verse, 'How fondly I remember Konan in March; the partridges calling, the flowers so fragrant' strikes a further chord; please remember and make use of it. Many monks, myself included, when we have a little time to ourselves and with nobody around, like to recite this verse, slowly, savouring the feelings and the beauty that it conveys. The most important thing is to recall this constantly, always and everywhere.

Mumon's Comment: Mumon first praises Fuketsu, saying that in spite of being confronted with a very difficult, abstruse question, his response was brilliant, and likened it to a bolt of lightning. We must be careful, however, and not just take it to mean that the response was quick, like a flash of lightning, merely referring to the speed of Fuketsu's response. It has nothing to do with quickness, but Mumon rather points at the fullness of Fuketsu's insight which is fully 'embodied' in his response.

Mumon then adds that Fuketsu walks freely wherever he wills. Walking thus freely, he does not lean to one side or veer to the other, and so walks along a vast and living way. Why then, in spite of this genuine insight, does Fuketsu borrow a verse from an old poet? If you can clearly understand why, then you too can find the path along which you can walk with total freedom. But take care! Mumon's comment, rather than being an evaluation of Fuketsu, is intended to trick you. So do not be tricked or confused by Mumon, but come to your own insight. As I said earlier, the verse itself is by Du Fu, hence Mumon's reference to Fuketsu borrowing somebody else's words. However, the moment that Fuketsu uttered them, they ceased to be Du Fu's and rather became Fuketsu's own, expressing his insight.

For ages people have said, 'I love you', but when we ourselves say it to somebody, do we think we are borrowing a much-used, hackneyed phrase? If so, 'I love you' immediately loses any power to affect the heart of the person addressed.

So please be very careful not to fall into a Samadhi of Words, in which you are taken in by Fuketsu's wonderful response, using Du Fu's verse. I, or rather Mumon, now invite you to produce your own verse, here and now!

The Verse: In the records, Fuketsu is always presented as rather severe and stern in his teachings. But Mumon says on this occasion he uses no difficult words but replies without a moment's hesitation, without any wavering, showing immediately and directly. If, instead of seeing that, one gets entangled and is drawn into discussions of distinctions of *ri* and *bi*, etc., then inevitably any sense of direction towards insight (satori) is lost.

CASE 25 · THE SERMON FROM THE THIRD SEAT

THE CASE
Master Kyozan dreamt that he went to Maitreya's heaven and there was allotted the third seat. A venerable monk then struck the gavel and announced, 'Today's sermon will be given from the third seat.' Kyozan stood up and, striking the gavel, declared, 'The Dharma of the Mahayana is beyond the Four Propositions and transcends the Hundred Negations. Take heed and listen carefully.'

MUMON'S COMMENT
Just say, did he or did he not preach? If you open your mouth, you fail; if you keep it shut, you lose. But neither opening it nor keeping it shut makes you stray 18,000 miles away.

THE VERSE
白日晴天
夢中説夢
捏怪捏怪
誑諕一衆

Dreaming while the sun blazes down from a cloudless sky
He preaches a dream –
Dreamstuff of his own making,
Upsetting the whole assembly.

SOKO ROSHI'S COMMENTS
Kyozan is an early Chinese Master, founder of one of the major

lineages of Chinese Zen. He was a contemporary of Rinzai and once actually encountered him.

Once when Kyozan was resting, he nodded off and dreamt that he went up to the heavenly realm of the Bodhisattva Maitreya. Now Maitreya is the Buddha who is to follow Shakyamuni and will appear sometime in the future, delivering all beings. Until then it is said that he resides in the Tushita Heaven on Mount Sumeru. Maitreya Bodhisattva thus represents the hope and aspiration of Buddhism. The dream here presents the aspiration that the teaching of the Buddha will illuminate our lives throughout time, from Shakyamuni's entry into Nirvana until the appearance of Maitreya.

So in his dream Kyozan went up to the Tushita Heaven, into the great hall where Maitreya would deliver his sermon. With some five hundred other Bodhisattvas present, all the seats but the third from the top were taken. In his dream, Kyozan was led to it and took this seat. He seems to be very forward!

Then one of the Elders stood up, struck the gavel, and announced, 'Today's sermon will be given by the monk in the third seat.' Without hesitation, Kyozan rose and expounded, 'The teaching of the Mahayana transcends all words and philosophy.'

The text to the case of this koan mentions some doctrines of early Indian logic and philosophy, but the important thing here is to grasp that the teaching of Mahayana transcends all words, letters, and intellectual discussion. And then Kyozan adds loudly, 'Take heed and listen carefully.' Mumon in his comment asks whether Kyozan did or did not lecture? His proclaiming that Mahayana transcends words and letters – does that constitute a lecture, or not?

I also would like to stress to you: Listen carefully, listen carefully. Do you think you grasp what is being said by 'transcending the Dharma'? If you grasp it only in terms of these words, that is a mistake. When looking at this koan, all I see are the words, 'Listen carefully, listen carefully.' Only these words that Kyozan used. What do you listen to? Kyozan says, 'Listen to the truth of the Mahayana Dharma.' Where do you hear the sermon on the Mahayana Dharma? You can hear it here, now, everywhere. The wind may make a bell tinkle, a bird may chirp, leaves dancing in the wind; the grass, swaying in the wind, all lecturing. Mountains, rivers and trees – everything is giving the sermon of the reality of Mahayana teaching. So listen carefully, listen carefully. Perhaps that is already saying too much.

Mumon's Comment: If you open your mouth, you fail; if you keep it shut, you lose. But neither opening it nor keeping it shut, is also a great mistake. Yet this, too, is not the core of Mumon's meaning. If it were, then Mumon's level, and the level of the monk who asks about distinctions between *ri* and *bi* would not differ much. Out of kindness, Mumon is again trying to confuse you. You smile, but however Mumon may try to confuse you, you must pursue your training until you are able to see reality and hear reality.

The Verse: The sun is shining in a cloudless sky. In this bright sunlight Kyozan preaches in a dream. What kind of feeling does Mumon try to evoke by this expression? The sun blazing in that cloudless sky is not simply daylight; it also indicates that in this brightness there is nothing hidden. It is so bright, so clear, that every single thing can be seen – not only with your eyes, but whatever you might hear with your ears, etc. – that, too, is openly and equally revealed, clear. In that clarity, Kyozan then preached in his dream.

People who are not sleeping, who believe that they are looking at reality, are they truly looking at it? They may think they are looking at it, or may be trying to look at it, but in fact are not looking at it. They seem to be listening, but in fact are not listening. Because, looking at something, they are captivated by it, or listening to something, they are enthralled by that; thus they lose the ability to see everything else. The expression 'to lose oneself in dreams' is used in the sense of seeing things in dreams; in Japanese it also has the sense of samadhi.

Kyozan's sermon on Mahayana Buddhism, though he expressed it in terms of a dream, has a very deep and rich flavour. Even if you see something clearly in a dream, you are not bound by it. Some people go to specialists to have their dreams interpreted and then believe their interpretations. However, seeing things as if in a dream, one by one, each one clearly, and seeing other things passing by, like water flowing away, or like the wind blowing past, from moment to moment, and maintaining samadhi with oneself flowing, unbound – that Mahayana sermon surrounds us everywhere, constantly, in the world we live in. This is the sermon that Kyozan demonstrated. But be careful, do not be fooled. If you hear one thing mistakenly, everybody here will be fooled by Kyozan. With your own ears, with your own eyes, with your own heart, listen carefully to the Mahayana sermon!

CASE 26 – TWO MONKS ROLLING UP THE BLIND

THE CASE

The Great Hogen of Seiryo was giving teisho to the assembly before the midday meal. Hogen pointed at the bamboo blinds. Two monks simultaneously went and rolled them up. Hogen said, 'One has it, the other has not.'

MUMON'S COMMENT

Say, who has got it, and who has lost? If you should have the Single Eye, you will know how the Great Hogen failed. Be that as it may, but what I most detest is disputations about gain and loss.

THE VERSE

卷起明明徹太空
太空猶未合吾宗
爭似從空都放下
綿綿密密不通風

The blinds rolled up and the whole sky is radiant –
But this bright sky does not resemble our school.
Better to have no truck with the sky –
For then, not even the slightest breeze can waft through it.

SOKO ROSHI'S COMMENT

Once upon a time a woodsman was cutting trees in a forest. He worked hard; pausing for a moment and looking up, he saw a strange-looking deer such as he had never seen before. Astonished, he wondered what it could be. Instantly the animal replied, 'You have just thought, "I wonder what this is?" I am called Satori.' The Satori deer seemed to grin, as if making a fool of him. The woodsman got angry, and immediately the animal said, 'And now you are feeling angry, aren't you – and you're thinking of hitting me, aren't you, or of driving me away – you want to try to catch me, don't you – and now you're so angry that you'd like to kill me, wouldn't you!' And so on, one by one, Satori grasped what was in the woodsman's heart.

The woodsman gave it up as hopeless, there was no dealing with that strange animal; he turned away and started working again. But the animal called out, 'And now you think you'll just leave me here, and go back to cutting trees, don't you!' The woodsman, determined to have nothing more to do with Satori, just concentrated on whacking away at the trees; but of course, though working away furiously, all kinds of thoughts and ideas rose up inside him, and at each one Satori nearby would say, 'And now you are. . ., and now you are . . .' The woodsman now put all his energy into his work and at length completely forgot everything around him, fully absorbed in what he was doing. And Satori had nothing more to say.

Then suddenly the axe that the woodsman was wielding hit an unusually hard knobble in the tree; the axe-head flew off and squarely hit Satori. This was so sudden and unexpected that Satori did not see it coming, and so Satori died and peace reigned again.

Please taste and savour this story; see how it relates to your own situation. So turning now to our koan, the Great Hogen is Master Hogen of the Seiryo Monastery who in his youth was known as Buneki. Hogen was the title bestowed on him posthumously by the Emperor. He had diligently studied the sutras and sastras in his quest for enlightenment, had delved deeply into the Yogacara and Kegon teachings, and had come to believe that he thus had grasped the meaning of satori.

Once, on pilgrimage with two other monks, they ran into a rainstorm and took shelter in the temple of Jizo Keichin. There Hogen kept talking all the night, telling Keichin about Yogacara philosophy – that everything exists only in consciousness. In the morning, Keichin pointed out a rock beside the gate and asked, 'Is this rock inside your heart, or outside?' Hogen replied, 'Inside.' Keichin remarked, 'By what karma are you carrying such a big rock around with you on your travels?' Hogen was unable to respond.

He discontinued his travels and stayed on with Keichin to practise under him. He had become used to responding according to the teachings of the Buddhist school that he had studied; but each time he tried to present such ideas, Keichin simply dismissed them, 'Oh, that is only what you have learned.' Eventually, Hogen realised that there was nothing that he could explain, nothing he could do, and that, in fact, he was helpless. On being told this, Keichin said, 'If you want to express the very core of Buddhism, then everything just is as it is.'

This 'being as it is' is what we find so difficult to realise. If we could accept this hand 'as it is', there would be no problem. However, when we look at one hand, we also see five fingers, and then the palm and the back; one becomes more than one. Thus, unable to accept things as they are, we constantly create intellectual distinctions in order to try to understand them. These in turn cause us to suffer, because in our intellectual efforts to grasp things by creating these distinctions, we are led further and further away from the understanding of how things really are. Men and women clearly differ from each other, yet as human beings they are the same. We recognise that there are distinctions and then we wrestle with the problem of trying to reconcile them. The ceiling is above, the floor is below; there is no distinction between the quality of the floor and the ceiling, one is not better than the other. Even when we try to reconcile such differences rationally, in our daily lives we are pulled, first in the direction of discrimination, and then towards seeing sameness, uniformity.

This being drawn to and at the same time being pulled away could be called the Satori-deer in the story above. How can we break free from this? And how can we reach the state of accepting things as they are? For, whenever some object tugs on us, then our heart is entangled or bound by that object.

When Keichin told Hogen that the core of Buddhism is that everything is as it is, all things as they are, Hogen now saw into this, not with his intellectual understanding but directly, as such. What he previously had tried to accept in his heart, broke at that moment. The obstruction, satori, anything that attracts, cracked and crumbled like a pot or a tile that when smashed, returns to earth – or like an icicle that melts and returns to water. In this way his heart melted, and he 'saw' 'as it is'. In that seeing there is no distinction, no contradiction, between different and same, between front and back; they are there in perfect harmony from the beginning. Within happiness is unhappiness, within success is failure, within health is sickness, and within birth is death. These are not contradicting each other – they are simply as they are. We, however, always think that success is success, and that failure is failure, and that sameness is sameness and differentiation is differentiation, satori is satori and delusion is delusion. But in truth, satori is the afflicting passions (*klesa*), and the afflicting passions are satori. We tend to think that like dropping ink into a glass of water, satori is obscured by delusion. But no – it's just as it is.

With this state of spiritual understanding opening, everything that Hogen had learned up until then, the intellectual, scholarly understanding that he had acquired, simply disappeared. He became a great master and is remembered as the founder of the Hogen School.

While Rinzai Zen has been likened to a general, strong, vigorous, and robust, the house style of Hogen's Zen is said to be that of a night-watchman who robs the citizens while he is on watch! Not for a moment can we drop our guard because whatever is important to us may be stolen!

There was a young man in Hogen's assembly called Soko who was responsible for the administration of Hogen's monastery, but who had never come to Hogen for sanzen. One day, Hogen asked him, 'Why don't you come to sanzen?' Soko answered, 'You may not be aware of it but I have already realised satori.' Hogen invited, 'Tell me about it.' The monk, very full of himself, said, 'When training under Master Seiho, I asked him, "What is Buddha?" Seiho said, "The Fire-god has come to receive the fire." At that moment satori opened.' Hogen prompted, 'Yes, Seiho's answer is truly brilliant. But since your understanding of it may be mistaken, tell me more about it.' Soko said 'Well, the Fire-god returning to get fire, that I take to mean that originally one is Buddha; and so the Fire-god originally being Buddha anyway, striving to become Buddha is foolish. This is how I understand it!'

Hogen commented, 'I thought you had got it wrong!' Soko was furious, and, believing that Hogen was denying his satori, left. Hogen remarked, 'If he comes back, he will achieve something great, if not, then there is no hope.'

Soko had gone some way but then checked himself, thinking, 'Hold on! Hogen is a great master, with five hundred monks in his assembly, he would never say something irresponsible.' And so he went back. Again, he asked Hogen, 'What is Buddha?' Without hesitation, Hogen replied, 'The Fire-god has come to get fire.' At that instant, everything within Soko broke down and vanished.

Another of Hogen's great successors is Tokusho. He had trained under many famous Zen Masters, and was now confident that he had fully realised the state of spiritual insight. So, when he came to Hogen he did not go for sanzen. But then, one day, he heard a monk ask Hogen, 'What is a drop of water from Sogen?' Now Sogen is the name of the Sixth Patriarch's Temple, standing in a valley with a small stream running nearby. So asking about this drop of water from Sogen is a rather literary way of saying, 'What is the essence of the Zen of the Sixth Patriarch?' Hogen, without hesitation, responded, 'This is a drop of water of Sogen.' The monk who had put the question did not understand, but Tokusho at that moment had a direct and clear insight, without any rationalisation, simply as it is. The marrow of Zen is not far away and is always constant just as it is, in everything, including oneself.

Now in this koan, Hogen ascended the high seat and was about to give teisho. No sooner was he seated than he pointed at the blinds. With glass windows unknown, the blind itself is the only boundary between outside and inside. At that, two monks went and rolled up the blinds. Hogen stated, 'One has it, one not!' If we say good, we make a value judgement; so the one who Hogen pointed out as no good we see as of no value. All our judgements come about by our assigning values. The two monks performed exactly the same task, like a mirror-image. Yet Hogen asserted that what they did differed.

Mumon's Comment: 'Who has got it, who lost?' or Who is good; who is bad? 'If you should have the Single Eye, then you will know that Hogen failed.' The Chinese original literally has 'made a great mistake.' Though this seems like heavy criticism, in Zen parlance it is actually highest praise. So rather than seeing it as Hogen having made a mistake, it is better seen as Hogen pointing out the core of the problem. Buddha statues usually show the Single Eye. Our two eyes always see things in relative terms; but symbolically expressed the

Single Eye sees things absolutely, the way they are. However, the two eyes seeing relatively, and the Single Eye, must come together; then at that instant all things are seen as they are – that within success is failure, and within failure, success; within sameness is differentiation and within differentiation is sameness. Not being entangled or carried away by either, but rather seeing them as they are and accepting each of them, fully – this awareness Hogen points out by using a seeming contradiction. Do you realise that the height of the mountain and the depth of the valley are the same? They are, but the mountain soars up, and the valley sinks down. Mumon's comment points out the need to understand right and wrong; but if we become involved in arguments about it, or have only an intellectual understanding of it, satori will never open.

The Verse: Rolling up the blind, outside and inside disappear and everything is one. This is truly a wide and open expanse – the expanse of true emptiness. But if we then cling to this emptiness, that is also contrary to the Zen tradition. So what Mumon is saying is that if we think that this world of emptiness is the final goal to be reached, that too is a mistake. Both the world of complete emptiness, and the world of distinctions – of inside and outside emptiness and of inside and outside the blind – both these worlds have to be thrown away. And then, moment for moment, whatever is being done, must be done for itself, perfectly and fully. In that state then there is not even the slightest crack through which wind can enter, the wind of discrimination, good or bad, large or small, etc. This is what Mumon expresses in his verse. So it is good to roll up the blind; it is good to lower the blind. If you lift the blind, then out there in the wide world there are mountains and rivers, green trees and red flowers. If you lower the blind, with nobody who can see in from outside, you can stand up, or lie down, take off your clothes if you like and dance around; there is not a single element of contradiction – things are as they are. As they are, or as it is, in perfect peace and harmony.

CASE 27 • NEITHER HEART NOR BUDDHA

A monk asked Master Nansen, 'Is there a Dharma (Truth) that has not been taught?' Nansen said, 'There is.' The monk asked, 'What is the Dharma-truth that has not been taught?' Nansen replied, 'It is neither heart nor Buddha nor anything.'

MUMON'S COMMENT
Nansen was asked only one question but with that used up all his treasure in one go. How shabby of him!

THE VERSE
叮嚀損君德
無言眞有功
任從滄海變
終不爲君通

If overly courteous, you lose your virtue,
But neither is there merit in not saying anything.
Just let it be – even should the blue ocean change,
You cannot take hold of it.

SOKO ROSHI'S COMMENTS
Master Nansen is famous for his koan, the fourteenth in this collection, of killing a cat. In Koan 19, 'The Ordinary Heart is the Way', Master Nansen helped Joshu to awaken. Nansen was deeply versed in Buddhist doctrine, and learned in the Vinaya, the rules of the

Buddhist monk. He had then trained under Master Baso Doitsu and realised awakening. Doitsu said of Nansen that he was somebody who transcended the boundaries.

When Joshu asked him, 'What is the Way?' Nansen said, 'The everyday heart is the Way.' This everyday heart means not ignoring anything, and yet not being captivated by anything, the heart with which we are born, and which has nothing to do with our habitual discriminations or delusions. Nansen had attained to this spiritual state and now lived and acted in response to the ordinary events of everyday life.

Nansen was cutting grass one day when a monk asked, 'What is The Way?' Nansen immediately held up the sickle and said, 'I bought this for thirty coins.' The monk insisted, 'I'm not asking you about that sickle, I'm asking you about the Way, satori.' Nansen simply replied, 'The sickle cuts nicely,' and continued cutting. At that moment, in that place, Nansen's satori was just cutting grass.

Zen does not deal in speculations – 'if something were like that, then ....' What it deals with is the problem of here and now, this instant, right in front of the eyes. If you engage in training, expecting to reach something, sometime, somewhere, however distant, satori will ever evade you.

In this koan, a monk approached the great Master Nansen and asked, 'Is there a Dharma that has not been taught?' Is there a teaching that has not been taught because it cannot be taught? To go more deeply into this, from of old it has been said that Zen is a special transmission outside the teachings, not holding to words and letters. In this special transmission, then, the teachings of the Buddha as reflected in the sutras or the teachings of the Masters cannot express the 'This' which Zen looks at.

So, then the monk's question was whether Nansen could or could not express that teaching that is not taught in the sutras or by the earlier Patriarchs of the Zen school. No doubt this monk had expected that Nansen would answer, 'There is none.' However, Nansen very calmly said, 'There is.' Startled, the monk, then asked, 'What is this teaching that has not been taught – that cannot be taught?' Nansen said, 'It is neither heart nor Buddha nor anything.' Perhaps easier to grasp would be, 'Do not be caught by the heart; do not be captivated by the Buddha; do not be taken in by anything.' Everything is denied any value.

It is interesting that in response to this koan, the great Japanese Zen master Hakuin said, 'I would answer differently, and would say, "*Avatamsaka*, *Agama*, *Vaipulya*, *Prajna*, *Lotus* and *Nirvana*."' These are the sutras the Buddha taught during his life. Nansen, in denying and rejecting everything, focused on that. It is like the palm or the back of the hand, the important thing is not to make a problem out of Nansen's response. And trying to decide whose response was better, Nansen's or Hakuin's, is a sheer waste of time. You remember that in the fifth koan, Master Kyogen, having trained hard for a long time, eventually awakened on hearing a pebble striking a bamboo stem. The words of the Buddha, or of Nansen or Hakuin – and even without words, the mere sound of a pebble striking bamboo – can awaken to enlightenment. What expresses this directly is everywhere, flowing fully everywhere. There is absolutely no reason to feel dependent on words, particularly those of Nansen. The point is whether, at that moment of hearing the sound of the pebble striking the bamboo, or of hearing the words, there is a kind of ripeness within that allows the sound to enter, and respond to it.

'It is neither heart nor Buddha nor anything' – these words, though Nansen used them to respond, were not his own but were a favourite expression of his teacher, Baso Doitsu, 'Heart is Buddha.' One day a monk had asked Baso, 'You always say that heart is Buddha. Why?'

'In order to stop the child crying.' The monk asked again, 'When the child has stopped crying, what do you say then?' Baso said, 'It is neither heart, nor Buddha.' 'What would you do,' the monk then further questioned, 'if you met somebody who is entirely uninterested in religion, neither crying nor having stopped crying?' Baso said, 'It is not the heart.'

'It is neither heart nor Buddha nor anything,' but as said above, think of it as not being captivated by heart, or Buddha, or by anything. To a crying child you say, 'Your heart is wonderful.' When the child has stopped crying, you say, 'Do not be taken by heart, do not be taken by Buddha.' And for somebody who does not think of engaging in practice, who does not think about the Buddha, does not think about religion at all, you say, 'Do not be taken in by things,' because people who do not believe in anything are captivated, taken in by things. Baso had taught just this, and although Nansen's response in this koan was not something new, it nonetheless arose out of his own spiritual insight. And what is important is whether on hearing this response there is an explosive opening into awareness.

We shall meet Baso again in Koan 30, 'Heart is Buddha'. On hearing this, Hojo had a deep insight. He left Baso's monastery, and Baso heard nothing about him for quite some time. Told that Hojo was teaching on Mount Daibai, Baso sent one of his monks there to see how Hojo was doing. The monk arrived at Daibai and asked Hojo, 'What are you teaching here?' 'When I was studying under our Master Baso, I realised enlightenment on his saying, "The ordinary heart is Buddha." According to that insight, this is what I am teaching here, too.' As instructed by Baso, the monk now said, 'That's what he used to say; but recently he has changed his teaching to "Neither heart nor Buddha nor anything."' Hojo's immediate response was, 'Can't that tricky old fellow (that is, Baso) give up cheating people?' and then added, 'But whatever Baso may do or say, I continue to teach, "The ordinary heart is Buddha."' Now, Hojo on Mount Daibai (Great Plum) is also referred to as Master Daibai. On hearing the report about him, Baso was delighted and remarked, 'The great plum is really ripe.'

However, we must not understand this as Daibai's sticking stubbornly to 'The ordinary heart is Buddha.' When he was with Baso and had heard 'Heart is Buddha' – everything had burned away, nothing remained. On making a bonfire, putting a match to it will make it burn. But what has been completely burned away, if you then apply something like Baso's 'Neither heart nor Buddha,' there is nothing left that can burn. So Daibai is not stubbornly clinging to 'Heart is Buddha' – he uses this version simply because everything else was burned away and there was nothing left; this is the crux of the matter. But whatever firebrand you bring to it, if the heap to be burned – or you – are too wet, however powerful the flame, it will not burn; even if it kindles a little, it soon dies down.

Even so, the Buddha and the succession of patriarchs use all kinds of lighters and matches to make a fire that can burn away; and not only Buddha and patriarchs – the wind blows, birds twitter, flowers bloom, and on the sea the waves come and go; all of these are matches, available to burn up our delusions and point to THAT. But unfortunately, the material is wet!

Mumon's Comment: Nansen, questioned by the monk, immediately brought out all of his treasure. He is weak; how unpleasant, how ugly! 'How shabby' it is translated here, which is a good way of expressing it: how despicable it was. Of course, this is the highest praise in Zen parlance. Mumon is praising Nansen's kindness in his generous use of matches to produce a flicker of fire in this wet straw. But, from another point of view, Mumon feels some frustration: Couldn't you do more? You, Nansen, you are the one who killed the cat; why did you deal so feebly with this foolish monk, being so excessively generous and kind? You should have given him thirty blows!

The Verse: This also shows Mumon's vigour and vitality. Talking too much or too detailed, you may end losing your strength; perhaps being silent is best. Were the waters of the ocean to disappear, and be transformed into green fields, so great a change cannot be explained; likewise, a deep spiritual understanding cannot be explained. For even if the ocean vanished and land appeared and could be walked on, yet to convey spiritual insight is impossible. You yourself must explode, must burn away, must arrive at a great, perfect understanding. Human beings generally set up a screen over there, and on it they project their delusions. The husband throws his image of his wife onto the screen, the wife projects her image of the husband; and when these images do not perfectly match, they quarrel. They do not try to project themselves, or themselves become the screen.

However many splendid koans you may put forward, however many great patriarchs may be lined up – it is utterly useless if you make them into a kind of blank screen and project your own delusions onto it. Look at the sky, look at that big tree – even if I say that all things around are offering you the truth, you do not take it in. You rather make them into a screen and project yourselves onto it. Do you not, for example, project yourself onto the sky and the clouds? Try – go for a walk, just throw yourselves down into the grass and look up at the sky; do not make the clouds into a screen – just look at them. Although to begin with you may project your own particular feelings onto the sky, gradually you will stop talking to the sky; and then a little while after that, the clouds will come to see you – not you seeing the clouds. The clouds enter into you, and you become full with clouds, become clouds, become nothing but clouds. Not just with clouds, but with trees, with people, and so also with Nansen, Baso, or Joshu; if you can let them enter, then do so; you are Nansen, you are Joshu. Then, for the first time, you can deal with this koan, realise this koan.

CASE 28 • RYUTAN BLOWS OUT THE CANDLE

THE CASE

Tokusan went to Ryutan to ask for teaching, and stayed into the night. Ryutan said, 'It is getting late, you had better go.' Tokusan took his leave, and pulling aside the curtain, stepped out. Seeing how dark it was, he turned back, 'It is pitch-dark outside.' Ryutan lit a lantern and gave it to him. Just as Tokusan made to take it, Ryutan blew out the candle. At this, Tokusan was suddenly enlightened. He bowed deeply. 'What have you seen?' asked Ryutan. Tokusan said, 'From now on I will never doubt any of the teachings of the old masters.'

Next day, Ryutan ascended the High Seat in the Teaching Hall and said, 'Among you is a fellow whose fangs are like swords from the sword-tree, and whose mouth is a bowl full of blood. Hit him with a stick and he will not even turn his head. Some day in the future he will settle on a lofty peak and there establish our Way.'

Tokusan burned all his commentaries on the *Diamond Sutra* in front of the Hall and said, 'All the deeply profound comments are but like one single hair in the vastness of space. All the knowledge and wisdom of the world are just like one drop of water spilled into an abyss.' Having burned all his notes, he departed full of gratitude.

MUMON'S COMMENT

Before Tokusan had passed the barrier, his heart was eager and his tongue sharp; confidently he arrived in the south, bent on confuting the 'Special Transmission Outside the Scriptures.' On the road to Reishu, he asked an old woman at a tea house for a snack (lit., 'to point the heart and to nourish the heart' – a word-play here). The old crone asked what books he was carrying in his satchel. Loftily, Tokusan replied, 'These are my notes and commentaries on the *Diamond Sutra*.' The old woman then asked, 'It is said in the *Diamond Sutra*, "The heart of the past is gone, the heart of the future not yet come, and the heart of the present is not attainable." Which of these hearts does the Venerable Sir wish to nourish?' Unable to reply, Tokusan tightly shut his lips; but as he could not die the Great Death at the old woman's words, he finally asked her, 'Is there a Zen Master in this neighbourhood?' 'About five miles from here lives Master Ryutan,' the old woman told him. Arriving at Ryutan's, he experienced perfect defeat.

It has to be stated that his words before and after are inconsistent. Ryutan is like a mother who for love of her child does not notice its ugliness. Seeing that Tokusan had the seed of fire, he at once doused him with slop water. Looking impartially at this story, it is rather ridiculous.

THE VERSE

聞名不如見面
見面不如聞名
雖然救得鼻孔
爭奈瞎却眼睛

Better seeing the face than hearing the name;
Better hearing the name than seeing the face.
Even though he could save his nose,
He did lose his eyes.

SOKO ROSHI'S COMMENTS

In Case 13, Tokusan's Bowl, Tokusan is already a great Master. The present koan tells how Tokusan became a Zen monk, attained satori under Ryutan, and inherited his Dharma. The various stages of how Tokusan came to satori are outlined in Mumon's comment rather than in the case, and so we will start with the comment, and get back to the case later.

Tokusan was born at Shisen in the upper reaches of the Yangtse River. His family name was Shu. When young, he studied the sutras thoroughly, and was also learned in the Vinaya/Precepts. Particularly, he had studied the *Diamond Sutra*, lectured on it, felt himself to be an expert on it, and, indeed, was known as 'Diamond Shu.' He was proud of his deep insight into the sutra, and his grasp of the various precepts of the Buddhist life.

One day, he heard that a new teaching was emerging, called Zen, which claimed to be a separate transmission outside the sutras, and emphasised that heart is Buddha, and that this teaching was spreading in the south.

Tokusan, who was steeped in the sutras and committed to their teachings and the precepts of the religious life, could not accept a teaching which stressed sudden awakening to Buddhahood. The sutras teach of becoming a Bodhisattva, and then a Buddha, and this only after *kalpas* of time, by means of infinite study of the sutras, and painstaking observation of all the many precepts. Because he had studied both, sutras and vinaya, Tokusan had full confidence in them and decided to travel south to find out about this new Zen teaching and to refute it.

Mumon's Comment: This opens with, 'Before Tokusan had passed the barrier, his heart was eager and his tongue sharp; confidently he arrived in the south, bent on confuting the "Special Transmission Outside the Scriptures"'. So then, bent on defeating this teaching of a separate transmission outside the scriptures, Tokusan arrived at Reishu where the Zen teachings were already well-known. Being hungry, he went to a little tea house, and asked the old lady there, 'Could I have a light snack (tenjin).' In Zen, past and present, there are some ferocious old ladies! I specially remember the one with my old teacher, Goto Zuigan Roshi, who was also ferocious. I was training under Zuigan, and taking sanzen with him, but owe a great deal to her, too. Now, I can whole-heartedly thank her, whereas at that time, I hated her!

So, the old woman in the tea house noticed that this monk had a pack full of books, and asked, 'What books do you have with you?' Tokusan, very pleased with himself, answered, 'They are commentaries on the *Diamond Sutra*; but they are somewhat beyond your understanding.' The old crone smartly replied, 'It is said in the *Diamond Sutra*, "The heart of the past is gone; the heart of the future has not yet come; and the heart of the present is not attainable either." Is this true?' Tokusan, taken aback, said, 'You really have great understanding; yes, it's true.' Then the old lady said to him, 'If you can answer my question, I won't charge you for your snack; if you cannot answer, I'm certainly not going to waste good food on a stupid monk. So, tell me, if neither the past, nor the present, nor future heart can be grasped – which of these hearts do you wish to nourish?'

At that moment, satori could have opened; however, Tokusan missed it. But what is great about Tokusan at this point is that he shut his mouth. A monk of Tokusan's learning would easily have been able to set up an intellectual barrage to confuse this country woman; instead, he was honestly disturbed and troubled. Even if he could confound the old woman, he could not fool his own heart.

When my late Master Zuigan gave Teisho on this koan, he would always say, 'You fellows here, however much I provoke or torment you, you don't seem to feel it. You are like catfish wriggling here and there, and slinking away; however much I press, I cannot get you – you are no good. If I say one thing, you say something else. If I say this, you respond to that. You only spout intellectual abstractions and are never at a loss, never caught.' Now, this is not just something only we heard from Zuigan, he is saying it to you, too!

Anyway, Tokusan realised that in contrast to the scholarly Buddhism he was familiar with, the old woman had a direct understanding that came out of her daily life and her human experience. If an old crone in a teashop could show an understanding of Buddhism that confounded him, then surely there must be some great Zen teacher in the neighbourhood. Asking her about it, she told of Master Ryutan's Monastery nearby, and Tokusan at once made for it.

Although he had been reduced to 'biting his tongue' by the old lady, nonetheless on arrival at Ryutan's temple, Tokusan again launched confidently into a detailed exposition of the Buddha's Teachings.

'Ryutan' literally means 'dragon's abyss', the deep pool in which the dragon resides. And so, referring to this name, Tokusan started, 'The name Ryutan resounds throughout the world, but now that I come here in the flesh, I find that there is no dragon, and no deep pool.' Ryutan responded, 'For that very reason you have come to Ryutan.'

This, too, was a chance for Tokusan to realise satori. No dragon, no deep pool, nothing – in that, precisely, is the true Ryutan. That is really what Ryutan was saying to Tokusan. Anyway, having missed this opportunity, Tokusan continued to hold forth to Ryutan throughout the evening and into the night. With that we now come to the koan, the opening of the case.

The Case: Tokusan was quite determined, and kept spouting away at Ryutan till well into the night. Finally, Ryutan said, 'It is late

– you'd better leave.' Tokusan, who in his enthusiasm had forgotten the time, made to leave, and lifting up the blind, stepped outside. It was pitch dark; he turned round and asked Ryutan, 'It is pitch-black outside; I can't see my way.' Ryutan lit a lantern and handed it to him; but just as Tokusan stepped outside again, Ryutan blew out the candle. At that moment, satori opened for Tokusan. The term *satori hiraku* – literally means 'satori opens' and is usual in Zen texts. It is the opposite of grasping something, or getting hold of anything; rather, what hitherto has been clung to now disintegrates, and all that had been harboured in the bosom, or had been carried on the back, suddenly disappears, and one burns oneself out completely.

So, the instant the candle was blown out, all Tokusan's bonds were cut; he prostrated himself before Ryutan who saw that Tokusan had truly awakened. There is a saying in Zen, 'If you kill somebody, see that you finish it off properly.' Although Ryutan knew that Tokusan had had satori, it had yet to be proved. Ryutan therefore asked, 'Why do you prostrate yourself, what is it that you have seen?' Tokusan replied, 'From now on I will never doubt any of the sayings of the old masters.' This, however, was not a casual 'From now I will believe', but was said with complete confidence, because Tokusan had had genuine insight on a par with the Buddhas and the patriarchs, and there was now no element of doubt in his seeing.

The following day, Ryutan told the assembled monks, 'Among you there is a really great man. His fangs are like swords, his mouth is like a bowl full of blood. Hit him with a stick, and he will not even turn his head. Some day in the future, he will settle on some lofty peak and there establish our Way.'

This was his authorising of Tokusan; as thus predicted, Tokusan became a great master and ranks, with Rinzai, as one of the two great pillars of Chinese Zen.

A particular point here is Ryutan's reference to the future activities of Tokusan. For however deep a satori may open, to begin with it is a personal realisation. In order to make it useful for others, it is essential to continue working day after day constantly to refine that spiritual state. Zen stresses that satori opens suddenly and that one is Buddha as one is. At the same time of seeing into the True Nature (*kensho*), as satori opens, it has to be checked against the sutras. And there is also the need to constantly check oneself in one's day-to-day activities.

So, Ryutan confirmed Tokusan's satori. Tokusan then carried all his commentaries on the *Diamond Sutra* in front of the hall, set fire to them, and said, 'Whatever depth of truth one may realise intellectually, compared with the insight of satori, it does not even amount to a single hair set against the immensity of the sky. Though familiar with all the learning people prize, compared with this insight of satori, it is less than a drop of water in the vastness of the ocean.' When the books had been burned, he thanked Ryutan and left.

Mumon's Comment: As is typical of Mumon, he makes some rather sarcastic remarks. Tokusan had set out with great confidence and arrogance, but was completely routed by Ryutan. What he had held and said before is totally different from his words after he had been routed by Ryutan. Mumon is praising Tokusan. Please think carefully about this 'perfect' defeat. If you win, you must win perfectly; and if defeated, you must be defeated perfectly. That perfect defeat becomes a perfect victory!

Mumon then turns his barbs on Ryutan, and says that Ryutan had not behaved well. He was like a mother who, in her love for her child, does not see he is ugly. Of the many young mothers who come to see me with their children, all say, 'Isn't he/she a darling – which of us does he/she resemble?' What fools! But then, Ryutan, too, expressed this affection for Tokusan in the same way. Finding just a tiny spark of potential in Tokusan, he got quite excited and tossed a bucket of muddy water over him, and drowned him in it. Impartially seen, this encounter is rather a farce!

The Verse: Better seeing the face than hearing the name; better hearing the name than seeing the face.

While still in Shisen, Tokusan had heard rumours about Zen; and he had set out from home determined to confront Zen and crush it. But when he actually confronted the face of Zen, he underwent a tremendous defeat, and became a Zen monk. When satori opened, he realised that he had come back to his native place, which is different from mere ideas about satori. Through his encounter with Ryutan, Tokusan was able to open his nostrils which had been blocked, and through them could breathe the air of satori; this was fine. But he then also burned his commentaries and, as the Verse says, 'lost his eyes.' Thus, Mumon in this verse warns against the misapprehension that only satori is important, and all intellectual understanding, learning and progress is useless and to be rejected!

Tokusan had studied the precepts and the sutras; and then, by his own insight or satori, all the former learning was illuminated. He had studied the books, but what made Tokusan so effective and useful for many was his own insight, which allowed him to expound and illuminate the treasure of the Dharma.

CASE 29 • THE SIXTH PATRIARCH'S 'THE HEART FLUTTERS'

THE CASE

Two monks were arguing about the temple flag fluttering in the wind. One said, 'The flag moves,' the other said, 'The wind moves,' and they could not settle their dispute. The Sixth Patriarch said, 'Neither the wind moves, nor the flag; the hearts of the two venerable monks are aflutter.' The two monks were struck with awe.

MUMON'S COMMENT

Neither the wind moves, nor the flag, and not the heart either. How then to understand the Patriarch? If you can come to a really familiar insight, you will know why the two monks could get gold instead of buying iron. The Patriarch could not withhold compassion and so the story leaked out.

THE VERSE

風幡心動
一狀領過
只知開口
不覺話墮

The wind moves, the flag moves, the heart moves –
All these are mistaken.
Knowing only how to move the mouth
Without knowing that talking is wrong.

After his encounter with Myo, the Sixth Patriarch did not appear in public for about fifteen years. There was still the possibility of being attacked by jealous rivals, but more so, he wanted to prove and strengthen the insight attained, and to develop it in everyday life.

He is said to have spent that period in a fishing village, helping the villagers in their work. At about the age of forty he appeared again in his native province, Koshu; we may picture him like a beggar, with matted hair, long tangled beard, and rather frail. His Record reports that he attended a lecture on the *Nirvana Sutra* by Hinju Osho of Hosho-ji. Such a 'public' lecture on a sutra is usually advertised by flying a banner from a pole at the temple gate. The flag was flapping in the wind; two young monks began to argue. One said, 'The flag is moving', and the other maintained, 'No, it is the wind that is moving.' They could not agree and the argument began to be acrimonious.

Eno, who had overheard them, interrupted, 'Although only a layman, I suggest it is neither the flag nor the wind that is moving – the hearts of the two venerable monks are fluttering.'

Hearing this, the two monks were so startled that they began to tremble. Of course, the monks were familiar with Buddhist philosophy, particularly that of the Yogacara or 'Consciousness Only' School which expounds that everything is 'Heart Only', nothing exists outside the heart. But the 'Consciousness Only' that these two monks were arguing about was based on intellectual understanding and not founded on spiritual insight. Thus while arguing, reality had slipped away from them. In contrast to this, the Sixth Patriarch's 'It is neither the wind nor the flag, your hearts are moving' came out of his own direct experience.

He is said to have been illiterate, with no knowledge of Buddhist philosophy. His words express a natural reality that welled up from his heart; there is not the slightest difference between the Sixth Patriarch's words and the Sixth Patriarch's being, and it was this power that caused the two monks to tremble.

After the Sixth Patriarch, Zen Buddhism spread widely and in time the 'Five Houses and the Seven Schools' evolved, with branches all over China. Hogen, the founder of one of these Schools, had first been in the 'Consciousness Only' School. As a monk on pilgrimage, he one night put up at a Zen temple and throughout the night bombarded the Master, Jiso Keijin, with his exposition on 'Consciousness Only', that all phenomena exist in the heart/mind only, and arise from consciousness.

Now, Jiso Keijin had listened all night without saying anything; in the morning, when Hogen was about to leave, Jiso accompanied him to the temple gate. Near the gate, Jiso pointed to a large rock nearby, 'Last night, you were talking and talking about the heart; and this rock there, is it inside or outside your heart?' Hogen could only reiterate, 'The rock is in the heart.' Jiso compassionately said, 'What kind of terrible karma has forced you to carry such a huge rock in your heart?' Hogen was speechless. He stayed under Jiso, struggling very hard to break his conceptual understanding of Buddhism. One day Jiso told him, 'If you express Buddhism in a single word, then everything is itself.' When Hogen heard these words, a Great Satori opened; the Hogen School of Zen is named after him.

But to go back to our text, under no circumstances must you think that the two monks were wrong, arguing about whether the wind or the flag was moving, and that the Sixth Patriarch's saying, 'Your hearts are aflutter,' was right. Wind, or flag, or heart – look at it in terms of the earlier 'not thinking of good and bad' – just that. There is then no distinction between flag and wind and heart – and it is from that level that the Sixth Patriarch had spoken.

Mumon's Comment: 'Neither the wind moving, nor the flag, and not the heart either.' And then he asks how to find the Sixth Patriarch? You cannot find him in the wind; nor in the flag; nor do you find him in the heart; where is he then? Can you answer?

If the two monks could have seen through this problem, it would have been like setting out to buy iron and finding they had purchased gold; they had been offered an opportunity for their abstract understanding to become illuminated. But, Mumon says, the Sixth Patriarch was unable to contain himself, and flowed over with kindness; and, Mumon critically adds, therefore, 'He gave them foolish advice.'

This incident – the two monks arguing and the unkempt, bearded layman telling them, 'It is the heart that moves' – quickly spread around the monastery and soon came to the ears of the Master, Hinju. Next morning, Hinju had Eno summoned to his rooms, and repeated the question as to flag and wind. Eno responded with the same words. Hinju was greatly astonished and remarked, 'Although you look like a beggar, clearly you are not an ordinary person. I have heard that the transmission from the Fifth Patriarch had been carried to the south. Are you that person?' Eno admitted he was the Sixth Patriarch and carried the robe and bowl of transmission. Hinju affirmed before the assembly of monks that this man here was Eno, a living Buddha, and that robe and bowl of the transmission had been shown as proof. Eno then assented to have his head shaved, and taking on the semblance of a monk began to spread the teaching.

After him, the Zen School prospered and spread widely, and the Sixth Patriarch's transmission has come down to us. Because Eno could not contain himself and interrupted that dispute out of excessive kindness, he came to shave his head and wear the robes of a monk.

In a way, for him, this was an unnecessary, foolish undertaking; but thanks to it, over the centuries many thousands and tens of thousands have benefited by that.

The Verse: The wind moves, the flag moves, the heart moves. However you put it, the same great mistake. Those two monks and the Sixth Patriarch know how to open their mouths and use words, but they realise that once you put things into words, they are lost.

This should not be taken as criticism of the Sixth Patriarch. It rather expresses Mumon's grandmotherly kindness to us. To be bound by the wind, or bound by the flag, or bound by the heart, or bound by any of these, is a great mistake – not just abstractly in words, but actually separating ourselves from distinctions of good and bad. We must transcend, move beyond distinctions of good and bad, so that our True Face can act and respond freely and naturally of itself. And this vital activity of our True Face, is not making us act positively towards others, but rather is a state of understanding in which everything that is around is allowed to flow into ourselves.

On a walk in the country, or in a park, the trees flow into us, or the grass and the sky, or birds that are flying come to us. We talk to the trees, the grass or the birds without using words. That kind of vital activity is what Mumon is demanding from us, every moment of our lives. Do not try to grasp at things and say, 'This is reality.'

CASE 30 – THE HEART IS BUDDHA

Daibai asked Baso, 'What is Buddha?' Baso said, 'Heart is Buddha.'

If you could grasp what Baso said, you are wearing Buddha's robes, eating Buddha's food, speaking Buddha's words and, in fact, are Buddha. But though this may be so, Daibai has misled quite a few to mistake the calibration mark on the balance for the actual weight! He does not know that when uttering the word 'Buddha' we must rinse the mouth three times. Had he been a man of clear insight, he would have covered his ears and run!

青天白日
切忌尋覓
更問如何
抱贓叫屈

Under the blue sky in broad daylight,
Abstain from searching and seeking,
From enquiring about (Buddha).
Crying out one's innocence while holding
    on to the stolen goods.

The thirtieth koan of the *Mumonkan* deals with Master Baso, who is a 'grandson' after the Sixth Patriarch, Eno, in the line of descent from Bodhidharma. His full name is Baso Doitsu. Patriarchs are frequently known by the name of the mountain on which they settled and taught or were associated with; but in Baso's case, Ba is a family name. He is known as the great teacher of the Ba family. Literally, the Chinese character for *ba* also means horse, and his Zen was very vigorous, like a horse kicking away the illusions of his disciples. It is said that long before his birth there was a prophecy that in time a tremendously powerful horse would appear. But even if this is legendary, Baso played a tremendous role in the early development of Zen in China. He is said to have been a very big man who walked like a bull and had the eyes of a tiger. This description of him is also an attempt to convey something of the power of his Zen. More than eighty disciples came to be enlightened under him, and those disciples spread all over China, carrying his kind of Zen with them.

As a youth, Baso had trained under Master Ejo on Mount Nangaku. There, Baso had lived nearby in the sub-temple of Denbo-in, practising meditation day and night. Master Ejo heard about this and, thinking he might help this young man, went there and said to Baso, 'What are you doing?'

'Sitting zazen,' answered Baso.

'What do you expect from that?' asked Master Ejo.

'I am trying to become Buddha,' replied Baso.

This is not just relating a dialogue between Ejo and Baso; rather think that Baso, or Ejo, is putting the question directly to you. What are you doing here? zazen. Why – what do you expect from it? Trying to become enlightened!

Ejo picked up a brick and began to rub it. Baso, who could not help noticing the Master's action, asked 'Master, what are you doing?'

'I am polishing a brick,' replied Ejo.

'Why, why are you doing that?' asked Baso.

'I am polishing the brick to make a mirror.'

'But no amount of polishing will make a mirror out of a brick!'

'And no amount of zazen will make a Buddha.'

Baso was shaken. 'Then what should I do?'

'If a cart gets stuck in the mire, do you whip the cart, or the ox?' asked Ejo. Baso was silent.

Ejo kindly continued, 'You are trying to become a Buddha by sitting zazen. Practising zazen is not in sitting, nor in sleeping. Trying to become Buddha, you need to realise that Buddha does not have any particular form. Don't make distinctions, don't become captivated by anything; don't take reality and divide it into true and false. Trying to become Buddha by practising zazen is killing Buddha. If you are taken and captivated by the form of zazen, you will damage or destroy the teaching of the Buddha.' Baso, on hearing this, determined to stay with Ejo and continue practising under him.

Perhaps it is helpful to elaborate a little on Master Ejo's words. In Japan, people also make distinctions – 'Ah, this is a true Roshi,' or 'He is not a good Roshi.' There is nothing more stupid than an argument about true and false. All of us, including myself, everything is truth. In this world, there is nothing that is false, 'un-true'. So if we argue about truth and falsehood, we create those distinctions in ourselves. Sitting zazen we express ourselves in a peerless posture; but sitting on the toilet does not mean presenting ourselves in an ugly posture. There are no good and bad aspects to either of these.

The vital thing is that we realise that we ourselves are not false or artificial, not bad in any way, and that this awareness remains constant whether sitting or not sitting, whether the mind is clear, vague and wandering, or whether steady awareness is maintained in all our doing. However, we always tend to think in terms of my good aspects and my not so good ones, and so I have confidence in dealing with some problems, but no confidence in my ability to deal with other ones. We feel that there is a hole in us from which things leak out, and that unless we can somehow plug that hole, our good aspects will leak away, and we won't be able to live up to our best. But that is not the case; we are perfect as we are.

So after Baso had been with Ejo for a while, and had awakened, he eventually settled at Kose and came to be known as the Great Teacher Ba of Kosei. His teacher, Nangaku Ejo, heard rumours about Baso's activities, and sent one of his disciples to find out what Baso was doing, and gave him explicit instructions that when Baso ascended the high seat to expound the Dharma, he was to ask him 'How are things with you?' The monk did as told. Baso answered, 'In the thirty years or so since training under Master Ejo there has been nothing that disturbs me, nothing that I am wanting.' Metaphorically this could be expressed as saying that he did not want for either salt or condiments in all of the time since he left Ejo; now salt is essential for human life and spices give it flavour. So Baso saying he had no need for them, meant that every day his life was brimming full. When Ejo heard this he greatly rejoiced!

Daibai Hojo was one of Baso's leading disciples. In some of the koans we have discussed, the question, 'What is Buddha?' has already come up. Zen monks of that time had often studied scholastic Buddhism before they engaged in Zen practice. Asking, 'What is Buddha?', they did not expect a philosophical answer; however familiar we are with Buddhist Teachings, this alone does not satisfy the heart.

So by asking Baso, 'What is Buddha?', Daibai hoped for an answer that would help him to complete his understanding. Putting it in another way, he was looking for a trigger to open up a religious awakening or insight within himself. Baso's answer simply meant, 'The heart with which you asked the question, "What is Buddha?", that heart is Buddha.' The Japanese/Chinese term for this is *sokushin sokubutsu* – *shin* meaning *kokoro* or heart, and *butsu* meaning Buddha. But the nuance of *soku* in *sokushin sokubutsu* is extremely difficult to convey. The closest possible meaning for *soku* would be 'just as things are.' I am, just as I am; you are, just as you are; the trees are as they are. Emptiness, or nothingness, of itself as it is, is flowing; however distant things or individuals may be, they are intricately connected.

An experience last New Year, clarifies the meaning of *soku*. One of my students, a German woman, has been practising Zen more than ten years. As is the custom, she was ceremoniously preparing to write/brush the first calligraphy of the New Year. I said to Ursula, 'Please write the ideogram that most appeals to you.' She picked up the brush and wrote one character, *soku*. Usually Zen students tend to write the character *mu*, emptiness, or *ku*, also translated as emptiness. I was very pleased with her, but what I really should have done at that moment, was strike her. Instead, I smiled and complimented her, 'That is a good character.' A week later, I asked her again to write something. This time she brushed *kan*, meaning a barrier. There was now no need to strike her. There is no way to explain it, so I will stop here.

Anyway, Daibai, on hearing the words, *sokushin sokubutsu* – 'The Heart as it is, is Buddha' – was enlightened. But to think he was enlightened because of the meaning of these words is all wrong. Nor was it Baso who first coined these words, 'The Heart as it is, is Buddha.' They appear both in a text of the Pure Land School and in the recorded sayings of Fudaishi, a teacher who was active in China before Bodhidharma. So Daibai must have been quite familiar with these words, but only in an intellectual way. As such, the expression is not exceptional, there is nothing special about it; but in Baso's use of it, through his insight, it took on tremendous power and struck and shattered Daibai.

Mumon's Comment: If you can grasp Baso's words and intent directly without any explanation, then you are wearing Buddha's robes, eating Buddha's food, living the life of Buddha, and are Buddha.

But as I see it, Mumon said something extremely foolish. For whether enlightened or not enlightened, we are wearing Buddha's robes, eating Buddha's food, sleeping as Buddha, living as Buddha. The only difference is that we are not satisfied. And the one who feels this dissatisfaction tries to cover up or to plug the dissatisfaction with the expression 'The Heart as it is, is Buddha!'

Mumon, who seems to admonish Daibai, is actually warning all of us, saying something like, 'Daibai, it is true, your insight is certainly wonderful; but unless you are very careful, you will cause many to mistake the calibration mark on the scales for the actual weight.' Mumon thus says that if 'The Heart as it is, is Buddha' is erroneously taken to be equivalent to the mark on the scales, and people are led to believe that by simply having confidence, they will grasp 'The Heart is Buddha', they also are misled.

There is nothing that causes greater confusion than the word 'Buddha'. So, Mumon is saying to Daibai that by even uttering the word Buddha his mouth becomes dirty and needs to be rinsed for three days. Are you aware of that? Somebody with genuine insight, on hearing 'The Heart as it is, is Buddha', would feel his ears being sullied, and, covering them with both hands, would run away? These words of Mumon's are terrible! But in Mumon, who utters these words, there was no hole whatsoever that he had to plug up with Buddha!

The Verse: The sun is shining in a brilliant, cloudless sky. Even without trying to see, everything is fully visible. There, what are you looking for? Is it not that without looking, everything is there, clearly visible? If, in spite of this, you still insist on going around asking, 'What is Buddha?' – why, it is just like a thief who, carrying the stolen goods with him, keeps on protesting, 'I've stolen nothing; how unfair to accuse me of being a thief.'

CASE 31 · JOSHU TESTS AN OLD WOMAN

THE CASE

One of Joshu's monks asked an old woman the way to Taizan. The old crone said, 'Go straight on,' but when the monk had gone a few steps, she called after him, 'There goes another one!' When a monk related this to Joshu, he remarked, 'Just wait, I'll go myself to check out this old crone.' Next day he set out, and asked her the same question, and she answered the same way. Returned, Joshu told his assembly, 'I have checked out this old woman of Taizan for you.'

MUMON'S COMMENT

The old woman sat scheming in her headquarters, and did not recognise the famous robber. Old Joshu managed to steal into her camp and plunder her fortress, but was no great marshal. Considering the case, one comes to the conclusion that both were at fault. Say, what is it that Joshu saw in the old woman?

THE VERSE

問既一般
答亦相似
飯裏有砂
泥中有刺

Question and answer
Are like each other –
In the rice is sand,
Thorns are in the mud.

SOKO ROSHI'S COMMENTS

In teisho, the comments on the text reveal the teacher's own insight and thus try to help and stimulate trainees in their own practice. There is no need to attempt to understand, for that comes down to trying to grasp things in the head. But if instead some point in the teisho triggers your own insight, then the teisho will have served its purpose. If your own heart and the words of teisho match, that is excellent – but it is less likely to happen the more you try to understand it intellectually. This kind of encounter or confrontation, between what teisho is offering and your own experience, is not confined to elicit abstract understanding only. Perhaps when half asleep, or if at some time during the day a doubt or some other reaction will arise – this too is a valid reaction to teisho. So the purpose of teisho is to provide something that will help to break through the crust that you build up as you move through life.

Master Joshu has already appeared in some of the previous koans, so here we only need to recall that he came under Master Nansen at nineteen, and remained continuously at his side for some forty years. After Nansen's death, now sixty, Joshu set out on pilgrimage, and for the next twenty years travelled all over China, continuing his practice. He was eighty when at last he settled down at Kannon-in temple, and taught there until his death at the age of a hundred and twenty. Both in the length of his life and in depth of experience, he was truly remarkable.

The koan probably refers to an incident after Joshu had settled down. Kannon-in was not so far from Mount Godai, the 'Five-Peaked Mountain' sacred to the Bodhisattva Manjusri, who, it was believed, had actually appeared there in person. Monks and lay people came on pilgrimage from all over China, even from India, Mongolia, Korea and Japan. At the foot of Mount Godai, near the beginning of the pilgrims' way up to the sacred shrines, an old woman kept a tea house.

In Case 28, Ryutan Blows the Candle Out, Tokusan also met an old woman in a tea house, and got into difficulties with her. Zen stories tell of many such old women who are full of insight and who torment young monks who encounter them. I, too, when I was a young monk, came across such an old lady. She was taking care of Zuigan Roshi, but was very fierce and kept after me all the time; while she was alive, I hated her. Now that she is dead, I feel nothing but gratitude.

Anyway, when monks asked this old woman for the pilgrims' way up the mountain, she always answered, 'Straight on.' What road should they take to go straight on? Probably there were a number of paths, and they asked because they did not know which one to take. But she only said, 'Straight on!' When the monk then walked straight on, the old crone would call after him, 'Ah, that's a fine monk – he's doing it again.'

Where is Mount Godai? That is the first problem. The monks asking the old woman for the way had the pilgrimage to Manjusri at the top of the mountain in mind. Now, the old woman who told them to walk straight on was not thinking of Manjusri at the top of the mountain. And Joshu, when as a young monk visiting Mount Godai, had on the way there met another monk who, on learning that Joshu was on his way to Mount Godai, had said, 'In this wide world, wherever you are is the training hall; why then take up your staff and make for Mount Godai? On Mount Godai, should Manjusri manifest out of the clouds, the eye of genuine insight would not deem it so wonderful!'

Joshu had asked that monk, 'What is the eye of genuine insight?' The monk could not answer. Certainly, the monk's words 'Wherever you are is a training place' are correct but still, it is a generalisation and practice cannot proceed by generalisations. Here, now, in this very place, this is the training hall. Even if you say that the whole world is a training place, for me, here and now, there is no other place than this one. So that even if you say that everything is Buddha, the trees or the rain or the grass – yet if you really venerate Buddha, he is nothing other than within yourself, here and now.

Zen training is utterly practical, and a generalised understanding does not contribute, does not add up to practice. So the old woman's 'Straight on' did not mean that Mount Godai was here or there, but demonstrated that here, this very instant, within you, is Manjusri of Mount Godai. This is not just the problem for the monks who asked the question, but also for each one of us. But the monks did not understand and thought the old woman's answer capricious, and that she was making fun of them.

It is the same with those who come to see me in my temple. All I can do is listen to what is being said. The resolution of the problem is within themselves, dealing with it there and then, going 'straight on'. When in trouble, everybody thinks that their state, or the place that they are in, is hell and that if they could only go somewhere else, they would be in paradise. They look outside, always outside, and so forget the most vital thing – this time, this place, inside themselves. Master Rinzai warned, 'Do not look to the outside.' For if you look and seek outside, it will only cause suffering.

Anyway, a number of monks had met that old crone and word about her passed around. Joshu, too, was told about her and said to his monks, 'I'll go in your stead, and see through her,' i.e. test her.

So Joshu arrived at her tea house and, as other monks had done, asked her, 'What is the way to Mount Godai?' And as always she replied, 'Straight on.' Joshu returned and told his monks, 'I went in your stead and saw into the very depths of the old crone.' But he did not say how he had seen into her.

How did Joshu see through, or see into her? Do not think of her answer. Nor did Joshu see through the old woman – she saw through him! Why is it that somebody of Joshu's stature did not see through that old crone? Because he would have seen through her even if he had not troubled to go and see her. Why did he go then? What he had to see into, or see through, was not in her belly, but in his own.

Forgetting Joshu and the old woman for the moment, what is certain is that we will all die. Yet most of us do our best to live and continue living. So, ask yourselves what is it within you that makes you carry on? You know that you will get old, and will get ill, and eventually die. If you understand this, and in spite of knowing that you will die, why do you continue to sit zazen, to work, and strive and struggle to keep going? To think that you can avoid illness, and that by exercising your physical strength the body can be maintained, is merely foolish. Conversely, those who give up on life become a burden to society.

Why do you then put so much effort into living? Joshu troubling himself to go and see the old woman; she telling monk after monk, 'Go straight on!' And as for us, we give birth to children who are bound to die, we continue to produce and build up what we know will in time disintegrate and collapse. There is no difference between Joshu's exerting himself, the old woman's repeated 'Straight on' and our involvement in activities which we know will fall apart again. Nor does this apply to human activities only. The hallmark of all things in the universe is 'coming to be and ceasing to be'. And yet, the activity or the energy that gives rise to all the fleeting things never ceases to function. So what Joshu saw through was not simply the spiritual state of the old woman, his eyes saw through life itself, and through the workings of the universe.

Mumon's Comment: This old woman had the tremendous power of a great tactician, a military commander who remains at his headquarters at the rear and yet directs all. However, she did not notice that the great robber Joshu had stolen into the very heart of her fort. And though Joshu was able to sneak in like a thief at night, what he actually achieved was rather childish. If you look at it carefully both made mistakes.

These are Mumon's words. And I now ask, how are you trying to live your lives? Not in the belly of Joshu or of the old crone, but within yourselves, in what kind of spiritual state are you living your life? Of course, I am not referring to the life in your head; please look into the very foundation from which your life is functioning.

The Verse: Joshu asked the old woman the same question as the monks, and her answer was the same too. Yet within this simple question and answer something tremendous is concealed. If you are not careful, it is like finding grit in your rice, or like cutting your feet on thorns submerged in soft mud.

So once more, lots of people can and do make elaborate intellectual systems about life; but life itself, the living of life, is very easy – is like eating soft rice, or walking on soft ground. However, if you are not careful in eating or walking, you are likely to have some painful surprises! Yet rather than regarding these as painful, you can also say that they are quite wonderful. Again, just reflect on or review your life. If you think that you can make your life successful, then it will not be successful. And why not? Because you cannot take into death what you have acquired during life, nor can you taste the joy of having been born. How, bounded between these two extremes, can you live a life that has value? Having settled this for myself, I give this problem to you as a present!

CASE 32 · A NON-BUDDHIST QUESTIONS THE BUDDHA

A Non-Buddhist asked the World-honoured One, 'I do not ask for words, I do not ask for no words.' The World-honoured One just sat. The Non-Buddhist was deeply moved and said gratefully, 'The Great Compassion of the World-honoured One has burst open the clouds of my delusion and enabled me to enter the Way,' and prostrating himself, he departed. Ananda asked the Buddha, 'What did he realise that moved him to such admiration?' The World-honoured One remarked, 'A high-mettled horse gets going at the shade of the whip.'

MUMON'S COMMENT

Ananda was the Buddha's disciple, but his insight was not like that of the Non-Buddhist. Say, what is the difference between a disciple of the Buddha and a Non-Buddhist?

THE VERSE

劍刃上行
氷綾上走
不涉階梯
懸崖撒手

Walking along the cutting edge of a sword,
Running across splintered ice,
Without a ladder
Hanging on a cliff, let loose the grip.

SOKO ROSHI'S COMMENTS

From ancient times, asceticism and contemplation were common practices in India and so a variety of philosophical systems and contemplative traditions developed. When Prince Gotama became disenchanted with the life that he was living and began his search, he first joined such sects but found no satisfaction in philosophical discussions. Finally, rather than looking at things or people, he turned inward and worked through to finding the reality within himself.

'Awakened', he became the Buddha. The many schools of thought and practices prevalent at his time may be categorised into two main persuasions, whether or not there is a self-nature in things or whether 'I' has a self-nature, i.e., whether there is life after death, whether a soul persists. All these may be considered in affirmative or in negative terms, hence the two main branches of eternalism or nihilism, either affirming or denying reality. However, such theories should not be seen as just intellectual gymnastics. We human beings always have two problems. One is how to make our life as fulfilled, satisfying and prosperous as possible, the other is realising that our life is inevitably limited and that however much we may satisfy ourselves or amass prosperity, all ends with death. And the question is how to take this limited, physical existence of ours and connect it to something that is unlimited, eternal?

We constantly grapple with these two problems, the temporary and the eternal. If we want to resolve the second of them, it is essential that we have an understanding of the underlying, fundamental reality of things. 'Non-Buddhist' literally means somebody who follows an 'Other Way', apart from the Buddhist Way. The various other sects attempted by means of philosophical debates to clarify this question of existence or non-existence.

Our koan introduces a Non-Buddhist who approached the Buddha seeking insight. He did not come to confront the Buddha, or to challenge him to intellectual discourse, but rather hoping to get from the Buddha some indication of how to resolve the thorny question of existence or non-existence, eternalism or nihilism.

He actually said that he neither asked for an explanation in words, nor for one without words; but his real question, not concerned with words, was, 'I have been unable to understand myself and the universe around me in affirmative terms or in negative terms. How can I resolve this and come to genuine insight?' The Buddha's response to this was simply to sit. The Non-Buddhist then, seeing the Buddha simply sitting there silently, felt profoundly moved and exclaimed, 'Your great compassion has burst open the clouds of delusion that surrounded me and enabled me to awaken.' Then he prostrated himself before the Buddha, and left.

What was it that the Non-Buddhist found in the Buddha's simply sitting there silently? This is what our koan asks.

Although not in the text of this koan, undoubtedly this Non-Buddhist had gone through a period of intense personal upheaval. Such insight opening on his asking the Buddha implies that he was already powerfully charged.

Please ponder this very carefully. It cannot be taught; we ourselves must awaken to genuine insight. However great the teacher, all he can do is provide a stimulus. Confucius said that he would only teach a disciple sufficiently charged, ripe and receptive for what was to be taught, so that when shown one corner, he immediately would also know the other three. This may seem very stern, but study and practice are fundamental. We all have a basic urge to learn and find out for ourselves. In Japan nowadays, the main emphasis in education is on teaching; but when all the stress is on teaching, then the students' capacity to learn and to find out for themselves, begins to atrophy. What they learn is quick critical thinking, but the ability to find out and discover for themselves, to produce and create, cannot develop. Whether in education or in Zen training, a return to fundamental attitudes is required.

In an early chapter of the *Vimalakirti Sutra*, the wealthy Hoshaku comes to listen to a sermon of the Buddha. He is accompanied by five hundred equally rich men, all of high social standing and well-educated, and all bearing parasols as status symbols of their rank. When they arrived before the Buddha, they handed their parasols to the Buddha who, by his supernormal power, transformed all the parasols into a huge one, and under it was shown the reality of the world.

The deep meaning of this is that in presenting their parasols to the Buddha, they also handed over their wealth, their social status and their education to him. But over and above these externals, they also laid down their very being, their spiritual lives, presenting all to the Buddha. Why all their parasols could be transformed into the one gigantic parasol under which the truth of the universe was shown, was not because of the supernormal power of the Buddha, but due to their own receptiveness and their ability to rid themselves of the things that they possessed. What died within them was the need to see things as their possessions, like their social influence and their education.

Though many look for and ask, 'What is truth?', they do not look straight at truth. Instead of confronting truth straight on, they always try to fit truth into some kind of framework of their own; and when they have done so, and are familiar with it, then they say, 'Ah, now I understand, I have got it.'

I remember a foolish youngster who every morning looked at the thermometer, and according to the reading would put on warm or cool clothes. Do you laugh at this? Can you really laugh at this? If you had a voucher here, for ten thousand pounds, you would take it, of course, and treat it as treasure. But, if the voucher was for one pound only, would you then care how you put it down, or what happened to it? Actually, you are then not really looking at the things as they are, but only at the voucher. However, what we really want to know is what these things are in reality? We try to look for truth using a yardstick that we have created for ourselves from the way we live our lives, and do not see the heart as the one that produced all standards.

We refer to people who are studying or practising traditions other than Buddhism as followers of 'Other Ways' or Non-Buddhists. The difference between those who adhere to Buddhism and those who study Other Ways is the difference between looking inwards for the heart, or seeking it outside. However, the Non-Buddhist who asked the Buddha his question, was taking all the standards he had created by looking outward, and laid them down before the Buddha. Thus when seeing the Buddha sitting silently, he saw not only the Buddha but the whole of reality, in all its truth. Just as in the *Vimalakirti Sutra* the reality of the universe appeared under that great parasol, so in this koan the reality of the universe is also revealed by the Buddha's just sitting there. The Non-Buddhist was able to take this straight in. To repeat: the Buddha did not show; the Non-Buddhist received; even without the Buddha showing, it is always and everywhere present.

The Non-Buddhist, transformed, prostrated himself in gratitude and left. Ananda, who had been present, wondered why the Non-Buddhist was so overjoyed. Now, Ananda had attended the Buddha for some twenty-five years, so had heard more of the Buddha's sermons than any of the other disciples. When, after the Buddha's death, the teachings were recorded, and the sutras compiled, Ananda's part was essential; he had such total recall of the Buddha's words that those listening felt the Buddha himself was speaking and were moved to tears.

But at the occasion of the Non-Buddhist's visit, Ananda had not yet come to understand and asked, 'What was it that the Non-Buddhist saw that made him so full of joy?' The Buddha replied, 'There are four kinds of horses. The best respond to just the shadow of the whip. Not quite so superb, but still good, is a horse that will begin to run when the whip just touches its hair. The third kind will not run until the whip touches the flesh. And the fourth type only bestirs itself when the whip has cut into the flesh and the pain begins to enter the bones. The Non-Buddhist who came here is like the high-spirited horse that starts at the shadow of the whip.' The Buddha was not referring to the Non-Buddhist's enlightenment; he replied in a metaphor that was pointing at the spiritual state of the Non-Buddhist, encouraging Ananda to develop within himself the ability to move at just the shadow of the whip, which is the ability or power given to everybody as their birthright.

Mumon's Comment: Ananda was Buddha's disciple, but in spite of that, he seemed not to have the insight of the Non-Buddhist. What difference is there between Ananda and the Non-Buddhist? Speak, explain that difference directly, clearly!

This is Mumon's comment; but I would like to ask, 'What kind of difference is there between you and Buddha?' This is a second koan!

The Verse: 'Walking along the cutting edge of a sword, running across splintered ice' – both express praise of the Non-Buddhist. It is dangerous and extremely difficult to look at anything directly, in a straightforward way, without any kind of gauge. Especially so when we ponder the procedures by which we human beings have constructed our society. Instead of taking things directly, or simply exchanging them, we tend to deal with things indirectly. Our ancestors, if thirsty, would take up the water that was flowing in front of them. Or they could fish and at once eat the fish they had caught. They would pluck the fruit from a tree and eat it there and then. But today when most of us live in cities, which are considered as advanced society, we no longer see flowing water or fruit on a tree! Water comes through a pipe or a tap, and we have to pay for it with money. When we let that water run away, we are again involved in an indirect interaction, because we have to pay for sewage or plumbing. Food itself is also not directly available; we provide roads, lorries to transport food, and it all becomes a very cumbersome structure.

Long ago people lived simple lives. Today, we learn of all kinds of theories – hence the man who looked at the thermometer every day to decide what to wear! Yet within ourselves there is the power to directly grasp things as they are, without having to create intervening gauges.

Our Non-Buddhist had the great courage and strength to deal with his anguish, and rid himself of the fixed standards he had carried with him to the Buddha. So Mumon then is praising him and adds encouragement for other practitioners. For satori to open, it is not necessary to have a ladder on which to climb up rung by rung. We all cling to something as if clinging with all our might to something on the edge of a precipice. We may not know what it is, or may not be fully aware of it, but there is something which we feel we just cannot let go of – when all that is really needed is to just let go! But please, before letting go, get clear about what it is that you are clinging to! If you do not really penetrate this, you will let go of unimportant things, and continue clinging to the central problem.

Everybody thinks that life is important. But some people feel that pride is more important than life, and rather than have their pride hurt, they feel it would be better to throw away their lives. This is just one example but everybody has something, some precipice, to which they cling. Mumon gives us the advice to just let go – and at that moment reality manifests.

CASE 33 · BASO'S 'NEITHER HEART NOR BUDDHA'

THE CASE

A monk asked Baso, 'What is Buddha?' Baso answered, 'Neither Heart nor Buddha.'

MUMON'S COMMENT

If you can see into what Baso said, you have come to the end of Zen training.

THE VERSE

路逢劍客須呈
不遇詩人莫獻
逢人且說三分
未可全施一片

If you meet a swordsman, show him your sword.
Do not show your poem to a man who is not a poet.
Explain three parts when talking to people,
But never tell them the last quarter.

SOKO ROSHI'S COMMENTS

A monk asked Baso, 'What is Buddha?' Baso answered, 'Neither Heart nor Buddha.' Now this is the same question that Baso answered with 'Heart is Buddha' in Case 30. Since the present answer seems just the opposite, we have to look at it carefully.

Jizai Zenji, one of Baso's disciples, takes up this matter of Baso at one time saying, 'Heart is Buddha', and at another time saying,

'Neither Heart nor Buddha.' He explains that to somebody who is hale and hearty yet convinced of being gravely ill, Baso gives the medicine called 'Heart is Buddha', but to somebody already cured but who cannot stop himself taking the medicine, Baso gives the remedy called 'Neither Heart nor Buddha.'

Once Baso was asked, 'Why do you say, "Heart is Buddha"?' He answered, 'It is to trick a crying child.' 'Then what do you do when the child has stopped crying?' 'Neither Heart nor Buddha.' Though Jizai was a disciple of Baso, his explanation of the difference between these two sayings, or the relationship between them, or even Baso's own exposition, are too explanatory. A later incident, also involving Daibai, will help the understanding of this koan.

Daibai had already found enlightenment under Baso's guidance; he then went off into the mountains and in near solitude continued his practice, deepening his insight. In the course of years, as people began to hear about him, other monks joined him and eventually a monastery came to be established on Mount Daibai.

Baso then heard of this and just as Nangaku Ejo had once sent one of his disciples to see what Baso was doing, so Baso in his turn sent one of his monks to see what Daibai was doing, instructing the monk to ask how Daibai was training his monks. Daibai's answer was that he taught 'Heart is Buddha', by which phrase he himself had come to insight under Baso. Primed by Baso, the visiting monk informed Daibai that Baso was no longer teaching this, but had changed his teaching to 'Neither Heart nor Buddha'. Daibai laughed, 'That foolish old man, hasn't he yet stopped tricking people? Whatever he may say, however much he may assert, I for myself stick to "Heart is Buddha".'

The monk went back and reported to Baso who was delighted and declared, 'The Great Plum (i.e. Daibai) is fully ripe.'

But we must make no mistake here. Daibai was not stubbornly clinging to 'Heart is Buddha' as if it was a jewel casket that he had received from Baso. When he had asked Baso, 'What is Buddha?' Baso's reply, 'Heart is Buddha' was, at that moment, for Daibai, like a burst of flame which consumed everything within him; therefore, though you follow it up with another flame such as 'Neither Heart nor Buddha', in Daibai there was nothing left that could burn.

This does not, however, mean that 'Heart is Buddha' is appropriate for some and 'Neither heart nor Buddha' suits others. Whether the flames are fuelled by wood or coal or whatever, it is all fire. As that fire, it can utterly consume the one who asks; but unless the fire totally consumes the questioner, it has no meaning.

One day Nangaku, Baso's teacher, said to him, 'If the cart sticks in the mire, do you whip the cart or the ox?' So, on looking at these *Mumonkan* koans, what is more important, to analyse the fire in the koan or see the relation of the koan to yourself?

Mumon's Comment: If you understand what Baso said, your study of Zen is at an end! Briefly, satori is burning oneself out; if at this moment, in this place, everything is burnt, then the practice is perfected.

The Verse: 'If you meet a master swordsman, show him your sword. Do not show your poem to a man who is not a poet. Explain three parts when talking to people, but never tell them the last quarter.' The meaning of this is to place the problem at the receiving end rather than making what is given into a problem. Of course, if you are looking for understanding and insight, the teacher who does not have insight is useless. Still, however deep an insight a teacher may have and demonstrates, if you cannot draw it from them and burn up what is within yourself, then it is of no use to you.

People nowadays like asking questions, and having asked them, they try to understand the answer. They do not try to think for themselves, or see for themselves. For somebody who is already full to the point of exploding, with only a thin cover over it, a mere touch from the teacher will release it.

So when dealing with a koan, or with problems in your daily life, grapple with that problem yourself. It is a tremendous loss to us if we get angry and complain about our problems, seeing them only as a personal burden. Having a problem, and wrestling with it, is actually a good opportunity for us. And when, in trying to resolve this problem, our own answer begins to emerge, then we have to investigate whether this answer is correct, is a true answer. Having thus questioned and doubted again and again, and become convinced that, yes, this is right, we can then go for sanzen with that problem. And, when you have taken a problem to your teacher and presented your efforts and answer, but are sent away and told it is no good, do not accuse yourself or blame yourself for failing to understand. What the teacher is offering in sanzen is a reality that cannot change, thus offering you an opportunity that when taken may trigger a change in you. The teacher thus stimulates you, and you, changing direction, can go still deeper into the problem. When that problem gets to the point just before exploding, then something like the encounter between Baso and Daibai will occur.

People everywhere increasingly seem to suffer from getting angry. So when you feel anger, make that anger your problem and try to confront it. Then anger can become a powerful driving energy to resolve the problem you are facing. There is no need to repress the anger. Of course, this does not mean that you vent your anger on others, for if you turn your anger on others, you lose the opportunity to use its energy which is lodged in yourself. When in the course of training the problem that you are working on is expanding within yourself, it is not helpful if the teacher gives too much of an explanation. Nor does this refer to Zen practice only. So as a teacher or parent, be sparing with your explanations. If you believe that the person you are dealing with is Buddha, then they have the strength within themselves to resolve the problem. We all have that strength. So a very small amount of help may trigger a more simple joy; therefore do not overdo it. That is all.

CASE 34 · NANSEN'S 'WISDOM IS NOT THE WAY'

Nansen said, 'Heart is not Buddha, Wisdom is not the Way.'

MUMON'S COMMENT
Of Nansen it should be said that in his old age he knew no shame.
Opening his smelly mouth, he told others of the family feud. Few
appreciate his kindness.

THE VERSE
天晴日頭出
雨下地上濕
盡情都説了
只恐信不及

The sky is blue and the sun shines,
Rain falls and the earth is drenched.
With utmost kindness he explains everything,
But oh, how few believe him.

SOKO ROSHI'S COMMENTS
This is a seemingly simple and limpid koan; however, the spiritual state underlying it is extremely powerful. 'Heart is not Buddha,
Wisdom is not the Way.' Scholars hold that these words are not
Nansen's, but are supposed to be by Nyoe, a fellow disciple of Nansen
under Baso Doitsu. This is because in the patriarchal biographies like
the *Keitoku Dento-roku* or the *Goto Egen*, this koan does not appear

in Master Nansen's biography but in Nyoi Zenji's. Nyoi said, 'Heart is not Buddha, Wisdom is not the Way. We behave like travellers on a boat who have let a precious sword drop overboard. So they notch a mark on the side of the boat and as the boat sails on, call out to each other, "The sword is here, the sword is here!"'

It really does not matter whether this saying is by Nansen or Nyoi, or by someone else; what matters is that we can hear it and are stimulated by its power.

What is now called Buddhism developed from the Buddha's teaching after his enlightenment. Some nineteen hundred years ago, Buddhist texts began to flow into China; as they were translated, they probably were studied first intellectually, but the rituals and ceremonies of Buddhism also began to spread and attract attention. This then influenced and embraced many cultural aspects of Chinese life, giving rise to styles of Buddhist architecture and of the carving of cult objects. This form of Buddhism was spreading when Bodhidharma came to China. His way was completely different from anything that preceded it. He had nothing to say about the sutras, treatises, or about Buddhist rituals and Buddhist art. And when the monk Eka asked, 'My heart is anguished, not at peace, please pacify it for me,' Bodhidharma said, 'Find your heart and bring it to me.' By making Eka himself seek for the core of his own heart, he engendered Eka's awakening.

Bodhidharma's school has variously been called Dhyana School or Zen School or Buddha-Heart School. In other words, his teaching is 'Pointing directly to the human heart, seeing into its nature and becoming Buddha.' As that it came to be known as the way to direct insight.

As already mentioned, the saying 'Heart is Buddha' is not only Baso's but appears much earlier in texts of the Pure Land School.

The very core of Buddhist teaching is the understanding of the heart and to look outside the heart for satori is the approach of the Other Ways. Therefore the generations of the patriarchs throughout time have always stressed the heart as the essence. Accordingly, there are a great number of koans in which the central question probes, 'What is Buddha?', 'Heart is Buddha', and the like.

The *Heart Sutra* may be said to encapsulate the very essence of Buddhism and as that it is chanted daily in Zen monasteries. It belongs to the cycle of the *Prajna Paramita Sutras*, the Sutras of 'Great Wisdom Gone Beyond'. Truly the wisdom of the heart underlies and functions in everything. Just this is the essence of Buddhism.

The developing Zen tradition also incorporated some of the indigenous Chinese customs and thought, in particular the concept of the Dao, the Way; in time, Buddhism came to be seen as the Way, too.

So, looking at the first line of this koan, 'Heart is not Buddha, Wisdom is not the Way', and taking Nansen literally, he seems to reject what is at the core of human experience and human suffering, and at the core of developed Buddhism: Heart, Buddha, Wisdom, and Way. But what he is actually saying is that none of these are of any significance to me directly.

In Koan 33 Daibai's satori opened on his hearing Baso's 'Heart is Buddha'. Later, when Daibai himself was teaching, he always held to 'Heart is Buddha', and said he would go on using this in spite of being told that Baso was now teaching 'Neither Heart nor Buddha'.

Now, it might seem that Daibai felt somewhat like possessing a jewel with 'Heart is Buddha', and on someone else offering him another jewel, 'Neither Heart nor Buddha', had no need of it and so stuck to the jewel he had. But Daibai was not clinging to any jewel; because when satori had opened for him at Baso's 'Heart is Buddha', it was as if he had been set on fire and completely burned out. So what

Daibai meant was that whether 'Heart is Buddha' or 'Neither Heart nor Buddha', now that he was enlightened, neither of these had any significance for him.

What is called 'Zen' (zazen, or dhyana, or Sitting Meditation) is constantly in flux. That flux, that movement, is like a snake that sloughs its skin. Zen, then, is constantly shedding its surrounding, its cover, and being reborn as a new Zen. We use the word 'Zen' as a verbal convenience; the thing that we happen to call 'Zen' is this state of flux. It is, put into other words, our lives which, changing from moment to moment, never remain in precisely the same state. In our human bodies, there is constant cell regeneration, and yet in the midst of this constant flux, I remain I, and you remain you.

As a tradition, Zen has continued to transcend the individual. If you cling to anything, such as 'Heart is Buddha', and use that constantly, that is dead, defunct Zen. But if you then think that 'Neither Heart nor Buddha' is the key word and cling to that, that, too, is dead Zen. That is why Nyoe cautioned against notching the side of a moving boat to mark the place where the sword dropped overboard.

Grasping at something such as 'This is Zen' or 'This is I' or 'This is God' or 'This is salvation' or anything, such clutching binds you; let go! While you are clutching, the hand cannot be used for anything else. Let it go; then you can use your hand or hands for anything. This free movement, the ability to move freely, is what has been called Zen or satori or Buddha. So, to repeat, it always transcends the I, the self.

Mumon's Comment: Perhaps that has given some indication of the tremendous power of Nansen's so simple 'Heart is not Buddha, Wisdom is not the Way.' In this sense, my commentary, too, is superfluous. Mumon implies this when he says that Nansen is getting old and has forgotten shame. In his doddering old age, although his mouth is stinking, he keeps opening it and chirping away, revealing secrets of the house that should be kept secret. As for myself, I am now sixty-five but I feel that I am being criticised as the old man here. I have given away all the secrets.

Mumon then continues that in spite of Nansen's tremendous kindness, how many people do or can really appreciate his words? Rather than feeling gratitude, they tend to complain. There may be some (here at the Summer School) who think, 'I have given up all my time this week, and paid good money, and I really want to hear more about Buddhism!' What are you thinking and in what spirit are you saying that? What is Buddha useful for? In what way is the history of Buddhism useful? If you know most of the Buddhist terms, what good is it to you? What is the meaning, what is the point, when you are already burdened and your back bent with all the junk you carry around yet come and ask for still more junk? Somebody covered in mud had better go to the bathroom to wash it off. But there, instead of washing off all that muck, we foolishly apply paint and make-up on top of it. Cease from such foolishness and just let go, empty your heart! Do not worry because you have or carry nothing. Understand that because you are carrying nothing you are able to do anything.

Why is it that explanations are so much in demand? If there are no clouds, naturally the sun shines. And if it rains, the ground is wet. What kind of rationalising is necessary for that? We are born, feel hungry, evacuate, work, and when the time comes, die; what kind of explanation is necessary for any of these? We seem to feel that without some explanation, without attaching some explicit value to such natural things, we are like a dog or a cat. But that is mistaken; we need rather be concerned about the fact that we cannot live and act as freely as a dog or cat!

Mumon then says that Nansen has exposed everything in his great kindness, but probably you do not believe him. For Nansen, Heart, Buddha, Wisdom, Way – none of them are holes which he has to stop up; so he has confidence in himself. You do not trust yourselves because you feel there are all kinds of holes! And do you not feel that unless these holes are filled up you cannot be happy? So that is what is meant by not trusting, or not having confidence.

The Verse: Mumon says that although people may hear what Nansen said, many will not be able to trust him, will not believe him. If what has been said and what you have heard is still not sufficient, then put your load on your back and carry it. Then, muddy and dirty, put paint on all over, make up your face, and so live your lives!

CASE 35 · SEIJO'S SOUL SEPARATED

Goso asked a monk, 'Seijo and her soul are apart – which is the real one?'

MUMON'S COMMENT
If you have genuine insight into the truth of this matter, you realise that passing from one husk to another is just like a traveller putting up at an inn for the night. If you do not see, do not rush about blindly. Suddenly earth, water, fire and air fall part, and like a crab in boiling water, you struggle with seven legs and eight arms!

THE VERSE
雲月是同
溪山各異
萬福萬福
是一是二

Among the changing clouds the moon is ever the same.
Valley and mountain are different from each other.
How joyous, how wonderful –
Is it one, is it two?

SOKO ROSHI'S COMMENTS
The Goso of this koan is not the Fifth Patriarch, but Goso Hoen who lived in the Song Dynasty on Mount Goso on which the Fifth Patriarch also had his monastery. In China it became the custom not to use

the actual name of a respected master, but to address him or refer to him by the name of his monastery, or the name of the mountain on which his monastery stood. So all of the masters of the monastery on Mount Goso would be known as Master Goso.

However, the Goso Hoen of this koan was so renowned that when we talk of Goso we now usually mean Hoen. His birthplace was in the upper reaches of the Yangtze River. He only became a monk at thirty-five; perhaps remaining a layman until then gave strength to his later practice and teaching. It is not recorded what led him to become a monk, but the fact that Hoen lived an ordinary life for thirty-five years gave him a very direct and practical understanding of the sufferings and problems of ordinary people. So his practice, then, was not only confined to sutra study in a monastic environment, to monastic observances, or the merely intellectual study of Buddhism – it went deeper than that. Later when he began to teach, what stands out from his recorded sayings and the koans associated with him is his down-to-earth and practical approach, which could easily be grasped by ordinary people in lay life.

After he entered the monastic life, he also made a considerable name for himself in the scholastic study of Buddhism. He hoped and prayed that he would come to genuine insight not just intellectually, but with his whole self, his whole being. He visited and trained under various masters, but eventually awakened to satori under Master Hakuun.

One day Hakuun told his monks, 'The other day, a group of monks came from Mount Ro. When I asked them to make presentations, they gave wonderful speeches. Raising various koans with them, their responses to them were accurate. When I asked them to comment on a particular koan, they provided superb commentaries. However, they have not reached it.' On hearing this, Hoen was thrown into great doubt. He greatly respected Hakuun, his teacher; but he did not understand what was being pointed at and felt that if he were truly enlightened, he should clearly see what Hakuun meant. So without sleeping, he wrestled day and night with the koan. After some days, Hakuun's meaning suddenly burst open for him; he ran to Hakuun, and it is said that Hakuun, too, on seeing Hoen rushing in, danced for joy.

Zen constantly requires one to transcend Zen itself; it is the same with satori. There is a satori which transcends, or surpasses, satori; and then there is a satori that surpasses that satori.

Later, Hoen said of the moment of insight, 'It was like carrying a heavy burden, pouring with white sweat; and then suddenly this burden fell off and a cool wind blew.' He also liked to say that he had practised for twenty years, and so had now come to feel shame. This expression is extremely profound – instead of saying that he had awakened to satori after twenty years training, he stated that he had come to feel shame. What he was pointing to was that instead of having come to see reality, the obstacles to seeing reality had been removed from his eyes. The real problem is not seeking truth, or reality; the real problem is that in the face of truth, of the reality which surrounds us and is welling up everywhere, our eyes are covered so that we do not see it. And is it not the case that, if you are blindfolded and your ears are plugged up, even when a great teacher comes and presents you with still more truth, you cannot accept or understand it? Truth is not something that is presented by the teacher; truth is intrinsically there, everywhere. So the koans presented by the teacher are not meant to provide us with truth; they simply help to remove the blindfold from our eyes, and the plugs from our ears.

Now we can move on to Goso's koan. Having lived as a layman for thirty-five years, he does not use difficult Buddhist concepts.

Rather he has recourse to a simple story that was widely known from a popular Tang dynasty book called *The Record of the Separated Soul*. This is the story:

In the past, on the Yangtze River, there lived a man called Chokan, who had two daughters. Sadly, the elder of the two died when still quite small, and so he showered all his love and affection on the younger daughter, Seijo, who grew up into a very beautiful girl.

Chokan also had a nephew, Ochu, a nice boy of a of about the same age as Seijo. The two used to play together, they looked charming like dolls. Chokan once told them half-jokingly, 'It would be good if you got married later on.' When the two children heard this, they took him seriously. In their hearts they felt from then on that sometime in the future they would get married. As they grew up, so their love for each other also deepened. Seijo was an extremely beautiful young woman, and when she was old enough to get married, dozens of suitors asked Chokan for her hand. Chokan, who had long forgotten what he had said in jest to the children, chose as her husband the son of a statesman who clearly had a great future ahead of him.

In China at that time, it was unthinkable that a child would not conform to the wishes of its parents; but Seijo was in despair; and Ochu was so distraught at the prospect of her having to marry somebody else that he could not bear to even see her again, and left by ship up the Yangtze.

Sailing up the river, further and further from home, through the mist one evening, he heard a voice calling him from the bank. When he looked, he saw that it was Seijo. The two were delighted to be together again. They went right up the river and settled there, got married and had two children. But some five years later, Seijo began to wonder how her parents were and what was happening at home. Overwhelmed by homesickness, she discussed it with Ochu who also began to feel homesick. So they decided to return. They made their journey by boat down the river. At Seijo's home town, Ochu left Seijo and the children on the boat, while he went to talk to her father, Chokan, to explain and apologise.

On hearing this, Chokan was dumb-founded. 'I don't know what you're talking about. Seijo is inside, sleeping.' Now it was Ochu's turn to be struck dumb, and all he could say was, 'No, that can't be so. Seijo has been with me these past five years.' Chokan insisted, 'From the time you left here, Seijo has been sick in bed and not spoken a word; she has been here all the time.'

Chokan asked Ochu to fetch Seijo from the boat and he himself went inside to talk to the Seijo in the sickroom. But when the sick Seijo, who had been in the house, met the Seijo from the boat, Seijo became one.

This is a famous story that all the monks of the time would certainly have known. There is the Seijo of the flesh, the bodily Seijo who married Ochu, and gave birth to his children; and there is the Seijo who no longer said anything, in bed at the house of her parents. Which then is the true Seijo? This is the koan that Goso threw at the monks.

Of course, this problem is not really concerned with Seijo. It occurs to us every day. While doing zazen, our heart is somewhere else. At home, while talking to spouse or children, our soul is apart. While working at our job here, our heart is there in the south of France on holiday. An ideal self, and a real self; a self that is working and struggling, and a self that in thought lives in another dimension. Though our bodies grow older, our feelings cling to youth.

Once you start putting things into these terms, there are an endless number of examples. Which of them is really the true you? Look, for example, at your photograph album. Your face, that same face, appears in a variety of different aspects – many different faces. Which of them is the real you? Your photograph?

From morning to night, you have a serious face, or a smiling face, and sometimes you cry. Which of these is your face? What we are thinking in our hearts is changing instant by instant.

Mumon's Comment: If you can know what is the real you, from the time you are an infant until you are an old man or woman, or from the time when you are alive and the time when you are dead, it is like a hermit crab who moves from one shell to another, and then from that shell to another. Or it is like somebody who is on a pleasant journey, a happy traveller, who moves from one hotel to another. Can you live thus freely, in an untrammelled way?

Rinzai said very clearly that you can be free anywhere. Mumon then continues: If, however, you cannot see this truth, at least do not rush around trying to take in anything and everything. Instead of looking outside, trying to grasp and pull in things from outside, look inside and exert yourself to gain insight there. If you don't do that but continue to live in a vague, indifferent way, quite suddenly you will be confronted with the prospect of death.

The text says, 'Suddenly earth, water, fire and air fall apart.' In early Indian thought, these four elements were seen as the components of the universe and of life; this falling apart is death. Mumon then is saying that if you die without understanding, you will be like a crab in boiling water, its limbs moving around helplessly. Thus Mumon implies, 'If so, then don't turn around and complain, "Why didn't you warn me?"'

The Verse: 'Among the changing clouds the moon is ever the same' – but is it really the same? And the next line, 'Valley and mountain are different from each other' – but are they really different? For Mumon, clouds and the moon, the valley, the mountain, there is no difference or distinction. For him, the clouds, the moon in the sky, the mountains and valleys on earth, all are *fu-ni* – not two; and he takes them in as not two, just as they are. Therefore he is able to say in the last line, 'How joyous, how wonderful!' This 'joyous, wonderful' is Mumon's state of being. And your state? You and I – are we one, or are we two? Your heart and your body – are they one, or are they two? The heart that is striving in zazen, and the heart that longs to lie down and rest in a bed – are they one, or are they two? The living you, now, and the you that will one day die – are these the same, or are they different? The you that is walking in the woods and fields, and the world or the scenery around you – are these the same, or different?

CASE 36 • ON THE ROAD, MEETING A MAN OF THE WAY

THE CASE

Goso said, 'When you meet a Man of the Way, greet him neither with words nor with silence. Say, how will you greet him?'

MUMON'S COMMENT

If you can respond with easy familiarity, you deserve unstinted praise. If you cannot, be heedful about everything that meets your eye.

THE VERSE

路逢達道人
不將語默對
攔腮劈面拳
直下會便會

When you meet a man of the Way,
Do not greet him with words nor be silent.
Let fly at his jaw and split his face open
Grasp it right now, grasp it at once.

SOKO ROSHI'S COMMENTS

This koan is also about Master Goso Hoen. Addressing his monks, he said, 'When you meet a man of the Way' – that is one who has realised the Way, who is enlightened – 'greet him neither with words nor with silence. Say, how then will you greet him?'

Goso Hoen is not the first to raise this question, it goes back to Master Kyogen. But for us this is of no significance. If, looking at a rose, you think, 'Well, it has bloomed the year before, and the year before that,' and if you then let that influence how you see the rose now, you would fail to take in its beauty. The fact that a rose is blooming now, as it bloomed in past years, should have no influence on its beauty before your eyes now. What is wonderful is that it is blooming now, and that you are looking at it.

Thus in Kyogen's and again in Goso's use of the phrase, 'Man of the Way' takes on a new power. This Man of the Way, who has realised the Way, is one who does not veer either to the left or to the right, but goes straight on, he has grasped the reality of not-two. As that he is a man of the Middle Way who has transcended the opposites. If on meeting such a man, you reply verbally, the words veer towards the Relative. But if you keep mum and hold that silence, that is the Absolute; and then, rather than veering to the Relative, you now cling to the Absolute. So, how does a man of the Middle Way, of not-two, keep balance?

Goso raised this koan as a challenge to confound people and prevent them from mere intellectual understanding. So what he was trying to do for those listening to him was to stir up doubt about their aspiration and vocation, make them examine why they had taken the robe and tonsure and were doing zazen. This doubt would then lead them to deeper insight, and to the confidence that comes with such insight.

Whether or not we do zazen and/or sanzen, we cannot ward off old age and death. However, zazen is important for testing and checking our lives. By its means, a way will emerge along which we can live our lives with a sense of peace and confidence.

Although this points out the purpose of Goso's Koan, we must not take it abstractly, but should confront this koan directly as the reality of our daily life. So when Goso asks about meeting a 'Man of the Way', where in the course of our daily lives is that Way? It is the Way of our life. And who is this man? At times we encounter people we regard as truly superior, as great individuals. In the Zen school it is said that the first step in practice is to meet a good teacher. Meeting such a one is, indeed, great good fortune. On meeting them, we cannot but feel reverence, love, and the wish to maintain and cherish the relationship.

The longer this relationship continues, and the further it is cultivated and you invest yourself in it, the more it is likely that a feeling arises of not understanding them or not knowing how to maintain the relationship. In front of the teacher you become tense, hesitate to say anything for fear of making a fool of yourself. You try to respond in a creditable manner, and the more you try, the more your body and words stiffen and you lose your freedom. Then, in such circumstances, how do you respond?

Many youngsters come to Daishu-in to train for varying periods, and they invariably get into that state. Desperately trying not to make a mistake, they cannot speak freely or act naturally, and so they make a mess of what normally they would do without difficulty. They cannot help themselves and always are tense and hesitating. The same also applies to Zen trainees everywhere. But this stiffness differs from the respect and veneration one feels for God or Buddha; it is caused by the fear of making a mistake and is inevitable when hesitating between veering to the right or to the left. So when Goso advises, 'Greet him neither with words nor silence,' what he means is, 'Do not hesitate.'

Of the hundreds of young people who have stayed in my temple, a young woman came out with something quite wonderful. She had become engaged just before entering Daishu-in, and had agreed with her fiancé not to contact him, so as to devote herself for one month just to her practice – and she really did so wholeheartedly! Taking leave she told me, 'I am deeply grateful. In all my life I have never had a whole month in which I could live with such a sense of ease and be so relaxed. Here I knew that if I made a mistake, you, Roshi, would correct me, and so could relax completely and grow and flourish here.' She is married and lives a full life. Now, did she respond to me with words, or did she respond to me with silence?

Perhaps you now can see that the problem is not about responding with words or with silence, but whether, on meeting a Man of the Way, you don a suit of armour and defend yourself, careful not to make mistakes – or whether you let go of everything and leave yourself open, completely naked.

Let us go still further. This Man of the Way is not only a roshi or one who has awakened to satori. Within our consciousness, even within our conceptualising, however much we may stray, everything is this enlightened one – the trees, the grass, flowers, the clouds in the sky, water in a stream, all are this Man of the Way. Then on meeting him, wherever the encounter, how do we customarily respond to him? Do we take off our armour and become open and naked? It seems that all great teachers of the past were thus naked, and so in response to a given situation they were as pliant and natural as a baby. They never assumed any kind of pose, gave themselves no airs, and never treated others with arrogance.

Having expounded on this koan in great detail, it should now be very clear. But these are only words, and the real question is whether we can realise it ourselves in our daily lives, responding to whoever or whatever, without any kind of armour, cover-up or pose, and doing so with our naked heart, without thinking moment to moment, without being swayed by gain or loss, without attempting to change the relationships we are in. The real test is whether we can actually and concretely act like this.

A monk asked Master Seppo, 'Goso says, "When you meet a Man of the Way, greet him with neither words nor silence." How then should I greet him?' Seppo said, 'Have a cup of tea.' The monk was deflated. On hearing this simple, direct response, 'Have a cup of tea,' the armour he had been wearing fell off; and with it the weight he had carried on his shoulders. Thus the koan that until then had been but a concept in his head, was resolved and became a simple act of everyday life.

And now a suggestion for practice. When sitting zazen, do not try to attain anything, neither hoping to understand something, nor expecting to produce a you that is better than you are at the moment. All you need do is just sit on a cushion or chair, and be at ease. Let go of every kind of pose, of every ornament. It is extremely difficult not to wear self-decorations or maintain poses; but if you simply sit on the cushion, without thought, simply sit there at peace, then how easy it all is! Just sitting there with a naked heart, and then on getting up from zazen, confronting what meets you with that naked heart. Your life will change; and your problems will change of themselves, without any need for you to try to change them.

Mumon's Comment: If you can respond with easy familiarity, that is indeed admirable, and your daily life will be full and complete. If you cannot respond, then every day carefully confront everything you meet, in samadhi.

This is what Mumon actually means. 'Samadhi' implies 'being one with'. On meeting a tree, you are one with the tree; on meeting a cloud, one with the cloud. This 'becoming and being one with' happens when you dissolve and the cloud comes into you. Such dissolving is tantamount to being empty, is having become naked and opening up, so that the cloud can come in and pervade. With however much concentration you look at a tree, if there is even the tiniest shred of self-consciousness, of interpreting, 'the tree is laughing' or 'the tree is suffering,' then this is not samadhi. Rather than trying to understand the other, just allow it to enter. We are all born with this power to open up. In these small, frail bodies of ours, we have the power to take in the whole universe. So, I suggest you make yourselves completely at ease, allow yourselves to become naked.

Contrarily, although you may attempt to fashion a coat of armour from your experience and knowledge, or strike a pose with all your resources, this will not amount to even the tiniest fraction of your potential. If you still doubt that you have the ability to take in the universe, just look! Our eyes are only about three centimetres wide, yet a vast scenery – mountains, sea and sky – pours into this small space. How then should the whole universe not easily enter an empty and receptive heart?

The Verse: The rose is beautiful each time it blooms. If somebody cannot become naked and take in its beauty as it is, then, Mumon says, he will slap his face and box his ears. If you understand it, then understand it right now.

CASE 37 · THE OAK TREE IN THE FRONT GARDEN

THE CASE

A monk asked Joshu, 'What is the meaning of the Patriarch's coming from the West?' Joshu said, 'The oak tree in the front garden.'

MUMON'S COMMENT

Looking at Joshu's answer with easy familiarity, there is no Shakyamuni in the past, no Maitreya to come.

THE VERSE

言無展事
語不投機
承言者喪
滯句者迷

Words do not stand for things,
Speech does not set the energy going;
The one who clings to words is lost,
One who clings to phrases goes astray.

SOKO ROSHI'S COMMENTS

Joshu has already appeared in previous koans. He was one of the great Chinese Masters of the golden age of Chinese Zen, during the late Tang dynasty (9th century). According to the surviving records, Joshu's Dharma lineage did not continue and it might thus seem that his influence was but slight. But although his lineage didn't continue, the koans that are recorded in our collection – the first and this Case

37 – are great and powerful expressions of Zen. They have been treasured through the generations and have assured Joshu's reputation as one of the great Masters.

Indeed, for Mumon, the compiler of the *Mumonkan*, satori opened with his insight into Joshu's Mu-Koan. Today's Zen trainees, too, especially in Japan, have almost all worked on the Mu-Koan. My own first religious insight also opened while working on the Mu-Koan. And so, although Joshu's lineage may not have continued, it may be said that he, nevertheless, has many thousands of disciples today.

Now, a monk came to Joshu and asked, 'What is the meaning of the Patriarch's coming from the West?' Although his question referred to Bodhidharma's coming from the West, on another level, however, the question, 'What is the meaning of the Patriarch's coming from the West?' had taken on the sense of 'What is the meaning of Zen?' or 'What is the True Nature?'

This particular question had often been asked before. In the koan of Case 30 a monk asks Master Daibai the meaning of the Patriarch's coming from the West. And Daibai's response indicated, 'There is none.' And when Master Rinzai was asked the same question, he said, 'If there were a meaning to Bodhidharma's coming from the West, Bodhidharma could not even save himself, still less others.'

We tend to look for a meaning, and attach a meaning to our actions; likewise, we assume a meaning in the activities of others. But in our limited understanding we have to grasp that there can be a freedom to act which transcends our efforts to attach meaning to things. So the monks who asked this question, whether of Daibai or Rinzai, were able to grasp the workings of emptiness, of the empty heart, and to attach a meaning to this. This was not worthless; but in most cases the monks who asked this question only understood the answers intellectually. In your own case, if you have some understanding of the workings of the empty heart (*mushin no hataraki* in Japanese), does this have any significance for you unless you actually put it into practice in your daily life? Likewise, however much the monks thought they had grasped, for example, Daibai's response of there being no meaning to the Patriarch's coming from the West, if they could not resolve the problem for themselves, this question was repeated again and again.

In this way, the question was eventually asked of Joshu whose response was tremendous and powerful, and up-turned everything. Throughout all his teaching life, from the age of eighty to a hundred and twenty, Joshu was the incumbent of the Kannon temple, known as the 'Oak Tree Temple,' because of the many oak trees around it. So, when Joshu was asked the meaning of the Patriarch's coming from the West, he simply looked at the oak trees outside and responded, 'The oak tree in the garden.'

If, on hearing this answer, you are hit by this tremendously powerful response and react to it directly and strongly, then you can get up from your cushion and need no more zazen. But, while you have the slightest sliver of doubt, and begin to wonder why Joshu said this, you need to continue zazen until your bones crack.

Here this koan is presented tersely, in a simple form, but in *The Recorded Sayings of Master Joshu*, it is told in a longer version. According to that, the monk was disappointed with this answer: he thought he had asked a very personal question, a problem from the depths of his heart, the question about satori, and it seemed to him that Joshu was talking about externals. So he said to Joshu, 'Do not talk about the external environment, or about objects.' But Joshu calmly replied, 'I am not talking to you about externals.' The monk then repeated, 'What is the meaning of the Patriarch's coming from the West?' Joshu answered him steadily, 'The oak tree in the front garden.'

When we are in love, we hold hands, hug and kiss. However, the love or the affection that can be expressed in these ways is still a very small love. Joshu did not take the monk's hand, did not hug or kiss him: but in his response, 'The oak tree in the front garden,' Joshu expressed the highest kind of love.

To help the understanding of this, some further exposition may be useful. Love is to completely realise the unity of oneself and other. In one sense this is all that can be said, but more can be added to make it explicit. Thus, it is taught, 'God is love,' and in Buddhism we talk of the Great Compassion of the Buddha. The love of God, the Compassion of the Buddha is not something that is put on like face-powder. Even if separated, one is still united. Whatever happens, we cannot be parted because originally and fundamentally we are one. That itself is the highest form of love.

So the monk who asked Joshu believed that things were separate, and that somehow they could or should be brought together, and did not understand how the oak tree in the garden could be identified with himself. Everybody can understand with their heads, abstractly, intellectually, that all things can be one with oneself.

But while thus intellectually understanding, we firmly believe that it is by means of our will, by sheer will-power, that we can achieve this unity. Those so convinced are inevitably split in two. But for Joshu, Buddha, enlightenment, the tree – these were not separate. The heart within himself and the oak tree were not two, and so he needed no effort to make them one. Masters Daibai and Rinzai, likewise, when they were asked, 'What is the meaning of the Patriarch's coming from the West?' could answer, 'There is no meaning.' Their reply arose from the same understanding as Joshu's.

However explicitly this may be expounded, we continue to live lives in which we plan, try to arrange things and to overcome duality.

We have a habit of contrasting things, as well as wanting to plan everything, and we need to have the itch to plan taken out of us. This koan of Joshu possesses the power to draw it out.

The founder of Myoshin-ji, Kanzan Egen (14th century), was a great Zen master. In *The Inexhaustible Lamp* he is reported to have said, with reference to this koan of Joshu, that it was the work of a great robber. There are no collected sayings of Kanzan, nothing that survived him. About three hundred years after Kanzan, the Chinese Master Ingen came to Japan. When visiting Myoshin-ji, he was surprised to learn that no recorded sayings of their founder existed; the lack of such a collection might be misinterpreted as there being no tradition preserved. So Ingen wondered about the eminence of Kanzan and mentioned it to one of the Myoshin-ji monks. The monk told him, 'Although there are no collected sayings, we have a tradition that Kanzan called Joshu's koan about the Patriarch's Coming from the West the work of a great robber.' Ingen was greatly impressed, went to Kanzan's grave, bowed reverently and avowed that this one sentence of Kanzan's was equal to a hundred collected sayings.

This anecdote cannot really be understood by someone, who has not had everything stolen by Joshu's response. Kanzan and Ingen both had everything that they possessed stolen by Joshu's koan. And as for you, are you not hoping to steal something, from this book, or from me? Do you not think that you may be able to pick up what is offered here and keep it as a treasure? Is it not the case that, although you already carry pounds and pounds of treasures on your shoulders, that you are hoping to still add to them? Would it not be better if, on reading this, all you have would be stolen from you?

Mumon's Comment: Mumon says that if you can really grasp the essence of what Joshu is saying, then for you Shakyamuni, the

Buddha of the past, and the future Buddha, Maitreya, will disappear. Probably the notion that you yourself are somehow in between Buddha Shakyamuni in the past and Maitreya in the future – this self will disappear. What Mumon is saying is that then a self is realised that is as infinite as space and time; in other words, seeing into Joshu's koan is having everything stolen, taken away by this insight.

As human beings we are frequently lonely or sad, and we long to be loved by others. Please think and realise the spiritual state of Joshu's awareness of this 'Oak Tree in the Garden'. Even if you try to cut yourself off from the sky, the grass, the trees, the clouds, you cannot do so; all of them are part and parcel of you. When you realise this, you are empty. The more we stuff ourselves with things, and the more we consequently know, the sadder and lonelier we become.

The Verse: This verse is not really Mumon's. It goes back to Master Tozan, who appears in Koan 15. Here it is used by Mumon. Reality, truth, cannot be expressed by words. In case of a fire alarm, do your lips burn when you hear the shout 'Fire'? You cannot convey the reality of fire or burning lips in words. And however much you talk about it and try to explain it, you just cannot convey to another the reality of insight. And so to be pulled by words or to be bound by sentences leads only to loss of insight and to confusion. This is what Mumon indicates in his verse.

However, one of Joshu's disciples had realised this in practice. This was Kakuteshi, famous also for his encounter with Master Hogen. Hogen asked Kakuteshi, 'I understand that your Master Joshu made the koan of the Oak Tree?' Kakuteshi said, 'My Master made no such thing. Do not make fun of him, do not debase him.' Hogen praised Kakuteshi, saying, 'The lion cub has its own great roar.'

So please do not take up or collect bits and pieces from your reading, but make sure that everything is taken away from you and that from within yourself you can let out this great roar of your own, your own words from your own heart. Decisively express, and speak in your own words, within which there are no expressions like 'Zen' or 'satori' or 'emptiness', and always be aware of the unity of yourself and all that is.

CASE 38 • A BUFFALO PASSING THROUGH A WINDOW

Goso said, 'For example, it is like a buffalo passing through a window. Head, horns and the four legs have gone past – why cannot his tail pass?'

If you can get this at one glance of your single eye and can give one turning word, you can requite the Four Obligations above and assist the Three Realms (of existence) below. If you cannot yet grasp it, go on whole-heartedly pondering that tail and surely you will get it!

過去墮抗塹
回來却被壞
者些尾巴子
直是甚奇怪

If it passes, it will fall off into a ditch,
And if it turns back, it will he destroyed.
This waggly wisp of a tail,
How magnificent, how magnificent!

There are no prerequisites for starting Zen training. No knowledge of the historical background of Buddhism or Zen is needed, no reverence for any particular God or Buddha. Once started, you quickly realise that the forms of practice can be accepted and used by everybody. Probably, on reading these koans, you come across the great Patriarchs of Zen, and they seem to be unique. Zen trainees in Japan, as well as in the West, are attracted by such individuality. Yet this can also be a source of confusion and misunderstanding, and can lead us astray.

Just because there are no prerequisites, those who have been in training for a while may either try to assert their egoity, or they may become entrapped in the forms of Zen practice. There are still others who, attracted by the strong personalities of the great Zen Patriarchs, think that it is sufficient to copy them. And still others may misread such Zen sayings as 'No reliance on words and letters' as the essence of Zen, and become very argumentative about Zen.

Reflecting on your own training, should you find any of these tendencies in yourself, then you should recognise them as mistakes that are taking you away from true Zen practice. Once more, in Zen training there is no set form. What in your practice you may see as form, or forms, is merely a convenient means of correcting mistaken and misleading tendencies in your practice.

From the time we come into this world, we co-exist with other beings and things. There are men and women; some things are big, others are small; we are brought up to be aware of ourselves as different from others, and in this way we come to know ourselves and others. From this basic assumption we then discriminate between self and other, and make value judgements of better or worse which then become habitual.

Yet this phenomenal world in which we live is constantly changing; it is a limited world, not an absolute one. Unless and until we accept this, when faced with some great change or tragedy, we suffer from a sense of loss or completely disintegrate. Death exemplifies the ultimate state of being locked into such misunderstanding; we just cannot think except in terms of the polarity of life and death.

And yet, although we may lose contact with it or even forget it, in this universe in which we live, there is something that is absolute and unchanging. The nature of religion may be defined in various, even differing ways, but the first step into a religious perception is to shift the direction of our gaze from the finite world around to a world of infinite reality. Thus religion does not prescribe a person's way of life, or their character; rather, it is the realisation that in beholding the infinite world one can live easily, freely and comfortably in this our finite world.

Joshu's Mu-Koan serves as a powerful lever or catalyst to transform our vision from the everyday world of phenomena to this other world of infinite reality. In these commentaries, many koans and diverse examples are presented, but looking at Joshu's 'Mu', however well it is understood with our intellect, it is and remains quite useless to us until it is realised that while living in this phenomenal world, we are yet linked to a world of infinite reality. Until the full realisation of this dawns, the Mu-Koan does not answer and remains useless.

As with the previous Koan of the Oak Tree, for those who perceive only a world of phenomena and of distinctions, the oak tree will always remain separate. Trying intellectually, without actual experience, to establish union between yourself and the oak tree, is merely creating more delusion for yourself. And when realising the infinite reality of all things, the connection comes about by itself.

Since this may seem difficult to apply to the koan, a hint or example may bring things into focus. Master Gudo, a Japanese Zen master, was in charge of temples in both Kyoto and Edo (Tokyo), and frequently had to travel between the two cities. Long Jaw, a famous highwayman so named because of his long chin, observing the frequent journeyings of Gudo, thought of robbing him. So one evening when Gudo put up at an inn for the night, Long Jaw did likewise. During the night, when he judged Gudo asleep, he stole into his room. But he saw no Gudo, only a huge oak. Startled and frightened, he hastily left, closing the door behind him. Shortly afterwards he heard the door, and saw Gudo come out to go to the toilet. Long Jaw was overcome by awe as he realised that Gudo had been in the room all the time! All notion of stealing from such a man vanished; rather, he went to Gudo, confessed all his sins and crimes and asked him to take him as his disciple.

He trained with utmost determination and when dying said to his own disciples, 'Look, here within this body is the true Long Jaw,' thus showing that in addition to the physical form that was disintegrating, there was a true Long Jaw who would continue to live. But do not think of this true Long Jaw in terms of a soul. He did not assert that 'within this body is the spirit of Long Jaw'; what he meant was that within each of us is a true self, a true Long Jaw within each of us.

The stress here is not on Long Jaw, but on Master Gudo sitting in his room as an oak tree. He was known in Japan as the greatest master of his day. Even though no longer a monk in training, and even while travelling, he continued koan practice. The point here is that he did not 'think' about a koan, but rather he himself faded out and the koan remained. Or expressed simply, his heart was always empty and open, and into this heart then entered koans, men, women, mountains, all kinds of different phenomena while he remained in this infinite and timeless world. Experiencing this infinite realm does not then mean ignoring the phenomenal world around us. One who is captivated by the phenomenal world, but who on turning his eyes towards the infinite world then rejects the phenomena of ordinary life, such a one cannot truly enter the infinite realm. Thus the infinite, timeless realm and the finite, everyday world of phenomena, are like the palm and back of the hand. Goso Hoen's koan is to help us to deepen our understanding of this.

Out of the more than 1,700 koans, the great Japanese Zen master, Hakuin, selected seven or eight that were regarded as being particularly difficult, and this Buffalo Passing the Window is one of them. 'Difficult' or 'easy' are not qualities inherent in the koan, but lie rather in the person who is working on it. So please understand this koan as not being intrinsically difficult, but as particularly appropriate for the finer polishing and deepening of experience.

With regards to koans in general, when reading them together with their commentaries, one after the other, it becomes increasingly difficult to take them all in. In a training monastery, too, many monks doze during teisho, and those who sit up alert and respond to every sentence, have already seen into that particular koan or several koans. These then delight in listening, and seeing how freely the insight of the master presents the koan. Those who have not yet resolved Joshu's 'Mu' Koan and still grapple with the problems of duality and of the phenomenal world around them, however much they may try to intellectually grasp such expositions, for them even the most wonderful presentation is just so much hot air and only adds to their confusion. In that case, it is better to close eyes and ears and not let any more garbage in.

Now to the koan itself. Reading the text, it is difficult to understand. This difficulty lies not in an inadequate English translation; the text of the original also lends itself to misinterpretation. On reading the case, it may be taken that the buffalo is walking past the window; however, the true meaning is that the buffalo is going through a narrow window, from inside out. According to that, on Goso's behalf, this commentary is offered.

But first, the Goso of our koan here must not be mistaken for the Fifth Patriarch (also Goso), but is Goso Hoen, a famous master who lived several centuries later in the Song dynasty and takes his name from the same Mount Goso. Mumon must have admired this Goso because of the forty-eight koans which make up his collection, four are Master Goso's.

So, one day Goso said to his monks, 'A buffalo is stabled in a dark barn. There is just one tiny window, and even that is barred. Then out of this dark shed, through this very narrow, barred window, out into the world of light, come the horns and the head of the buffalo, and then his body. All can be perfectly seen, horns, hooves, even the expression on the buffalo's face, his colour, and the markings on his body. The whole of him emerges into the light, only the tip of his tail is stuck in the darkness of the shed. This tip of the tail always remains in darkness!'

On Goso's behalf, I ask you, what on earth is Goso's meaning in telling this story? Horns, head, body, legs and all come out into the light, only the tassel at the end of the tail remains in the darkness of the shed. Somebody of quick intellect but without any Zen training, might 'explain' it thus. 'The narrow, barred window must be the training. Horns and head that come through must be one's own ego with its ingrained habits. The four legs then must stand for the four desires and corresponding resentments, those things that we resent not having but desperately want, think beautiful and feel we cannot do without. All these, all the attachments that we have, can be removed by training; but the final grain of attachment that we have to self, that cannot be removed, and that surely must be the tip of the tail that remains in the dark!'

This hypothetical 'explanation' serves as an example of a hopeless misunderstanding of this koan. One who reasons along such lines rather than pondering the koan, needs to undertake work on Joshu's Mu Koan. This koan has nothing to do with limited human attachments or concerns. So first of all, do we think that there are desires and attachments that have to be got rid of? No! What needs to be changed is our own attachment to the phenomenal world. The shape of the bull that comes out through the window into the light is very clear. Only the tiny tip of the tail remains behind, is invisible in the dark. And there it remains, without any blemish at all, a whole buffalo!

Long before Goso, Rinzai remarked, 'There is one who is eternally on the way, yet has never left home – and another who has left home, yet is not on the way.' Ponder this 'being at home' in terms of your everyday life. When alone and at ease in your home, do you then need to discriminate? If you do not need to compare, there is neither inferiority nor superiority – you are truly at ease. And however busy we may be in our daily lives, at the root of things there is a deeper level where this ease always prevails. Think of yourself as on a journey; you may become ill on the way or at your destination, and various problems may arise. What makes your travels enjoyable is a home to which you can return; if you had no home to return to, would the joy of travelling not rather turn into a sense of unease? Thus those who within even the phenomenal world of change, duality and contrast, find, at a deeper level, this infinite realm, they experience a very different flavour to life. That is what Rinzai meant by being at home while on the road, or in the midst of the city.

For Christians, in happiness or unhappiness, if they have faith and so feel constantly enfolded in the love of God, would they then not feel this to be a wonderful life? The formulation is different, but Rinzai's 'being at home in the midst of the city' comes from the same spiritual state. However, Rinzai's insight goes still deeper: not being at home, not being in the market place, means neither to be taken in by the infinite, nor to be captivated by the phenomenal. So you believe in the love or compassion of God, but are not captivated by that love. Though expressed somewhat starkly, this nonetheless presents the essence of Zen.

Mumon's Comment: A turning word means an expression that brings about a 'turning' from lack of insight to true insight. If with a single glance or with a turning word you can indicate your own full understanding, you are requiting all your obligations, and at the same time you will be of assistance to others; in short, you can live a life without regret. If, however, you cannot make a direct and clear response to Goso's question, then, he says, continue to work constantly on that tip of the tail that could not go through the narrow window.

To add my own comment to this, if you came to me for sanzen and although your response concerning the tail was a good one, I still would not let you off the hook there, but would question back immediately, 'O.K., the tail is all right. But is that buffalo male or female? What does it eat? Where does it live? How old is it?' If you hesitated in your response to any one of these questions, then as a parting gift, I would probably give you some twenty blows with my stick; for Goso is not simply telling tales about buffaloes – he is talking about the reality of things.

The Verse: Paraphrasing the verse: If not only the horns, head, legs and body pass, but the tail too, then you will fall into a ditch! Do you understand? For everything, even the tail, to go through the window, is for everything to enter into and be the phenomenal world; this means to see nothing but the phenomenal world of distinction and so to fall into the hole of dissatisfaction.

But if, contrariwise, afraid of thus falling, you pull back horns, head and body into the dark shed and do not go through the window at all, that is to deny the phenomenal world; and to focus only on the world of the infinite, holding that it alone is important, that is falling into a kind of nihilism.

So this tiny tail, then, what a big problem it is! And yet, at the same time, how very wonderful it is!

Too much has been said already. Enough!

CASE 39 · UMMON AND A SLIP OF THE TONGUE

THE CASE
A monk asked Ummon, 'A brilliant light irradiates the universe....', but Ummon interrupted him before he had finished the first line and said, 'Are these not the words of Setsu Shusai?' 'Yes,' said the monk. Ummon said, 'You are off the mark!' Afterwards Shishin raised this matter and asked, 'Tell me, how did the monk make a slip of the tongue?'

MUMON'S COMMENT
If you can grasp Ummon's unapproachable function, and where the monk was off the mark, you are in a position to be teacher of men and heavenly beings; if you are not yet clear about it, you have not even saved yourself.

THE VERSE
急流垂釣
貪餌者著
口縫纔開
性命喪却

Angling in a swift river,
Greedy for bait, he is caught!
You have but to open your mouth
And have lost your life!

SOKO ROSHI'S COMMENTS
Zen has no set form, but this does not mean we can do what we like

and behave quite arbitrarily. There is a world of difference between the intellectual understanding of Zen as having no set form, and actual insight into the underlying reality that Zen has no form.

Zen practice is often described as very severe, not because the practice is harsh, not because of the form of practice, but because it demands the actualisation, our own full realisation of the underlying reality.

One day a monk came to see me. He was dressed in a Western suit, wearing a French beret. Before I had time to open my mouth, he already began defending himself, 'Zen is a teaching that has no form, so it is quite all right to wear suit and beret.' I said, 'That is perfectly true. Zen has no set form. Just that is why I wear traditional robes rather than Western clothes.' Do you understand? That is freedom! And so in just a few words the spiritual state is clearly revealed. But if you grasp my saying that Zen has no form in your head only, then you are in trouble.

Although his training methods, were severe, Zen Master Sekiso Keisho had many disciples who sat zazen with such determination that they were known as the 'Grove of Withered Trees'. After Keisho had died, the monks expected the head monk, Shuso, to be the successor. However, one monk, Kyuho Doken, objected strongly. In front of the whole community he asserted that Shuso did not have genuine satori. But the head monk said that to show he had inherited the true transmission, he would light an incense stick and before the smoke had disappeared, would follow his master in death; he further said that in his zazen, life and death would be completely free. Truly, sitting in full zazen posture, he passed away before the smoke of the incense had disappeared. At this Kyuho Doken, who had asserted that he had no insight, tapped him on the shoulder, 'Certainly you can die, but you still do not have satori.'

You smile at this, but when I first read this, a cold shiver crept up my back: here, a live human being had thrown down his very life! We need to look at the feelings of such a person, recognise one ready to commit himself in such a way. He was faithful to the Dharma, but not according to ordinary human feelings. Anyway, Kyuho Doken became the new master and his reputation spread all over.

It is very easy to enter Zen practice; there is nothing that binds us. But at the same time, and for this very reason, we must remember that just because it is so easy to enter, it demands that we maintain a severity towards ourselves and our practice. It is of no use to say, 'I have done my best!' What matters is the resulting spiritual state.

A young government official, Chosetsu Shusai, came to Master Sekiso Keisho asking to be taken on as a disciple. 'Shusai' was the title for someone who had passed the old Chinese state examination system and could hold rank in the civil service. This Shusai was highly intelligent, and when Keisho asked him his name, he answered, 'My family name is Cho, and my personal name is Setsu.' Now, this contains a pun, for the Chinese character *setsu* suggests lack of skill, (the *setsu* in Suzuki Daisetsu's name is the same character) and for the Chinese, if something is done very skilfully, it reaches a transcendent point where it seems unskilful. A Chinese proverb says that a really brilliant man often seems like a fool. In the extreme, skilful and unskilful, clever and foolish, all pairs of opposites basically disappear.

Master Sekiso now retorted, 'Although we make great efforts, we still fail to become skilful; how come that you have already become unskilful?' With this question, Sekiso transcended the opposition of skilful and unskilful; and at that instant Chosetsu Shusai likewise transcended it. To show Master Sekiso this new state of understanding, he presented his spiritual insight in a verse:

'A brilliant light irradiates the universe containing worlds as
    innumerable as the sands of the Ganges.

In this our world of the senses, we rate people as ignorant
    or wise,

Yet all sentient beings are within the one circle of this light
    which is our home.

If no thought arises, all truth is revealed; but attachments,
    however tiny, obscure truth like clouds the sun, and so
    sight of it is lost.

Trying to cut off the attachments only increases the disease;

And trying to become one with truth is mistaken.

Living in this world, smooth response to its circumstances,
    encounters no obstruction.

Talking about Nirvana or life and death from such a spiritual
    state is like talking about seeing flowers in an empty sky!'

This verse of Chosetsu Shusai became well known. One day a
monk came to Master Ummon and started quoting, 'A brilliant light
irradiates the universe.....' But before he had finished even the first
line, Ummon, showing his wonderful activity as a Master, interrupted
him, 'Isn't that Chosetsu's verse?' The monk, foiled in his intention
to ask Ummon about Shusai's poem, stammered, 'Yes.' Ummon
again immediately retorted, 'You're off the mark.' In this Ummon
was perhaps a bit too kind. He should have taken up a thick stick
and hit the monk with it!

Later, Master Shishin, also taking up this encounter, used to
ask (his monks), 'Where was it that the monk missed the mark?'
Shishin was a great Master, well known for his quick mind and skill
in dialogue. While still in training, he was always ready to argue and
propound his views, on Buddhism, on Zen or anything. His teacher,
Master Maedo, worried about this tendency and one day when he again

happened to be in the heat of one of his disputes, Maedo suddenly rounded on him, 'Shut up! However skilful you may argue, it does not fill a hungry belly.' Shishin bowed, 'Master, I know you are right, but however hard I try, I cannot stop myself grasping at concepts.'

Shishin showed that he was aware of this weakness and had tried to overcome it; but as in the proverb, 'Swords and arrows are broken,' he felt that though he had done his utmost, he was still stuck, and now asked how he could come to peace of heart. Master Maedo sternly told him, 'Then die! Just kill off all knowledge and experience you have accumulated from birth.' On hearing this, Shishin was panic-stricken and rushed out. Why? He knew his own weaknesses and shortcomings; and when he heard them pointed out aloud, he could not bear it. It did, however, result in his giving himself into the practice with total dedication and to thus being able to eliminate his ingrained head-only attitude.

When at last genuine insight opened, he changed his name to Shishin. The *shi* of Shishin means death, and the following *shin* stands for heart, indicating a heart that has been reborn in death. Thus the Shishin, who was highly gifted but also polemical and argumentative, had entered into a much deeper insight and directly saw into Ummon's comment.

Suppose some of you meet me on a morning stroll. One of you says, 'Good Morning' and passes by; then the one following behind also says, 'Good Morning.' If I then ask, 'Isn't that what the one before said?' would you answer, 'Yes'? You should not, however, because you have greeted me with your own words! For when you meet me in the morning, you are not greeting me with 'Good Morning' because it is a fine morning, or copying what another had said before. And although saying, 'Good Morning' may be what you have been taught in the past, when you meet me now you are using it as your own response to express your feelings of that moment. Just as 'I love you' has already been spoken millions of times, but every time it is used, it is new and therefore has the power to transform people's lives.

Thus Ummon in challenging that monk was looking for that type of response. But instead of expressing himself in his own words all the monk could do was to quote Shusai's verse. Please ponder this, and work on it later.

Mumon's Comment: To paraphrase Mumon, if you can immediately see the peerless activity of Ummon's Zen, and see where the monk was off the mark, then you can help all beings who suffer from delusion. If not, you cannot even aid yourself.

To take it still further, neither Shishin nor Ummon ask for a logically correct answer – what is demanded is whether your own spiritual state is truly itself. If you live in your own house, yet believe it to be rented accommodation, whether trying to reduce the rent or bestirring yourself to earn sufficient money to pay for it, it is all off the mark! Yet in this world of ours, most people busily pursue just that kind of delusion; they go on working and earning from the outside in order to keep some stability in their lives. Much better is to realise that this is your home and be at ease within it.

The monk who carried this poem of Shusai's like a pack on his shoulders, also did just that – trying to raise money to pay the rent for what in fact was his own home.

The Verse: Like casting a fishing line into a very swift river, Ummon hurled a barbed question at the monk. And like a foolish fish the monk opened his mouth wide and gulped down the bait. Or, although for the short 'Yes' no more was needed than tiny movement of his lips, yet because of that he lost his life!

In a way it may be said that he lost his life because of his still immature practice. On the other hand, if able to recognise the barb in Ummon's question, then on the monk's behalf we should rejoice at the death he has gone through. However, this is not that monk's problem, but our own.

CASE 40 · ISAN'S JUG

When Isan was cook in Master Hyakujo's assembly, Hyakujo wanted to find a master for Mount Dai-i. He had the head monk call the assembly and told them that only someone of superior insight could go there. Then he put down a water jug and asked, 'Without calling it a jug, say what it is?' The head monk said, 'It cannot be called a stump.' Hyakujo asked Isan, who kicked over the jug. Hyakujo laughed, 'The head monk is not going to the mountain,' and ordered Isan to open the monastery.

MUMON'S COMMENT
Isan was whole-hearted and valiant, but he could not jump out of Hyakujo's cage. However, Isan leaned towards the difficult and away from the easy. Why do I say so? He takes off the block from his head (from the stocks) and instead puts on an iron cangue.

THE VERSE
颺下笊籬并木杓
當陽一突絶周遮
百丈重關欄不住
脚尖趯出佛如麻

Tossing away the bamboo utensils and the wooden ladle,
He immediately cuts off obstructions.
Hyakujo's heavy barrier did not stop him,
From the tip of his foot emerge Buddhas as innumerable as seeds
of hemp.

Master Isan had entered the religious life at fifteen, but in his twenty-third year placed himself under Master Hyakujo. Hyakujo at that time was already seventy-four, but continued to teach until he died at the age of ninety-four. Of all the great Zen Masters, Hyakujo is particularly important. For some generations after Bodhidharma there were no specific temples for the Zen School and his followers accordingly practised within the community of the other Buddhist institutions. Therefore Hyakujo established monasteries for his followers and organised rules for community life and practice. These are observed to this day in Japanese training monasteries and we revere Hyakujo more than any of the old patriarchs.

Hyakujo was past eighty when the monk Shiba Zuda called. This Shiba Zuda was a somewhat odd monk; he roamed all over the place observing the landscape, specialised in geomancy (the auspicious features of land and mountains) and was also expert in reading physiognomy (the reading of people's faces). Meeting Hyakujo, he told him that he had recently travelled in the south where he had come across a wonderful mountain, Dai-i, and knew at once that it would be most propitious for a large training monastery with an assembly of some fifteen hundred monks.

Hyakujo was very interested and said that he himself would go there and set up such a monastery. But Shiba Zuda objected, 'That mountain is auspicious for establishing something very rich and ample but looking at your face, I only see a poor monk: so it is not for you.'

It is heartening to hear that a poor monk yet became famous in the history of Zen Buddhism. But if you habitually rely on horoscopes, palm-reading, or looking into crystal balls, etc., you may as well give up! If you are poor, then a poor Buddha. If rich, then a rich Buddha. There is nothing to worry about.

Anyway, Hyakujo accordingly decided to send one of his senior disciples; among these, Shiba Zuda also declared Zenkaku, the head monk in Hyakujo's community, as unsuitable.

At that time Isan, who was to become co-founder of the Ikyo School of Zen, was the monastery cook. As the cook is responsible for the catering, he is always of senior rank and well advanced in practice. Food sustains the whole community in their practice and is to be handled and prepared with skill and devotion. Often also a gift from others, food must never be wasted.

When I was first put to kitchen duty, I was told the following story. A dedicated practiser of Zen Buddhism heard of a great Master living in solitude somewhere in the mountains beside a little brook. He set out to find him and as he walked up along the brook, he saw a cabbage leaf floating down. So he decided to go elsewhere because one who allowed vegetables to go to waste could not be much of a teacher. At that moment, a monk with a long stick came running along the path beside the stream, trying to fish out the leaf! The seeker realised the monk was indeed a great teacher and settled down to practice under him.

Actually at this point in his career the cook was known as Reiyu. Only after he had established a community on Dai-i-san, (Great-I-mountain), did he become known as Isan, the Master of I-san. To avoid confusion with other masters of Mount Dai-i, all known as Isan, this story refers to Isan Reiyu. Indeed, when Shiba Zuda set eyes on Isan Reiyu, he told Hyakujo, 'This is the one to establish a community on Mount Dai-i.' Hyakujo agreed. With regard to this, one might be inclined to think that Hyakujo just blindly accepted Shiba Zuda's suggestion, but not so. In Japan, we call this being a badger – someone who on the surface seems to be one thing, yet is managing things from beneath. Naturally, being the head of his community,

Hyakujo knew all his monks intimately, and no doubt had already decided to send Isan to open a monastery on this great mountain.

When the head monk, Zenkaku, heard that Hyakujo was about to send Isan Reiyu to Mount Dai-i, he complained, 'Just on the word of a geomancer and physiognomist you overturn the order of the community, and send Isan Reiyu instead of me, his senior.' This is why Hyakujo devised a test, well aware of what would happen. In that he showed his whole nature – sure of the outcome yet conceding to fair opportunities. He had the community assembled and in front of them placed a jug (literally *jimbin*, a flask or jug of the type the Bodhisattva Kannon is sometimes portrayed holding) and asked, 'Without calling it a jug, (calling it by its name), what is its true essence?'

At that time koans were not yet in use; the question arose from Hyakujo's authentic insight. 'Without calling it a jug, say, what is it?' This may seem to be a simple question, but actually it goes right to the heart of things. When you encounter this kind of situation, do not think in terms of 'cup,' or 'jug,' or 'saucer'. I am addressed Roshi, my name is Morinaga Soko; but such names and titles are merely temporary. Then what is the problem, our problem?

The wonderful activity or functioning of Hyakujo in presenting this problem is truly inspiring. The head monk, Zenkaku, was the first to respond. 'We cannot call it a jug, but we also cannot say that it is a wooden stump.' It is not much of an answer – you probably feel so, too. So Hyakujo asked Isan Reiyu, who came forward, gently toppled over the jug with the tip of his foot, and then stepped back again.

Here and now, without calling me 'Roshi' or 'Soko', but confronting the essence of me, say one word! By thus working deeper into the own essence, mere names are inadequate. The true response arises when we forget the self we are seeking. Master Dogen, the founder of Japanese Soto Zen, said that to study the Buddha's Way, the Dharma, is to study oneself; knowing oneself is forgetting oneself; forgetting oneself is allowing everything, just as it is, to enter oneself.

But be warned! If you forget what has just been said and merely focus on Isan Reiyu's smartness and fasten on his kicking over the jug as important or meaningful, then you are a fool. It is easy to kick over a small flask but if asked, 'Without calling it Mount Everest, what do you call it?' then what will you say?

On seeing Isan Reiyu kick over the jug, Hyakujo burst out laughing and, turning to Zenkaku, said, 'You've been worsted by Isan Reiyu, haven't you!' So Isan Reiyu was sent to establish a new community on Mount Dai-i.

It would, however, be a gross mistake to consider Isan being sent as great promotion. As yet, there was nothing there, all just virgin forest and wild beasts, not even a hermit's shelter. Also, he was all alone, no help, no companionship. Thus he struggled for some ten years, without a teacher to guide him, nor any friends, only wild animals for companions and eating what he could find. In a way it could be said that his real training began on that mountain. In time, however, news about a great hermit attracted some to come and train with him, and finally this grew into a community of some fifteen hundred monks.

In this story, the head monk Zenkaku's understanding seems to be shallow in comparison with Isan's. But Zenkaku, too, had great potential and later became a famous Master in his own right. After he left Hyakujo's monastery, he went into solitary retreat on Mount Karin. As his reputation spread, a senior official, Haikyu, who had practised under Master Obaku, heard of him and set out to visit him. Finding him all alone, Haikyu asked, 'Don't you have an attendant?' 'Oh, yes, inside,' Zenkaku said, and called, 'Come here, come here.' Two great tigers came out and roared! Haikyu was terrified but

Zenkaku ordered the tigers, 'You see we have a special guest, sit, be quiet!' and they curled up beside him like two cats. Zenkaku had named them Great Emptiness and Little Emptiness. As tigers, they lived struggling to find enough food and eating as much as they could get; so it is interesting he called them 'Emptiness'. As an aside, in Japanese monasteries to this day, the attendant of a Master is often referred to as 'Two Emptinesses' (*niku*). When writing a letter to the Master, it is thought impolite to address him directly. A letter to me might be headed, 'Soko Roshi, Two Emptinesses' – that is via the attendant.

Thus both winner and loser in the 'jug-contest', as their practice continued and deepened, became great Masters.

Mumon's Comment: When tested by Hyakujo, Isan showed great ability, yet he was not able to escape from Hyakujo's trap. Hyakujo had dislodged Isan from his senior position as cook in a thriving community and sent him off to establish a new monastery in wild and remote mountains. Mumon seems to be poking fun at Isan, but he is, in fact, praising the energy and power of Isan's insight.

The Verse: Here, instead of seemingly criticising Isan, the poem praises him directly, saying that he threw away his bamboo (cooking) utensils and wooden ladle. That is, Isan was not bound by his senior position as cook; freely he cut through the obstructions of Hyakujo's test, and although a heavy barrier, it could not block him. Thus, from the tip of his foot emerge Buddhas as innumerable as seeds of hemp.

The jug he kicked over represents the many problems that bind us. Each one has his or her own collection of problems; each one of us no doubt thinks that ours are serious or heavy problems. But is it that these problems bind us, or is it that we, in creating these problems, want to be bound by them? Mostly the latter! Thus, the more we are devoted to ourselves, the more importance we attach to ourselves, the more attachments we have and the more our problems multiply. Isan did not kick over the jug, he kicked over himself – and then, for him, all existence was Buddha. Whether fallen leaves or pig-swill or what-not, there is nothing that is not Buddha. Mumon is praising this state of spiritual insight when he says that innumerable Buddhas sprang from the tip of his foot.

In Zen there is no form. In order to treat all Buddhas as Buddha, an infinite, limitless practice is essential. But saying that Zen has no form does not give license for acting arbitrarily. With regard to each single thing in our lives, we have to practise dedicatedly day by day.

CASE 41 • BODHIDHARMA PUTTING THE HEART TO REST

THE CASE

Bodhidharma sat facing the wall. The Second Patriarch, having cut off his arm, stood in the snow and said, 'Your disciple's heart is not at rest. Please, Master, put it to rest.' Bodhidharma said, 'Bring me your heart and I will put it to rest.' The Second Patriarch said, 'Though I have searched for it everywhere, I have not found it.' 'There,' said Bodhidharma, 'your heart is finally at rest.'

MUMON'S COMMENT

The broken-toothed barbarian came specially from a hundred thousand *ri* away across the sea. It is like whipping up waves when there is no wind. Daruma had only one disciple and he was disabled. Shasanro does not know number 4! Phaw!

THE VERSE

西來直指
事因囑起
撓聒叢林
元來是你

Coming from the West and directly pointing
All the trouble comes from this.
Stirring up trouble among all the monks,
Goes back to those two fellows.

SOKO ROSHI'S COMMENTS

Counting from the Buddha, the 28th Patriarch, Bodhidharma, crossed the seas and came from India to China. Although it was more usual in those days to travel along the Silk Road, Bodhidharma chose the sea route and his voyage took three years until he arrived in Canton.

In his day, a kingdom called Ryo spread along the Yangtze River. Its ruler Butei (Chinese: Wu) was so devoted to Buddhism that he was also referred to as 'Emperor of the Buddha Heart'. Now, Buddhism in those early days was concerned with knowledge of the sutras, religious observances and rituals and keeping the precepts. Only a few thought about their own state, how to ease their own heart.

When Emperor Wu heard that a monk of the true line of the Buddha had just arrived from India, he had him brought into his presence and asked many questions about the Buddhist teachings. But the Emperor wasn't able to grasp Bodhidharma's replies and came to no real insight. The first koan in the *Blue Cliff Record* describes this encounter in detail. Bodhidharma then crossed the Yangtze and went north into the kingdom of Gi. He settled in the temple of Shorin-ji where, facing a wall, he sat in zazen for many years. The Japanese Daruma doll derives from that story, without arms or legs but when pushed over, always coming upright again.

As Bodhidharma was sitting in meditation one day, a middle-aged monk, Shinko Eka, arrived. Shinko had been very bright from childhood, was well-educated in the classics and in spiritual matters, and he was familiar with the Daoist and Confucian tenets. Gradually his heart was drawn towards Buddhism and he entered the religious life. Diligently studying the Teachings and observing the Precepts did, however, not bring him real peace of heart. Then he heard that in the nearby temple of Shorin-ji Bodhidharma was sitting gazing at the wall.

Here we have to remember that when Shinko came to Bodhidharma, he was already a well-seasoned monk and did not just ask idle or theoretical questions. Indeed, those desirous of undergoing Zen training must first start practising in their everyday lives. Equally important is that, instead of reading the latest fads or current cult books, they devote themselves to the corpus of literature with weight and spiritual insight from the past. Only when having read and digested these texts and pondered their own lives, when their 'sword is genuinely broken' and they have come to the end of their resources and cannot proceed any further, then when they go to a teacher, it will likely be beneficial and fruitful.

In Japan, and I suppose in the West too, there is a tendency in some Zen training places to indulge in trivial questioning, purely personal or psychological, and so the truly sharp questions which go straight to the heart of the matter are rare.

Think for a moment about the Buddha himself. He was born to wealth and power, with family connections and many attendants. He had all that ordinary people wish for, and no doubt used and enjoyed those things to the full, seeking his own happiness. Yet he was unable to escape a sense of unease and doubt. Finally he left home and lay life and, devoting himself to religious practices, sought out the greatest teachers without, however, succeeding to resolve his sense of unease. Next he underwent austerities so severe that they brought him to the point of death. Few before or after him could equal such devotion; illustrations of the Buddha, especially in the Gandhara style, show him emaciated, with nothing but skin and bones. They are all too real. However, when even these extreme austerities did not bring him the peace of heart he was seeking, he settled himself under the Bodhi-tree and remained there until finally he came to that genuine insight he had been seeking.

So what Bodhidharma brought from India to China was just that same one thing that the Buddha had gone through. Bodhidharma had also passed through the same stages and so had Shinko. Two thousand five hundred years have passed since the Buddha, one thousand five hundred years since Shinko. Although so long ago, they yet demonstrate this process so clearly and directly that one wonders why, in spite of these examples, so many of us are still entangled in problems and still stumble around. True happiness, the peace of heart that we all long for, is not to be found in economics, wealth or social status, nor in knowledge or even physical austerities. The Buddha showed that peace of heart is found only by truly understanding oneself. This we have to bear in mind when looking at the present koan.

So Shinko came to Bodhidharma but however much he entreated him and asked for his guidance Bodhidharma did not even look up at him and sat on unperturbed. Shinko bethought himself of the stories where seekers gave up even their lives for the Dharma, such as in the Jataka Tales where the Buddha in a previous life offered himself to hungry tigers, etc. and so he remained determined not to go away.

During a cold December night a blizzard raged and when by dawn the snow had piled up to above Shinko's knees, Bodhidharma seeing this at last spoke to him. Still today, when monks seek entrance to a training monastery, they are expected to stay and wait for days at the entrance. This endurance creates tremendous energy and provides drive once admission to the monastery is secured.

Shinko then, having at last drawn Bodhidharma's attention, shed tears of joy and asked, 'Please, with your great heart of compassion, show me the truth.' Bodhidharma responded sternly, 'Endless, infinite truth, time without boundaries, will only be seen into by enduring the unendurable and attaining the unattainable. For you of little faith and shallow heart, satisfied with little things, such insight is not attainable. Better to give it up.' I myself frequently repeat this for myself; and when Zuigan Roshi gave Sesso Roshi *inka*, transmission, he did so with these same words.

Shinko, on hearing Bodhidharma's harsh words, whipped out a knife, cut off his arm and presented it to Bodhidharma as proof of his sincerity, at which Bodhidharma accepted him as disciple. A poem by a later Zen Master says the snow stained with Shinko's blood shines in matchless beauty.

The koan gives the impression that all this took place at one and the same time. But obviously Shinko had to attend to his severed arm, and no doubt continued his training under Bodhidharma even after it had healed. Then one day he asked a question that went to the very limits, 'My heart is not at ease. Please put this heart of mine at rest.' This question arose out of Shinko's own experience: throughout his life he had studied diligently and as a monk he had followed the Precepts of Buddhism and had struggled to understand himself. Now middle-aged, after continuous effort at self-examination, he had arrived at his very limit. So Bodhidharma's answer, too, came from that very limit. If you do not understand this state of Shinko, then neither his question nor Bodhidharma's answer, 'Show me your heart and I will put it at ease,' will mean anything to you. You know anyway that this heart has no form and that it is not the physical organ which can be presented for inspection. If you do not fully understand the long process of preparation leading up to this exchange, you cannot fathom the gist of Bodhidharma's answer.

To Bodhidharma's 'Show me your heart and I will put it at ease,' Shinko at once replies, 'Though I have searched for it everywhere...' But in real life as well as in the training situation, a certain interval must have elapsed; after Bodhidharma's 'Show me your heart,' Shinko must have continued his practice to find his true heart and show it to Bodhidharma. It may have been for a week or a month or a year, but there must have been an interval of intense search. The Chinese text has 'finally' which also means 'in the end'; this is perhaps its most important factor.

Shinko's answer, then, does not come from desperation in the sense, 'I have searched for it everywhere but have not been able to find it'; rather, that he has searched for it, and has realised that this heart is everywhere and universal, active and vital, and in that sense cannot be grasped. He is expressing his joy at this realisation.

When your heart feels darkened, does not the whole world seem dark? And you then feel this to be an ineluctable fact. Or when you think something evil, do you not think that your heart itself is evil? But one who believes his or her heart to be hopelessly evil cannot believe that Buddha dwells within this heart.

So what Shinko had realised was this responsive heart which is always and everywhere, and vibrantly alive, now joyful, now sad, now active, now passive. If you recognise this just as it is, then the heart of unease becomes itself a heart at ease. Unease does not continue indefinitely. Shinko's response, 'Though I have searched for it everywhere, I cannot find it', was an expression of this insight, satori. That is why Bodhidharma gave him *inka*, transmission, saying 'I have put it to rest.' Without a training tantamount to the breaking of bones or flaying of your skin, this exchange will seem like an empty wordplay.

Mumon's Comment: He praises the wonderful activity of both. First the old fellow with broken teeth, hailing from India – not a complimentary description! But are there not times when you want to praise somebody very much and find that words of praise somehow cannot convey what you mean? A Japanese then will just say, 'Oh this old rascal!' and pat him or her on the shoulders. In Zen, the highest esteem is frequently expressed in terms that would seem derogatory.

At the time of Bodhidharma, Buddhism in China was either scholastic or based upon the precepts. Bodhidharma brought a completely different version that disregards the intervening process but fully and directly expresses the Buddha's insight as it is. Monks of other Buddhist persuasions regarded Bodhidharma as a rival and some historical records of the time tell of animosity, even of attempts at poisoning him, which, were futile and he only lost a few teeth. This, however, is unlikely because Buddhism avoids conflict; with Bodhidharma sitting and gazing at the wall for nine years, there was little contact with others for him to get poisoned. But even without poison, Bodhidharma was by then over a hundred years old. It is not known when he died but the common date given is 527, and it is said that he was then getting on for a hundred and fifty. It is certain he would have lost one or two teeth by then – more likely he had lost them all!

So Mumon is saying that this toothless old fellow got on a boat and made it all the way from India to China and stirred up waves in spite of the fact that there was no wind. Yet when you sum it all up, and ask what he achieved by all that, it boils down to one disciple; and if you ask how great was this disciple, it can but be said that he was someone who had cut off his arm and was thus disabled.

In the Chinese text, Mumon puts in an expression of energy: Hoi! Also, 'Shasanro does not know number 4' is unintelligible to a Western reader. *Sha* is one of the most common Chinese family names, especially among fishing people. *Sanro* means 'third son' – and a third son of such a family would not be educated, might not even be literate. The Chinese coins of that period showed four characters arranged in a circle and Shasanro could not even read the four characters on this ordinary coin. By saying Shasanro, Mumon is referring to Bodhidharma, or perhaps he is also pointing at Shinko who received the transmission from Bodhidharma. And he is saying that these two know absolutely nothing. There are many who do things by half measures, and nobody in human history has been able to do everything absolutely, but a few who, knowing absolutely nothing, have made history. Finally by saying, 'They know absolutely nothing,' Mumon praised and accepted these two.

The Verse: But his praise in the commentary seems not to have been sufficient for Mumon, and so he added more praise in the verse. 'Coming from the West, from India, and pointing his finger directly at Shinko's heart,' giving Shinko the transmission, is the reason why now in Zen institutions and training monasteries so many are suffering and are in such turmoil. And Mumon adds, 'You are the one who caused all the trouble for those gathered here, too!' With these words Mumon expresses the most profound gratitude to Bodhidharma.

CASE 42 · BUDDHA AND THE WOMAN IN SAMADHI

Long, long ago Manjusri came to the Buddha; the entire assembly of all the other Buddhas had returned to their realms, and only one woman remained, close to the Buddha's seat, in deep samadhi. Manjusri said to the Buddha, 'How can this woman be so close to you whereas I cannot?' The Buddha said to Manjusri, 'If you know how to awaken her from samadhi, you may ask her yourself.'

Manjusri walked round her three times, snapped his fingers once, took her up to Brahma's World and tried all his magic powers but could not rouse her from her absorption. The World-honoured One said, 'Even a hundred thousand Manjusris could not get her out of her absorption. But down there, past countries as numerous as the sands of the Ganges, is the Bodhisattva Momyo. He can make the woman come out of her absorption.' At that, the Bodhisattva Momyo rose up from out of the earth and bowed to the World-honoured One; told what to do, he stepped in front of the woman and just once snapped his fingers. At that, she awakened from her absorption.

MUMON'S COMMENT

The performance old Shakya puts on the stage is pitiful indeed. Manjusri is the teacher of the Seven Buddhas; so say, why could he not awaken the woman from her absorption while Momyo, a newly fledged Bodhisattva, could? If you can truly and deeply (intimately) understand why, then however busy your life, you will always remain in the Great Absorption.

出得出不得
渠儂得自由
神頭并鬼面
敗闕當風流

One could awake her, the other could not;
They both are quite free.
Head of a god as against the face of a devil
Oh, for the refined elegance of this botched performance.

SOKO ROSHI'S COMMENTS

This koan is given only in the later stages of training; insight into it
encourages a deeper understanding of the sutras. Perhaps Christians,
too, cannot always clearly understand certain passages of the Bible
without help from a priest. Certainly in Buddhist Sutras there are
passages and stories which cannot be understood logically or rationally but demand a going beyond logical reasoning, to a transcendent
way of seeing.

The universe the sutras deal with is vast. In past ages the world we
live in was assumed to be a horizontal plane. However, the universe
of the sutras contains not only the human realm in which we live
but layers upon layers of worlds or realms above us and also beneath
us. And further, the sutras tell us there are still other such universes
beyond this multi-layered universe of ours.

The world or realm in which we are living may be thought of as a
kind of solar one in which one transcendent Buddha provides light or
teaching. One thousand of such realms make up a 'Small Thousand-
Realm Universe' or the *Chiliocosm*. One thousand of those small ones
are then one 'Middle Thousand-Realm Universe'. One thousand of

these combined are the 'Great Thousand-Realm Universe'; these three together are sometimes also referred to as the Threefold Great Thousand-Realm Universe.

This universe then is incomprehensibly vast. In the sutras this vast realm is represented by one Buddha, Vairochana Buddha. So there is this one great Buddha, and behind him light emanates. In that radiating light there are countless middle-sized Buddhas from each of whom light also emanates; and in each one's emanating light there are also countless smaller Buddhas. Space or the realm of the universe, is thus reflected in the light emanating from Vairochana Buddha. Mysteriously, in this vast universe of Buddhas, the Buddha has only to blink and instantaneously any of those Buddhas can be called into presence.

This is a realm that modern people with their rational understanding of the world find quite impossible to grasp. However, think of this as something from the heart. I happen to be sitting beside you now. If I see you in contrast to myself and try to specify the differences between us, I am facing an impossible task and we become infinitely distant. But if I try to take you in, to accept you just as you are, or, changing the metaphor, if you are enfolded in my love, then the distance between us is naught, and it takes no time at all to come about!

Whether reading the sutras or in zazen and especially in our everyday life, what is important is that our approach is made with this in mind. As to the sutras, without this approach we will not get anything from them.

Mumon has taken this koan from a long sutra, the *Shobutsu Yokyu Sutra* in Japanese, which translates as the 'Sutra of the Essence of All the Buddhas'. This sutra enumerates the various qualities of all the Buddhas in great detail. There are some differences between the sutra and Mumon's presentation of the relevant part of it, but here we are only concerned with Mumon's koan.

One day the Buddha was engaged in a discussion with the Buddhas of the various realms or universes. Manjusri (Monju, Jap.) then joined the assembly; the moment he appeared all the other Buddhas returned to their own realms and the place was almost deserted. 'Long, long ago, Manjusri came to the Buddha; the entire assembly of all the other Buddhas had returned to their realms.' The point is that they disappeared the moment he arrived; when Manjusri appears, they vanish. Mumon himself does not make a point of this in his koan here, but I would like to ask, why do all the other Buddhas leave when Manjusri appears?

Anyway, after all the Buddhas had left, one woman remained sitting in deep samadhi. Manjusri asked, 'Why is it that although I cannot approach frequently and easily, this old woman is allowed to remain so close to you?'

To some women this query may feel unfair, but in ancient times women were thought inferior and more sinful than men. And what is interesting here is that in spite of that assumption in the background, there is this woman sitting here close to the Buddha! Thus in an age in which the distinction between the sexes was very strict, the Buddha obviously made none. Hence the issue here is not whether it is man or woman, but that person's spiritual state.

The Buddha said to Manjusri, 'Wake her up from her state of samadhi, and ask her.' But although Manjusri walked around her several times snapping his fingers at her, he was not able to rouse her from samadhi. Walking around somebody was an ancient form of respectful greeting but we need not make a problem of it here. Nor need we be distracted by trivialities such as wondering why he walked round her three times – that is not important either. Also, in the India of that time there were two meanings for snapping the fingers. One would be to attract someone's attention or to wake them up, the other would be to purify them; here the former meaning of opening somebody's eyes is being referred to.

So when Manjusri could not arouse the woman from samadhi, he took her up into one of the heavenly realms and there, using all his skills, tried to waken her from samadhi but again failed. His taking her into another realm indicates taking her out of the everyday life we know, into another state of spiritual reality.

The Buddha, seeing Manjusri's futile efforts, said, 'Even a hundred thousand Manjusris could not get her out of her absorption. But down there, past countries as numerous as the sands of the Ganges, is Bodhisattva Momyo who can take the woman out of samadhi.' So, then the Buddha – and this is not made quite clear in the text – called up Momyo who instantly appeared and paid his respects to the Buddha. This instant appearance was faster than any jet or rocket! Does this not sound interesting? Now, the first character in Momyo, *mo*, is the same as for *mu*, meaning emptiness. As that it is the same as *mu myo* – meaning 'not clear,' or not understanding (Skt.: *avidya*, usually translated as 'basic delusion'). Buddhism teaches that all attachments emerge from this lack of clarity, and thus Momyo Bodhisattva is working within all the attachments – love, hatred, desire, resentment, etc. This Momyo, following the Buddha's instruction, then went to the woman and at the flick of his fingers she awoke and came out of samadhi.

Mumon's Comment: Mumon took this incident from the above sutra and used it for his purpose. He says that old Shakya (the Buddha) put on a performance, but it was a very poor one. Bodhisattva Manjusri is said to be the teacher of the Seven Buddhas before Shakyamuni whose names are recited every morning in the Transmission. Although the teachings refer to many Buddhas and Bodhisattvas, Buddhism must not be mistaken as being polytheistic, for all the names refer to various aspects of the heart, and are thus an expression of truth. It especially needs to be stressed here that we must not think of 'heart' simply in terms of the working of our own spiritual state, but to perceive it as the power that lies at the source of every activity of our heart. Manjusri is the Bodhisattva who symbolises fundamental wisdom, which is not a wisdom that responds to momentary changes but is an underlying, infinite, unchanging wisdom. All who have arrived at this fundamental understanding are, called 'Buddha', and in this sense Manjusri is described as the teacher of the Seven Buddhas.

So Mumon then asks why Manjusri, the teacher of the Seven Buddhas, could not awaken the woman from samadhi? And why should Momyo, one of the lowest ranking of the Bodhisattvas, who, as his name indicates, lives and operates in the desire-realm of attachments, be able to rouse her from samadhi? Case 38 of this collection asks about the buffalo getting through a window-grill. If you can see into that koan, you can directly respond to Mumon's questions.

Mumon then says that when that depth of insight is reached, the everyday activities are seen to be the Buddha's realm of *Daizenjo* – of Great Samadhi. To put it more simply, we are Buddha as we are, without doing anything, without thinking, just as we are.

The Verse: One could arouse her from samadhi, the other could not. However, both the one who could and the one who could not, were acting freely and without constraint.

Earlier in his commentary Mumon suggested that this whole incident was a kind of play. In a play the actors appear wearing masks, of gods and of demons, of successful and unsuccessful persons. Mumon says that he sees it all as a quite fascinating show!

At the very beginning of my own training, before any insight had yet arisen, I read of an old Master who had said, 'If one wants to ask questions twenty-four hours a day, ask on, and I will answer without ever emerging from satori.' I was quite shaken and wondered whether he would still give a clear response if his pillow were jerked away from under him while sleeping? Surely he could not assert that without always being clear in mind and spirit? In fact, until satori had opened, I used to think people of deep insight could be graded into those of clear understanding and those of unclear understanding, and made up my mind that I would always try for clarity of understanding.

Now, however, I can confidently suggest that if somebody snatches away your pillow from under you and you drowsily awake, then be drowsy with ease of heart. If you feel angry on that occasion, then be angry; if you feel sad about something, then be sad with ease of heart. You can do that because within you there is the fundamental wisdom of Manjusri. To say, 'Don't be angry, don't be drowsy, don't be upset' is to be miles away from Manjusri's wisdom. Manjusri symbolises fundamental wisdom. The working that comes out of that fundamental wisdom is the working of Momyo. In the sutra, as in the koan, Manjusri and Momyo seem to be different entities, each with a name of his own, but ultimately they are the same. Fundamental wisdom does not stay still but is a power or energy that is constantly responding and working.

So, however argumentative or given to anger somebody may be, however hot a temper, that temper cannot flare twenty-four hours a day. Even if you try to stay in a temper all day long, that temper will come and go! However one may lust or long for something, neither lusting nor longing can be kept up constantly. However lonely you may feel, you cannot feel so all day long. Manjusri is within everybody. Therefore, be angry with peace in the heart. Long for things with an easy heart, and be sad with an easy heart. Then, the next instant, you can change brilliantly into another spiritual state – no problem at all. The world of the senses, of Momyo, is of itself Manjusri's Great Realm of Samadhi.

CASE 43 · SHUZAN'S BAMBOO STAFF

THE CASE

Master Shuzan held up his short, curved staff (*shippei*) and said, 'You monks, if you call this a staff, you make it a mental concept, and if you do not call it a staff, you go contrary. Then tell me, what will you call it?'

MUMON'S COMMENT

If you call it a staff, you make it a mental concept; if you do not call it a staff, you go contrary. Without having recourse to either words or silence, what is it? Speak, speak!

THE VERSE

拈起竹篦
行殺活令
背觸交馳
佛祖乞命

Raising up the staff
Commands giving or taking of life!
Concept and contrariness alternate
And Buddhas and Patriarchs beg for their lives.

SOKO ROSHI'S COMMENTS

What do these koans and the commentary really mean to you? Some may consider them as a kind of ragbag, others may find them to be useful information, and still others may take them as interesting curiosities that have little, if anything, to do with our own life. Yet the forty-eight koans in the *Mumonkan* relate directly and personally to your lives. Even the story of a Chinese monk from a thousand years ago, who raised a finger – if you do not take that incident as here and now, in this place, for yourselves then it will not amount to Zen training. The path of Zen training is the path of making ourselves the problem. However much I may expound on it or you may think about it, at the core of it, it simply relates directly to ourselves.

All human beings feel anxiety or fear. The path to overcome this fear is not by developing greater external strength, because this fear is to be found within oneself. Breaking through this fear is the practice of Zen. So whatever the subject matter in the stories, treat them all as relating directly and immediately to yourselves.

The protagonist in the present koan is Master Shuzan, also known as Shonen. The name Shuzan comes from the monastery he opened on a mountain of that name. When still a young man he left home to become a monk. He visited various monasteries and practised under their masters but he did not undertake real sanzen, the intense relationship with a master, but was devoted to reading and chanting the *Lotus Sutra*. Among all the Mahayana Sutras, the *Lotus Sutra* is venerated as the distillation of Buddhist wisdom, and is sometimes called the King of Sutras. Shonen may have thought that the essence of training and practice was the mastery of the *Lotus Sutra* and for many years saw no reason to change this view. Although he was very diligent and serious in his practice, in essence he was off the mark because he was studying the sutra rather than looking into the one who was reading the sutra.

And why was he reading the sutra so diligently? Why is it that you give time and money and energy to come to the Summer School? It is not a question of what you hear or what you learn. Unless the inquiry is directly pointing at yourselves, nothing will come out of it.

Shonen continued his reading and wandering for many years. He was already a middle-aged monk when he joined the assembly of Master Fuketsu Ensho, a spiritual grandson of Rinzai. There, he became known by the nickname 'Lotus Reader', but eventually rose to be Master Fuketsu's attendant. One day when Fuketsu was sitting in zazen, Shonen was close behind him and saw him crying and overheard him murmuring, 'How is it that Rinzai Zen has deteriorated so much these days? Why? Why?' For Rinzai Zen which had been so powerful and influential only a few generations before, was by his time in sad decline. Shonen who saw the many monks in Fuketsu's monastery, and vigorous and flourishing religious practice, asked, 'But here in your assembly surely there are many fine disciples? Why are you lamenting?'

Fuketsu, still crying, replied, 'True, many good and learned monks. Only, none have genuine insight, none are aware of their Buddha-nature.' Shonen asked, 'Might I be able?' Fuketsu denied it, 'No. To begin with I had high hopes that you might, but you are enthralled by the *Lotus Sutra*, unable to cut loose from it.'

On hearing this, Shonen vowed, 'I will let go of the *Lotus Sutra*, I will throw it away! Please, teach me.' From that time on he devoted himself to deepening his understanding of himself.

One day Fuketsu addressed his monks from the High Seat. He took up the koan of the Buddha Holding up a Flower (Koan 6 in the *Mumonkan*). It comes from one of the very late sermons; the Buddha was just mounting the platform when a wealthy patron handed him a wonderful, golden flower. Having taken his seat, the Buddha silently held up the flower. All the assembled thought the Buddha was going to speak about this flower. However, he just held it up without saying a word. One of his monks, Kasyapa, quietly smiled to himself. Seeing his smile, the Buddha announced to the whole gathering that Kasyapa inherited his teaching. This is the gist of that koan.

So Fuketsu told this story from the High Seat and asked, 'What was the Buddha talking about? What did he say? Do not assert that he said nothing, gave a sermon without giving a sermon. If you say that, you bury the Buddha in the ground.' None could utter a word. But Shonen who was sitting at Fuketsu's feet, shook his sleeves and without a word got up and left the hall. At which Fuketsu threw down the staff in his hand and went back to his quarters.

Later one of the monks asked Fuketsu, 'Why did the Lotus Reader get up and leave without saying anything?' Fuketsu said, 'Lotus Reader had satori.' Fuketsu then passed on the transmission to Shonen, or Shuzan as he came to be called.

On reading or hearing this story, do you not ask yourself what it is all about? And just because you do not quite understand, do you not marshal all your intellectual resources to grasp what is happening? That is the mistake!

Lotus Reader, shaking his sleeves, left the hall. And Fuketsu, having thrown down his staff, also went back to his quarters. So both the teacher, Fuketsu, and the disciple, Shonen, threw everything away. In that spiritual state when everything had been cast off, Shonen attained the transmission. What a mistake, then, to assemble a pile of informational garbage to grasp this all-important spiritual state in which everything is thrown off!

Over the centuries Zen Masters traditionally carried a staff of office, about two feet long, called a *shippei*. It is sometimes also used during sanzen interviews to strike a trainee. But do not think now that Zen is rough. Only few monks are ever hit like that, for those who need it are few, and for those few, even hitting has no effect!

After Shuzan had attained insight and received transmission, he became master of a monastery himself. One day while addressing his monks, he held up his staff and asked, 'What will you call this? If you call it a staff, you cling to that and are deceived by the name. This one is made of bamboo. You can use it as fuel or whatever, and so it is something that can change in hundreds of ways. Therefore, just because all the world calls it a staff, if you cling to the illusion that that is all it is, you might as well give up training! But if you do not call it a staff, although the rest of the world calls it so, and hold it is just a thing that is changing moment by moment, and that because it is ever-changing it has to be seen as empty or void, then you are making the error of falling into nihilism. So what are you going to call it then?'

Out of grandmotherly kindness we shall go over this again. First of all, it's not a talk about a staff.

At the time when Shuzan raised his staff, his brilliant disciple Kisho was in the assembly. He later inherited Shuzan's Dharma and became known as Master Kisho of Sekken. The moment Shonen held up his staff, Kisho grabbed it, threw it down and asked Shuzan, 'What do you call it?' Shuzan yelled at him, 'Blind!' At that moment Kisho attained to insight.

Do not think that this will or can be explained – if you do, you might as well give up! When you read such stories as this about the staff, or Isan's kicking over a water jug (Koan 40) they are exactly the same. Hyakujo placed a water jug on the floor, and asked his monks, 'What do you call it? If you call it a water jug you are inclining towards it, caught by it. If you do not call it a water jug, you are negating the fact, turning your back on it. What then will you call it?' On that occasion, Isan toppled it over with his foot and quietly left the hall – and thus passed the test Hyakujo had set them. Let us get quite clear: this was Isan's response. The one who grabbed Shonen's staff and threw it down was Kisho, and that was his response. As to Isan's toppling over the jug, yes, you can topple over a water jug. But if told, 'You cannot call it a mountain' – can you then kick over the mountain? If I say, 'You cannot call me Soko,' and then just like Kisho grabbed and threw down the staff, can you grab me like a staff and throw me down? Perhaps I do have the strength to throw somebody down; but if told, 'Throw yourself down' – then can you throw that down?

To repeat yet again: the staff is only a symbol. It stands for myself, and for yourself. Why then, rather than referring to a staff, is it not said, 'I myself' or 'you yourself'? Zen is a training which does not explicitly say, 'yourself' or 'myself', but instead, when a glass is picked up, or a finger is pointed, or a staff is thrown down, it is directed at oneself.

Mumon's Comment: In this case Mumon adds nothing in his comment, but instead, like a parrot, he simply repeats the koan, and then challenges, 'Without having recourse to either words or silence' – or, as said, you cannot remain silent and you cannot speak – 'speak, speak quickly, say what it is.'

Latent in this is Mumon's great kindness. He says that you cannot talk about it. But he is not just referring to words; you cannot move your hands or feet, you cannot think and you cannot not think. And Mumon then is warning, saying that all intention misses the target.

When faced by Mumon in this way, what do you do? In spite of Mumon's great kindness, faced with this and not doing anything, do you not ask, 'What shall I do?' Do you not go on again and again in the same way? But now you cannot go on in the same way, you must do something. And it is in that state, when thinking about what you might do, that Mumon challenges, 'Speak quickly, say now!' These words, short as they are, carry the essence of Mumon's own long training, deep insight and great kindness.

The Verse: Mumon repeats that Shuzan raised his staff before the assembly. We must bear in mind that the staff is not a staff and so this tremendous staff has the power to resurrect the dead, and the power to kill what is living.

Can you see the staff that kills you and gives you life? If our eyes are captivated by the temporary form of the staff or if we are caught up in a conception of emptiness and say, 'No, the staff is not a thing, not just a temporary changing form, but is the underlying reality of all changing phenomena,' then if we cling to that notion we are deceived by dualistic contradiction, and there is no kind of answer we can put forward, no resolution for this contradiction. While we are in the thrall of such dualistic thinking there is no way out. We human beings have developed it and even if we brought in the Buddhas and the patriarchs to help us they could not respond.

So when we assert that we have understood something merely on the basis of our learning, such understanding is defined or circumscribed. When asked, 'Who are you?' and I answer, 'I am Morinaga Soko' – this is only a name, I am just being defined by means of a name. If I say, 'I am the Roshi', this only describes a position. What I am trying to do is to grasp myself within some kind of temporary status or form. Surely you recognise that that is not the real me? If I say I am a man, that, too, is inadequate, and my stating that I am an old man on the verge of death, that is also inadequate. Saying I am a Zen monk or whatever else I describe myself as, will always be a limited description. So I, myself who appear as a phenomenon, and the life of *my self* which is eternal, how are you able to put them forth completely without any definition or circumscription at all, how do you answer that? That is the core, the crux of this koan. And when you have reached the point of being able to respond to this, then whatever you meet you will not be affected by it, and so you will not be hurt; and equally, whatever may happen, you will not be sullied. But if you only understand yourself in limited terms, there will be many times when you will feel humiliated or wounded, or feel that you have been wronged, and will suffer accordingly. But the self that cannot he sullied and cannot be hurt, the self that in its temporary, changing form, or in its underlying, unchanging reality, cannot be limited or defined – what do you call that?

That's all.

To repeat again, almost to over-state it, when you hear the koan of Shuzan and the staff, you must not ponder how to answer it, but instead just listen while thinking, 'How should I sit zazen?' Answers to koans are not necessary. What is important is that you are able to sit zazen and as an individual can be aware of, 'Hmm, hmm, this is my self.'

CASE 44 · BASHO'S STAFF

Basho said to the assembled monks, 'If you have a staff, I will give you one. If you do not have a staff, I will take it away from you.'

MUMON'S COMMENT
When the bridge is broken, the staff helps you to ford the river; it is your companion when you return to the village on a moonless night. But if you call it a staff, you go to hell swifter than any arrow.

THE VERSE
諸方深與淺
都在掌握中
撐天并拄地
隨處振宗風

The Deep and the Shallow everywhere
Are held in the palm of the hand.
Holding up the sky and supporting the earth,
Spreading the Dharma in all directions.

SOKO ROSHI'S COMMFNTS
The previous koan, 'Shuzan's Staff', was frequently used by Master Daie, one of the very great Zen masters of the Song Dynasty. The revival of the Rinzai tradition is attributed to him and he is known for his formalisation of 'Kanna Zen', or Zen training by use of koans. All contemporary Rinzai practice may be traced back to Daie of whom it

is said that once during a fifty-day retreat period he brought thirteen trainees to enlightenment by means of this koan of 'Shuzan's Staff'.'

Daie's master, Engo, is the commentator and compiler of the *Blue Cliff Record*, a collection of a hundred koans taken from the writings and records of the great Zen Patriarchs, originally collected by Master Setcho who had appended a verse to each koan.

This collection turned out to be so popular that it became available in all Chinese monasteries and was used by monks as a guide in their training. Although this was a compilation of his own master, tradition says that Daie collected as many copies as he could and burned them. From this we note that although the Rinzai tradition stresses the use of koans, Daie's action is a warning to be careful with koan practice.

When I hear the responses to a koan during sanzen, I do not concern myself to a great extent with the words or actions used in presenting insight into the koan. Rather I look at the person who is giving the answer. However splendid an answer may seem, perhaps even gleaned from the sayings of one of the great Patriarchs of Zen, I would not accept it. Why not? Because real joy never shines on the face of one who is quoting parrot-fashion or borrowing another's understanding. For such a person, even though the answer may have the correct form, the koan is not a source of energy or power. A koan is not something that you carry around in your handbag or walk about with it slung over your shoulder. When really seen into, the koan is a means of expressing joy and vitality while the koan itself disappears. There is no 'answer' to a koan. All that is there is a joy the trainee cannot suppress, a sense of total ease and relaxation. Daie placed such emphasis on koan Zen because he wanted his followers and monks to experience this joy for themselves. The koans are simply the means.

Another great Master, contemporary with Daie, was Wanshi. His way was to just sit silently. Widely known and respected throughout China, he utterly rejected the use of koans. There was great controversy among their followers as to which was the greater, Daie's Koan Zen (Kanna Zen) or Wanshi's Zen of Silent Illumination ('Mokusho Zen'). Daie, by giving a koan to those who practised with him, smashed everything that they carried with them, whereas Wanshi's way was to take up everything that the person was carrying and smash it by Silent Illumination. To those not practising themselves, only the differences of method became apparent and so they failed to realise that whether Daie or Wanshi, the end result was that both were smashing everything that the individual trainee brought along. So although their means were different, the end was the same.

Even today the debate continues between their respective advocates as to which is better, Koan Zen or the Zen of Silent Illumination. Never, never indulge in this kind of silly discrimination. If you have an opportunity to do koan training, then use that opportunity to smash the last thing that you think is important to yourself. And if you do not have the opportunity, then simply sit zazen and use the sitting as a means of breaking down whatever is the most precious thing that you still cling to. If you find that although you want to try to do so but cannot because other things get in the way, then the problem is not that Zen is difficult, but that you have the habit of clinging to some last shred of whatever seems to be precious or important to you, and you cannot break or shed that habit.

Anyway, while all of this debate was going on about who was the greater, and which way of Zen was the most effective, Daie and Wanshi themselves were indifferent to this and were, in fact, close friends. Wanshi died about seven years before Daie; on his deathbed, he sent a letter to Daie, in which he asked him to take care of all that might have to be done after his death – from which we can see their deep relationship, almost like mirror to mirror. Do you get the meaning of two mirrors face to face? Do not imagine that if you look into this mirror, you will see a whole line of hundreds of mirrors!

After this long preface we now look at Master Basho's koan. In the early centuries, many Japanese and Korean monks went to China in search of Buddhism or Zen training, some of them achieving considerable renown in China. Basho was from Korea. The name is that of the mountain his monastery stood on; his monk's name was Esei. He had already been to many different monasteries when eventually he came to the monastery of Master Nanto Koyo, a successor of Master Kyozan. In the previous koan mention was made of Isan kicking over the water jug. The lineage of Isan and his successor Kyozan is known as the Igyo line of Zen.

On arriving at Master Koyo's, Basho listened to his sermon. The Master was saying, 'All you gathered here, if you are true human beings, then roar like a lion that has just been born from its mother's womb.' On hearing this, Basho felt his whole body dissolving. It is said that he continued for five years in this spiritual state. The realisation of that moment formed the basis for his subsequent practice and later for his own teaching.

As to the staff, Zen teachers still use it. Now rather short, originally it was a kind of walking stick with a curved end. It does not matter whether curved or straight, long or short. Originally such staffs were carried by monks during the travelling season, as an aid for walking, or to sound the depth of a river or to move things out of their path, etc. In China, a shorter, curved version then came to be carried as a staff of office. Zen masters always had one at hand and at times would wield it to hit a monk or to present the essence of their teaching.

So one day, Basho raised his staff before his assembly and said, 'If you have a staff, then I will give you one. If you do not have a staff then I will take it away from you.'

Hearing this statement, if you feel only an instant's doubt at the contradiction inherent in this, then you are in trouble. Yet is there not some contradiction in giving the staff to someone who has already got it and taking it away from somebody who has not got it? If you see it in this way you are fooled by what he held up, by the staff, on which your attention is focussed. In the previous koan (Shuzan's Staff) it was stressed repeatedly that what Shuzan held up was not a staff. Yet if nevertheless you still see Basho's staff as a thing, an object, you are indeed in a sad state!

Leaving Basho's koan aside for a moment, let us look at an encounter between the famous Master Joshu and the monk Genyo. Before Genyo attained insight, he asked Joshu, 'What do you do to somebody who comes bearing nothing?'

In his practice Genyo seems to have grappled with the saying, 'Originally there is nothing', and came to understand it in an intellectual way. This he presented to Joshu. Though now knowing it intellectually, it had not really become part of his experience. So he came to Joshu, clinging to this 'I have nothing' and presented it to Joshu who yelled at him, 'Throw it away!'

This came as a real shock to Genyo. Convinced he had brought nothing, it hurt his pride to be told to throw away nothing! He responded angrily, 'What should I throw away when I haven't brought anything!' Quick as lightning, Joshu replied, 'Then carry it away!' The Chinese characters have the connotation of carrying something on the shoulders or on the back, loaded to exhaustion until the bones break!

So what did Basho take and what did he give? Is it the most

important thing that is taken away or given? But this giving and taking is surely not Basho's or anybody's function!

Mumon's Comment: 'When the bridge is broken it helps you to ford the river.' The translation has 'the staff helps you,' but it might be better not to focus too hard on the staff. So 'when the bridge is broken, it helps you to ford the river and it is your companion when you return to the village on a moonless night. But if you call it a staff, you go to hell swifter than any arrow!' The Chinese text is a beautiful verse but is without a subject. 'Always together, it helps me to ford the stream, on a moonless night. It kindly leads me back to the village.' Mumon simply cites this old poem and uses it to paraphrase and comment, and then adds, 'If you call it a staff – limit it as being a thing, the staff – you will fall into hell swifter than an arrow.'

The Verse: 'The Deep and Shallow everywhere are held in the palm of the hand. Holding up the sky and supporting the earth, spreading the Dharma in all directions.' Traditionally in Rinzai Zen training, the first two lines are interpreted as follows: If you have truly understood what Basho and Mumon are saying, you will clearly see whether the insight of the teachers you encounter is shallow or deep.

In my view, however, whether aware or unaware of recognising and knowing the staff for what it is, whether having insight or not, that person knows the shallows and the depths of human life. In walking through life – they know exactly where it is deep and difficult and where it is shallow and easy, and they do so as intimately as seeing the lines on the palm of their own hands. The problem is that we do not 'incline our ears towards it' and do not attempt to listen to it. Sometimes we do indeed hear that voice which is intimating just this, but we do not listen to it. And so in spite of knowing that the ford through the river is shallow, and though everybody crosses at that point, we end up walking into deep waters! Is it not so? Why? Because we want to be special. If somebody says we are unusual, or unique, we are pleased! This is why people do not want to walk in the shallows; they do not want to do what is the most natural and ordinary – however easy, people do not choose that way, and so suffer in trying to be special. But 'this one' knows everything, not just my own individual life but also the great working of heaven as heaven and of earth as earth, knows that you are you, and that I am I! We know this through this vigorous working. When we forget or when we are asleep, without any special effort to show or to be or to assert myself – this one – makes me, and in that presents the vital and true self – not a self that is an actor playing a role but the true self.

That is how I see it.

CASE 45 – HOEN'S 'WHO IS HE?'

THE CASE

Master (Goso) Hoen of Tozan said, 'Both Shakyamuni and Maitreya serve someone else. Tell me, who is this someone else?'

MUMON'S COMMENT

If you can clearly see who this 'someone else' is, it is like meeting your own father at the crossroads. No need to ask anybody whether it is he or not.

THE VERSE

他弓莫挽
他馬莫騎
他非莫辨
他事莫知

Do not draw another's bow;
Do not ride another's horse;
Do not speak ill of another;
Do not enquire into another's business.

SOKO ROSHI'S COMMENTS

We have already met Goso Hoen in Koans 35, 36 and 39. Mumon was in the sixth generation of direct succession after Hoen. As that he may have felt especially close to Hoen and included a number of his sayings. If so, he did so not only out of veneration, but also because Hoen was one of the greatest Masters of the Song dynasty.

The monastery of the Fifth Patriarch had been on Mount To (Tozan) and thereafter came to be known as the Mountain of the Fifth Patriarch (Gosozan). Since Hoen, too, was Master of that mountain monastery, he is referred to as Goso Hoen, the Hoen of Mount Goso.

Hoen once addressed his monks, 'The Buddha who is popularly revered is the Enlightened One of some thousand years ago and the future Buddha, Maitreya, will appear in fifty-seven million *kalpas* and deliver all those not yet awakened. These two greats venerated Buddhas are slaves at the beck and call of someone else. Do you know who *he* is?'

Before going into this koan, a few general remarks may serve as pointers. As human beings we are constantly beset by fears and anxiety. The Buddha felt this so keenly that he tried by all means to dispel them, from intellectual enquiry to practising the most severe austerities. Then in meditation he found the path to genuine insight and the spiritual state of satori which goes beyond one's own desire or need and, taking in absolute reality, is as such inexpressible. He further realised that since beings inevitably must die, the way to escape from the fear of death or any fear is to open oneself up to it, to accept it and take it in.

Not only Buddha, but all founders of the great world religions have recognised this universal truth, however different their approaches may seem. But whenever such universal understanding is accepted, it becomes a system of thought and as such it begins to take on particular characteristics, depending on the God you worship, or what observances and rituals are considered important and performed. Then these various systems begin to assert their own uniqueness or the rightness of their own tradition, and begin to compete and even feud with each other. History shows how often fanaticism, strife and violence arise in the name of religion. The same root still gives rise to the various regional wars going on in the world today when God has simply become a cheer leader for the various factions. Even worse, because there are cheering factions, it becomes extremely difficult to back away from confrontation. Not surprisingly, many people then lose hope and refute that kind of religion.

Yet from ancient times and all through the Middle Ages religion played a central role in all cultures. To begin with, much of religion was expressed as mystery. As time passed and consciousness developed, these earlier forms of religion were gradually replaced by philosophy and/or science with the result that in the so-called advanced countries today, religion has all but lost its spiritual connotation.

Why has belief in the efficacy of religion been lost? In the face of absolute reality, we must not deny our own mistakes. We have made this universal truth into a kind of slave, and use it to satisfy our wants or demands. Thus God, or Buddha, are treated like a slave for the satisfaction of our desires and wants. 'Please help me. Do this! Do that!' On all such occasions, our own needs are stated first, and God then is simply the figure who satisfies those demands. When praying, at the end we express our heartfelt salutation, reverence and love of God, but perhaps in our hearts already lodges the caution, 'If you do not grant my prayers, I will no longer believe in you!'

There is also an intimation nowadays that God is dead. Science has emerged in his place and has won our faith. True, the fruits of scientific enquiry have opened doors in many directions and to such an extent that if we use the word 'scientific', it almost equates with 'trustworthy'. However, in this case, too, we only have confidence in the absolute truth of science in the laboratory. Most of us come into contact with science only as it is applied, either in industrial production or in the manufacture of convenient consumer goods. So in the case of science, here too, we do not put ourselves face to face with the truth or the reality of science and test ourselves against it. Rather, we like to use the many conveniences that derive from science.

When looking at religion, or what is discovered by science, we mostly tend to treat them as slaves for our own needs and desires. As a result of this, faith in religion and faith in science has been destroyed, and consequently anxiety and fear become ever more widespread. We may think that the only thing that can relieve this situation is love, but love seems buried in a deep fog out of sight.

Now we are ready to look at the koan. Both Buddha and Maitreya, and not only those two, but also the God of Christianity and all the Gods and Buddhas – someone uses them freely and at will. If you know 'him,' show! This 'him' that Hoen and I, too, are talking about, is not to be understood at the word level. This is a 'him' we can and may absolutely trust. For those today who have lost all faith, we can confirm trust in *him*. But where is *he*? What is *he*?

Mumon's Comment: If you see clearly who this someone is, then wherever you meet 'him,' even on crowded crossroads, you will recognise him as you would your own father. Even if we cannot confirm this beyond doubt, yet we have never been apart from him. Wherever we may travel, there is no place where he is not. And therefore if you meet him, without asking anybody, you will know. Do not complain that you have no guide, no teacher. Even without confirming with a teacher, when you meet him from whom you have never been separated, you will recognise him instantly.

But sometimes you may make a mistake and think that you have seen him, or recognised him, and then, of course, it is important to confirm this with somebody who has experience and can guide you, to make sure whether indeed you have found him or not. However, before having anybody confirm anything for you, it is still more important that you first find him for yourselves. Even if you come to me asking where your father is, I cannot tell you. All I can say is, 'Look for yourself.' Anywhere, everywhere, whatever you may be doing, look immediately, directly there. He is not hidden in some secret or special place, or in a particular training centre.

The Verse: Do not criticise others. Do not be too concerned about what others are saying. Behind this verse is the urge, the warning, to look to yourself. After you have denied your present self, and denied it again and again, when he then emerges, that is an existence in which he and I and trees and you and mountains are all transcended. If he then truly appears, there is no other's bow, only your own; there is no other's horse. If there is anybody to criticise, it is yourself. If a problem arises, it is not somebody else's problem, it is your problem. In such a state we may indeed speak of love. While in opposition to others, or criticising others we are stuck in one-sidedness, if we try to use the word 'love' as a glue to repair that, that is not love.

CASE 46 · SEKISO'S HUNDRED-FOOT POLE

THE CASE

Master Sekiso asked, 'How can you go further from the top of a hundred-foot pole?' Another old master said,

> 'One who sits on top of a hundred-foot pole
> Has entered the Way, but it is not yet real.
> He has to go on further from the top of the pole
> Revealing his True Nature in the ten directions.'

MUMON'S COMMENT

Going beyond the top of the pole and up-ending the body, there is nothing to dislike or to praise. But tell me how to go beyond the top of the hundred-foot pole? Bah!

THE VERSE

瞎却頂門眼
錯認定盤星
拌身能捨命
一盲引衆盲

If the Single Eye in the forehead is blind,
The mark on the balance is mistaken for the weight.
Body is lost and life thrown away,
The blind leading the blind.

SOKO ROSHI'S COMMENT

Master Sekiso raises the Sayings of an old Master. We shall begin by looking at this Master. It refers to Chosa Keijin, a Dharma-heir of the great Master Nansen Fugen. One day, Keijin told one of his monks to visit a Dharma-brother, also heir of Nansen, and to sound the state of his spiritual attainment.

The young monk arrived safely and as instructed asked, 'What were you like before you started training under Master Nansen?' The other remained silent, just sitting zazen. Keijin's disciple probed further, 'Then how was it after you had trained under Nansen?' 'Nothing much has changed,' came the answer.

Perhaps what was shown was that there is no before or after, and that he was in a state without transformation or change or discrimination. The young disciple reported this to Keijin who composed the above verse and sent it to his Dharma-brother.

'One who sits on top of a hundred-foot pole' is sometimes also referred to as 'Sitting alone on a mountain peak', one that towers above all others or soars above the plain – this latter simile is also often used. These expressions, then, intimate entering the realm of absolute enlightenment, far transcending our everyday discriminations and problems of good and bad, more and less, winning and losing. Zen Buddhism has as its purpose the opening of enlightenment, of satori, and satori transcends the relative world of discrimination. Transcending that relative world, you sit in an absolute realm. But to the extent that you continue to sit in that absolute realm and come to rest in it, this is not full or true satori. Please do one step beyond, then a place will surely open where the satori can be used and turned back into the world.

So Master Keijin sent this verse to his Dharma-brother to encourage him to further practice.

Of course, 'the top of a hundred-foot pole' does not indicate a pole lying flat on the ground. If it did, it would not be difficult to do the next step. What does it take to do another step from the top of a pole that is soaring up vertically? If you were an ant, it would be very easy to take that step!

You may have made a wonderful pie but if you then leave it sitting on the side-board, it will only go bad. Zen has satori as its purpose but you cannot remain or stop in that absolute state of realisation. Rather, satori constantly involves the dissolution of self.

The Bull-herding Pictures were compiled by Master Kakuan who also added the poems. They are characteristic of Zen. The first picture shows a young man with a rope searching for the bull. Looking everywhere in mountains and on the plains, he eventually finds the traces of him. Then he actually sees the bull and gradually gains control of it. In the eighth picture the seeking man and the sought-for bull have both disappeared, and what is left is an empty circle. This is the world of satori in which all opposites are cancelled out. However, the picture series does not end there; the ninth picture shows 'Returning to the Source' and the tenth 'Returning to the Market with Bliss-Bestowing Hands'. It is easy to think of this last picture as of someone rich and powerful compassionately doing good to less fortunate fellow beings. But what the picture portrays is the state of someone who after enlightenment truly returns, to be and share with others and who accepts others fully and completely just as they are – to laugh with them and cry with them and share all their feelings. And while laughing and crying with those who have not yet found their way, in his heart there is always compassion and hope for others. So in the tenth picture there always appears an older big fellow and a young man setting out in search of the bull. The picture shows two figures, but are they not one form? It may be surprising that the series does not end with Picture 8 but goes on to No. 9 and No. 10. However, this is not really surprising, for when attaining enlightenment, this world in which we laugh and cry does not die.

This koan, too, stresses that satori is not the end of training. So we return to Sekiso who sets this koan. As usual, Sekiso is the name of a temple, and the successive incumbents were all known as Sekiso. Two among them are outstanding, one is Master Keisho of the Tang dynasty and another is Jimyo of the Song dynasty who is also known by the religious name of Soen. It is not absolutely clear which of the two is the protagonist in this koan, the Tang or the Song Master. Most scholars now believe that it is the second, Soen Jimyo of the Song dynasty. This Jimyo was a powerful master, renowned for his determination in Zen training, to the extent that when sitting, especially at night, he would hold a sharp awl over his thigh, so that if he dropped off to sleep, the awl would pierce his flesh. It is said that the great Japanese Zen Master Hakuin was much impressed by Jimyo's zealousness and vigour, practised it himself and introduced it into the training of his monks.

Although I myself feel a particular proximity to Master Jimyo, I would also dare to differ from the scholarly interpretation and treat the Master Sekiso who appears here not as Jimyo but Master Keisho, and this because of the following story associated with him.

Keisho's monastery was well known for being extremely strict. In training his monks, he insisted that in the meditation hall they always were to sit as if they were dead and would exhort them, 'Sit as if you are dead ashes or a stone pillar,' thus encouraging them to transcend the world of relativity. So day and night, the whole of his community sat as if they were withered trees, and did, in fact, become known as 'The Grove of Withered Trees'.

After Keisho's death, a dispute arose as to the succession. Almost all felt that the natural successor would be Shuso, the head monk.

Shuso himself also expected it. However, a fellow monk, Kyuho, declared that only one who had fully inherited and embodied his teaching could be Keisho's successor; otherwise the succession would become meaningless and would demean the Dharma.

Shuso confronted Kyuho, 'Are you saying that I have not inherited Master Keisho's Dharma?' Kyuho retorted, 'If you have indeed inherited the Dharma, show me!' Shuso said, 'Get an incense burner and light some incense. I will sit in zazen and before the smoke from the incense has died away, I will myself die.' And truly, before the smoke had faded away, he entered samadhi and died. The other monks were awed and frightened by the incredible feat, but Kyuho tapped the dead monk on the shoulder, 'Magnificent! But, nevertheless, you have not inherited the Master's Dharma!'

Of all the stories transmitted by tradition, this one is truly awe-inspiring! When I first came across it, I shivered and had gooseflesh creeping all over.

The koan itself is not really hard to understand intellectually or philosophically but it is still most difficult because of the incredible intensity in which the practice of these early Masters culminated at that moment. And this is also why I expounded on Keisho, the earlier of the two Sekisos.

So this Sekiso Keisho asked, 'How do you take another step from the top of a hundred-foot pole?' Perhaps you now understand how horrendous and awesome it is to take that single step.

Mumon's Comment: Stepping forward or moving on with utmost effort from the state of satori, you return to the everyday world of the senses. That to which you return, be it paradise or hell, at that moment becomes the wonderful realm of no regret at all. It may be easy to get the surface meaning, but Mumon asks,

'How do you take that further step from satori' – how do you do it?

But let me warn you! The koan insists that from the state of satori you must take a further step and return to the world. Zen Masters in the past often stress that dying is easy, coming to rebirth is difficult. But for us living today, before we can even think about coming back to rebirth, how difficult it is to die! It is difficult for us to overcome the world of discriminations and oppositions in which we live. Before we can be like Kyuho who tapped his fellow monk on the shoulder, we must first come to experience the state and the understanding of the head monk who had the incense lit and died while the incense was still burning. If we ignore or try to short-circuit this process or think we can do without it, we will find that Zen does not help in dealing with the problems around us and we will only give rise to further problems. For not only will we fail to find ease or compassion for ourselves, but will cause trouble to all around us.

So let me caution you, before taking that step from the top of the hundred-foot pole, first of all sit on it!

The Verse: The 'single eye' mentioned in the first line is frequently mentioned in Buddhism. Metaphorically as an eye, it stands vertically in the middle of the forehead. Our ordinary two eyes are the eyes of relativity and discrimination. The vertical eye in the centre of the forehead sees the Absolute. But even if that central eye has opened, unless you proceed from there, the eye is useless and it is as if it had been blocked up again.

There is a type of scale with a bar and a little weight moves along the arm. What is to he weighed is put on the tray and then by moving the weight along the arm, the scale will work. So this weight is only useful as long as it moves. If it sticks at any point along the balance arm, the scale is useless. Thus even if you have the single eye or 'Eye of Satori', if you stop at the mere opening of that eye, it is just like the weight that got stuck on the balance-arm. Then you willy-nilly fall into some kind of conception, your own notion of things, and the eye then becomes a rope that binds you! Even those who after many years of training and attaining to satori then stop there, cannot be said to have fully realised satori. Worse, since such individuals cannot even help themselves, they are more likely to lead others astray. Mumon's Verse ends here. It cannot be said too often, do not worry about the stopping at the attainment of satori. First of all, climb that hundred-foot pole and sit down on top of it. If it truly is the hundred-foot pole, without you needing to think about it, the next step will take place of itself!

CASE 47 · TOSOTSU'S THREE BARRIERS

Master Tosotsu set up three barriers and asked his monks:

'You pull out the weeds and study the profound so as to see into your True Nature. Where, at this moment, is your True Nature?

One who has realised the True Nature is free from birth and death. When the light of your eyes falls to the ground, how will you get free?

One who has escaped from birth and death knows where he goes. When the Four Great Elements fall apart, where will you go?'

MUMON'S COMMENT

If you can say the turning words to these three, you are master wherever you go. If you cannot, coarse food easily satisfies; finely chewed it keeps hunger away.

THE VERSE

一念普觀無量劫
無量劫事即如今
如今覷破箇一念
覷破如今覷底人

One instant of thought fills boundless *kalpas,*
And myriads of *kalpas* are just this instant of thought.
If this moment of thought is broken through,
The thinker is also seen through.

SOKO ROSHI'S COMMENTS

As is often the case, Tosotsu is the name of his temple and the master's name was Juetsu, so he was Master Juetsu of Tosotsu.

When still a boy, he decided to become a monk and began his studies in the Precept School. Then he changed to Mahayana, and eventually studied Zen under Master Kokumon. Sadly, Juetsu Tosotsu died young at only forty-eight. On confronting death, he composed this poem:

'Forty-eight years; I have done with the ignorant and the wise.

No hero; the way to nirvana is calm and peaceful.'

But the Three Barriers he left for succeeding generations have kept his name very much alive even to the present. In Japanese training monasteries, a monk who passes Tosotsu's Three Barriers is regarded as being well along the way of training. It seems almost ironic that Mumon, the author of the *Gateless Gate*, should at the very end of his collection insert these Three Barriers of Tosotsu.

With regard to the first barrier, Tosotsu says that 'Brushing the way through the tangled undergrowth of hillside forest, people continue on such a difficult journey only to discover their True Nature. If you can thus discover that True Nature, here and now, right in front of me, show me where that True Nature is, and show me its true functioning.'

Although Tosotsu set up three barriers, this first barrier includes all three. If we can find our True Nature in this first barrier, then the other two barriers will open of themselves. And not only these barriers, but the whole *Mumonkan* and also the *Hekiganroku* and the countless koans in the various collections, all of them are directed at seeing into the True Nature, at finding one's True Nature. However, this True Nature is not the self that we see in our everyday lives as distinct from others around us; it does not mean the limited self that differs from others in form or in ability. It is rather the universal True Nature that we lose sight of or fail to see, because we are so absorbed in the temporary and discriminating self. In order to see that universal True Nature we must be able to cut down or cut through the limited, daily self that we live with. In the past, this has been described as the dropping of self. Commenting on taking another step from the top of a hundred-foot pole (Case 46), it was said that rather than thinking about the further step, sit on that hundred-foot pole until you have truly realised your True Nature. That is the issue that concerns us and is also the central issue of this koan. And you need to do this sitting down as if you were dying. Although that is a terrifying way of putting it, yet it indicates the level of importance.

Why so? From the time that we are born, we are accustomed and trained to develop a self that discriminates. Our physical being, our intelligence and our emotions have come to look for and see only a limited I/self. Out of all the world we have come to love just this self, and not only do we love it but we have become attached to it. Yet however much we may cling to it, however much we love it, from whatever angle we view it, it still is and remains something that is limited. When we are hurt or feel pain or anguish, we do so because we are clinging to this limited self. But while clinging to this limited self, we human beings have also reached a desire to transcend it, or to attach it to something that is infinite.

If we were unable to reach a point of merging that limited self with an unlimited True Nature, there would be no hope for us. The Buddha and all the patriarchs clearly state that the limited self and the unlimited True Nature are indeed one. Unless we, each of us individually, test for ourselves whether that assertion is true and are able to confirm this ourselves, the words of the Buddha and the patriarchs are only hearsay. As that they then utterly fail to provide compassionate solace and succour for us human beings. This is why in this first Barrier, Tosotsu said to his monks that 'The reason for the various struggles that you go through in your training is only for the purpose of testing and seeing for yourselves whether and how that limited self is one with the universal True Nature.'

And he presses them further by saying, 'Not only that, but if you have found the True Nature, then here and now before me, show me where it is, what it is, and how it is working.'

So he is urging them by saying, 'Don't bring me some conceptualisation of the True Nature but let it manifest in all its living vitality, here and now, before me.'

As to the second barrier, he continued, 'If you understand and firmly grasp that the phenomenal I/self and the True Nature are indeed one, then you will be truly free within the limited and ephemeral phenomena that pass before you. When the light of your eyes falls to the ground, when death comes, what kind of free working can you show?' Thus Tosotsu presses upon us with tremendous, driving energy.

In my own tradition, the monastery I am associated with is Myoshin-ji in Kyoto. It was founded in mediaeval times by Kanzan Egen. One day, a wandering monk approached Egen who asked the monk what he had come for. 'I have come to clarify the problem of life and death,' said the monk. Egen, hitting him and driving him away, stated, 'In my monastery, there is no life and death.'

When Egen was on the point of death, he dressed himself as monk setting out on a journey, took up his staff, and saying farewell to his followers, died standing.

Some centuries later, another great Japanese Zen Master, Bankei, was asked by an old man, 'I am getting old and am aware of my approaching death. Please teach me how to meet death with confidence.' Bankei said, 'There is no need for some special confidence.' Startled, the old man asked, 'Why not?' Bankei replied, 'When the time to die comes, it is sufficient to die.'

On the one hand, then, there is Egen's almost superhuman response, and on the other Bankei's bland and perfectly normal reply. Although their responses may seem to be clear opposites, yet we must not lose sight of both emerging from the same deep insight of seeing into True Nature (*kensho*).

Both responses are famous in Japanese Zen and have been handed down to us over the centuries. But they come from Egen's satori and from Bankei's satori, and so are not my answer, nor yours. You and I, asserts Tosotsu, are to provide our own answer from our own insight.

Confronting the third barrier, Tosotsu demands, 'The one who can find perfect freedom in and through death, will understand and know where they are going in death. Show me where you are going.'

Most Buddhists would hope and believe that they would go to the Western Paradise. And most Christians would hope to go to heaven. Probably most agnostics would hope that at the time of their death they would be able to die peacefully. But, as far as death is concerned, things rarely happen as human beings anticipate. So for Buddhists who hope to go to Amida's Western Paradise, the question arises, where is that paradise? Or for Christians hoping to go to heaven, do they know which direction heaven lies? Heaven in England is up here – but in Japan, it is down there! So, then, where are you going?

Still another view. The famous Chinese Zen Master Seppo one day was talking to Gensha, another Zen Master. He said, 'A few days ago, a young monk came to me and asked, "When monks change their sphere of activities, where do they go?" I answered that it is like ice returning to water.' When Zen monks die, the term is *sengei*, literally meaning 'to change the sphere of activities.' Gensha remarked, 'That is not bad, but if it were me, I would not put it quite in that way.'

Seppo asked, 'Well, what would you say?' And Gensha replied, 'It is like water returning to water.'

Nanzen-ji in Kyoto is a temple compound as large and ancient as Myoshin-ji. When the founder, Daimin, died, he composed a verse, 'I have not come from anywhere, and I am not going anywhere. Then what does it amount to, what is it in the end? I do not part from this place.'

This too is just another version. But it is not your satori.

Mumon's Comment: If you brilliantly pass Tosotsu's Three Barriers and give answers which show that your misunderstanding is transformed into true understanding, then in life or in death, you are master wherever you go.

Now, do not misunderstand this. It would be a fatal mistake to think that what is being recommended here is that wherever you go you can assert yourself, or hold yourself to be the example or standard for people and things you are dealing with. Most trainees train along lines they have conceptualised for themselves. They make an image of what training should be like, and then they seek to conform or fit themselves to that image, or make it their ideal. Many worry that they might somehow lose their individuality if they carefully observe the regulations of the training place or respond diligently and carefully to the demands of the teacher. In Japan, many criticise the training and wonder whether a monastery might not be a place for making 'yesmen'. Try for yourselves to test the standards that have been set up. Even though somebody else has set them up, do not forget that the one who has to test them, to respond to them, is yourself.

We did not choose our own lives. We cannot choose our own death. So the training within this life and death, which we have not chosen for ourselves, is not and cannot be a training based solely upon our own constructed image. The True Nature is and can be in anything. Make no mistake; I can assure you that the True Nature can be entered and lived. Then, whatever situation we may be in, whatever we may be confronted with, we can simply be ourselves as we are, which is never being apart from truth.

If you cannot yet reach up to that understanding, then taking one step at a time, throw your whole energy into that step. Do not act or behave as if you will be satisfied with something that is unfinished or rough and ready. Do not jump to conclusions. Do not say, 'Oh, isn't that the way the world thinks' or 'There is a saying that seems to justify this.' As Mumon here says, if you eat rough food, or eat quickly, then your stomach seems to be fill up quickly. But if you chew carefully and considerately, then what you have eaten will sustain you, and you won't easily feel hungry. Mumon uses this common proverb about eating to encourage careful and diligent practice.

The Verse: An 'instant of thought' is a Buddhist term and expresses both the movement of the human heart and the smallest moment of time. If our True Nature is really seen into, then one split second, one tiny instant of the working of this Nature encapsulates the infinity of time. And all the historical events through all times, are also embraced within this single instant, now. So look into and through this instant, and you will look through everything and also through the person looking.

This verse shows some influence from the *Kegon Sutra*, but someone of Mumon's insight would not just quote. Even though the words are the very same as in the Sutra, they also flow out of Mumon's own insight and experience. But by it Mumon expresses a warning, namely, to take every instant as vital. For those who are in training this is the most wonderful of warnings. If and when you try to find the True Nature or infinity, you still will not find it; but second by second, that Nature functioning without allowing extraneous thoughts and ideas to flow in, will there enter into samadhi/oneness. That is the meaning of finding the True Nature in an instant. So, in my own training, the expression that I mostly heard was *sammai*, 'samadhi, at-one-ness'. If you are getting into the bath, then it is the bath-entering-samadhi; when eating, then eating-samadhi, and on the toilet, it is toilet-samadhi. So hearing it so often it seems like a tickle in your ear (cannot forget it)!

In practice, then, Mumon is urging us to find ourselves in a single instant, which means the samadhi with whatever we may encounter, without judging whether it is good or bad. Therefore, do not pursue your training in the sense of, 'If I do this, how can I avoid being told off?' or 'What is the best way to navigate around this problem?' Do not try to put a price tag on whatever you may be doing at a particular moment. Important and the real test at any moment is whether you are in samadhi. In that case you will certainly find yourselves and that will be the True Nature that is unmoved by life or death.

CASE 48 · KEMPO'S WAY

A monk asked Master Kempo, 'The Bhagavats of the Ten Directions have one road to nirvana. Where, may I ask, does the way start?' Kempo drew a line with his stick and said, 'Here.' Later, a monk asked Ummon, who held up his fan and said, 'This fan has jumped up into the Thirty-third Heaven and hit the nose of the Deva there. The Carp of the Eastern Sea gives one stroke and it pours with rain.'

MUMON'S COMMENT

One goes to the bottom of the deep sea and raises clouds of dust. One stands on a lofty mountain peak and beats up waves that reach up to the sky. One grasping, the other releasing, each with his one hand supports the profound teachings. They are like two children running into each other. In this world, few can grasp the truth directly. And of these two great masters, neither of them knows where the Way is.

THE VERSE

未擧步時先已到
未動舌時先説了
直饒著著在機先
更須知有向上竅

Without raising a foot, already arrived.
Without moving the tongue, the teaching is finished.
Though each move takes the initiative,
The final checkmate has to be known.

SOKO ROSHI'S COMMENT

Kempo was the Dharma-heir of Tosan, founder of the Soto school
of Zen. We do not know much about Kempo but much more about
the other protagonist in this koan, Ummon. Ummon's Zen and his
practice have already been discussed, and so has the quality of his
enlightenment. He appears in many koan cases, whereas Kempo's
name has come down to us only in this encounter.

One day a young monk asked Kempo a question from the
Surangama Sutra. This sutra is in effect the response to the question,
'By which means do Bodhisattvas awaken to enlightenment?' It
sets out the training along the Bodhisattva Path and points out the
obstacles that may be encountered. In the fifth chapter of this sutra
the Buddha teaches Ananda about death.

Referring to this chapter, the young monk asked Kempo, 'The
Bhagavats, or the Bodhisattvas of the ten directions have one road
to Nirvana; where does it start – where is that road?'

From his question, it appears the monk held a notion that there
must be a single road that all the Bodhisattvas had taken towards
enlightenment. But not only that monk, everybody who has been
practising over the centuries has been prone to fall into just this
error, assuming that somehow there is a form of practice, a way that
has a particular value or that there is some especially great teacher,
and then believing that one's training will only really start when that
place or that teacher is found.

So we need to remember, as Mumon urges us in Koan 47 above,
to find truth and insight in this present moment here right before
us. This moment NOW, the place we are in, what is being confronted
now, that in itself is the way towards enlightenment. Our monk had
ignored that and came to Kempo asking for the special path that he
should follow. The essential point in this koan is to see exactly what

that monk's error of thinking and behaviour consisted of. We always want to be given or told the truth instead of reflecting on our own mistakes. But more important than grasping the truth is to find out for ourselves what errors we have made in thought, word and deed. If only we can grasp and fully realise these errors, the truth will appear of itself.

We must take great care because if we believe that rather than looking within to find our own errors, we can receive the truth from somewhere outside, we lay the foundation for all opinionated disputes about the value of the truth we claim to hold. And from there it is but a short step to quarrelling and warfare. But the truth emerging for those who note, ponder, reflect on and penetrate their own errors never becomes a source of friction.

Kempo, in response to the monk, drew a single line with his staff and stated, 'Here!' We may take it that Kempo simply drew that single line. Why should it be so simple? Because wherever the staff touches in the here and now, it is not possible to be separated from that. Kempo's response was from the position that the whole universe is one and that whole universe is here and now.

From the top of that hundred-foot pole (Case 46), Kempo points the direction. Whenever, wherever, and in whatever circumstances we may be, whoever we may be dealing with, here and now is the single path to enlightenment.

Reading of the exploits and efforts of the great patriarchs of the past, we may be led to believe that Zen training is only for young people, or only for those who are very strong and determined and are willing to go through very hard and difficult experiences. But that is a great mistake. Although physical strength and resilience are necessary to sit all night in zazen, that is only one method used in Zen and by no means represents all of it. Yes, some can find their way to satori in just that way. But for others who are ill and very close to death, there is the path to enlightenment in just that weakness. Please always remember that from the time we are born until we die – and even after we have died – we are in the very midst of that path that opens to enlightenment.

But the monk who asked Kempo for a special path could not understand what Kempo showed him. So, dissatisfied with Kempo's response he went off and asked Ummon the same question. And Ummon gave him a tremendous answer, raising up his fan. And this fan flew up so high that it went right into the Thirty-third Heaven, struck old Daishaku's nose, and then falling down again splashed into the pond and struck the head of a carp. That carp, startled, flicked its tail, and just at that moment buckets of rain poured down from the heavens. The querying monk was stunned and probably thought Ummon was teasing him. And you too, on reading this, may think that Zen monks are just tellers of tall tales. But many of you may watch some of the BBC's fine science programmes, the best of which are also broadcast in Japan. Having seen some of them, the almost incredible things shown there are exactly what Ummon was demonstrating to the monk. Things which to our limited way of thinking seem totally unconnected with each other are, nonetheless, working with tremendous vitality in their own harmony and order. The world that appears through the lens of a microscope and the world of space seen through a telescope are interconnected and their tiniest particulars show the One Way that is working in the universe. With his fan Ummon penetrated this one way of the universe. And so Kempo from a position of absolute equality, and Ummon by showing the teeming variety of manifest reality around us, both clearly pointed out the way to enlightenment for the young monk. He, however, probably went around for the rest of his life still looking for the one way.

Mumon's Comment: It is as if Kempo in the darkest depths of the ocean is stirring up a cloud of dust. But although the stirring is lively and vibrant, in these pitch-black waters the cloud of dust that has been thrown up is also black. It is a world of complete darkness which at the same time is also a world of absolute equality. And Ummon, standing on top of a soaring peak in brilliant sunshine, seems to whip up the spume of the ocean into a vast cloud that reaches to the heavens. This is the working of the world of phenomena which surrounds us, but which in its totality we cannot take in all at once.

So both masters, the one from the standpoint of absolute equality and the other from the standpoint of the world of phenomena and distinctions, are reaching out and grasping each other's hands. There, a most delicate world of truth emerges. It is like two small children rushing towards and into each other. Mumon says that few in this world of ours have grasped and embodied this truth. But while praising both Kempo and Ummon, he also adds a sting to that, saying that in his view neither of these two great Masters knows the way to enlightenment.

Please never mistake or be fooled by such wordplay. It is like the pose taken by a Kabuki actor, who makes a dramatic entrance with his arms raised! Do not be fooled by Mumon's posturing. Neither Kempo nor Ummon, and not even the Buddha or Bodhidharma, when asked, would know the way to enlightenment. Why not? Because they simply just walk the way. If there is somebody who knows the way, you would have to say he has fallen into the same hole as the monk looking for that one way.

The Verse: The path that you are standing on at this moment is the way to enlightenment. You do not have to walk that path and arrive anywhere. The Third Patriarch starts his wonderful poem with,

'The Great Way is not difficult.' He is referring to that one path, the way to enlightenment. If you think of some place that you want to reach, on the way towards it are difficult and easy stretches. But if the place you are aiming for is right here and now, easy or difficult have become irrelevant.

Mumon is saying that you arrive without taking one step. So this one way that Mumon expresses here as a single moment is of itself spread all around us. What explanation should be needed to see it? Hence in Mumon's verse, 'Without moving the tongue, the teaching is finished.'

Even though you have fully realised all this, and even if your actions display it brilliantly from moment to moment, take care! The path does not end here and beyond it there is an infinite road. This is the meaning of the verse kindly provided by Mumon. There is nothing other than to walk on the path that is here and now with you. A journey does not begin when the train pulls into the platform and you get on. Now, here, our precious lives are moving and working, moment by moment.

Further Reading

On the Mumonkan

Aitkin, Robert. *The Gateless Barrier: The Wu-men Kuan (Mumonkan)*;
San Francisco: North Point Press, 1990.
Blyth, R.H. *Zen and the Classics, Vol. 4 Mumonkan*. Tokyo: The Hokuseido
Press, 1966.
Lynch, Paul. *The Barrier That Has No Gate* (with additional comments and
questions from Seung Sahn). Boston: Before Thought Publications, 2010.
Sekida, Katsuki. *Two Zen Classics*. New York: Weatherhill, 1977.
Shibayama, Zenkei. *Zen Comments on the Mumonkan*. New York: The New
American Library, 1975.

Books by Soko Morinaga Roshi

Pointers to Insight. London: Zen Centre, 1985.
– *Novice to Master: An Ongoing Lesson in the Extent of My Own Stupidity*. Boston:
Wisdom Publications, 2002.
– *The Ceasing of Notions: Zen Text from the Tun-Huang Caves*. London: Zen
Centre, 1988. Boston: Wisdom Publications with the Zen Trust, 2012.

Books and translations by Venerable Myokyo-ni

Wisdom of the Zen Masters. New York: New Directions Books, 1976 (under her
pre- ordination name Irmgard Schlögl).
– *The Zen Way.* London: Sheldon Press, 1977; Zen Centre, 1987. The Buddhist
Society, 2021.
– *Gentling the Bull: The Ten Bull Pictures, a Spiritual Journey.* London: Zen
Centre, 1988.
– *Living Buddhism.* Square One Publications on behalf of The Zen Centre, 2000.
– *The Daily Devotional Chants of the Zen Centre* (2008). Reprinted as *The Great
Wisdom Gone Beyond*. London: The Buddhist Society, 2021.
– *Look and See*. London: The Buddhist Society, 2017.
– *Yoka Daishi's Realizing the Way*. (translation and commentary), London:
The Buddhist Society, 2017.
– *Towards Wholeness*. London: The Buddhist Society, 2018.

Translations

– *The Record of Rinzai.* Berkeley: Shambhala, 1976 (under her pre-ordination
name Irmgard Schlögl). Reprinting as *The Zen Teaching of Rinzai*,
London: The Buddhist Society, 2023.
– *The Ceasing of Notions* (1988) (with Soko Morinaga Roshi and Michelle Bromley)
– *The Discourse on The Inexhaustible Lamp of the Zen School.* (with Yoko Okuda),
London: Zen Centre, 1989.